ESSENTIALS OF
PUBLIC POLICY
FOR
MANAGEMENT

ESSENTIALS OF
PUBLIC POLICY
FOR
MANAGEMENT

second edition

Rogene A. Buchholz
School of Management
The University of Texas at Dallas

PRENTICE HALL, ENGLEWOOD CLIFFS, N.J. 07632

Library of Congress Cataloging-in-Publication Data
BUCHHOLZ, ROGENE A.
    Essentials of public policy for management / Rogene A. Buchholz. -
    -2nd ed.
      p.   cm.
    Bibliography: p.
    Includes index.
    ISBN 0-13-284100-2
    1. Industry and state—United States. 2. Business and politics-
-United States. 3. Industry—Social aspects—United States.
I. Title.
HD3616.U47B762   1990
338.973'0024658—dc19
                                                89-3692
                                                 CIP

Prentice-Hall Essentials of Management Series
Stephen P. Robbins, **editor**

Editorial/production supervision: TKM Productions
Cover design: Christine Gadekar
Manufacturing buyer: Edward O'Dougherty

© 1990 by Prentice-Hall, Inc.
A Division of Simon & Schuster
Englewood Cliffs, N.J. 07632

10 9 8 7 6 5 4 3 2 1

Printed in the United States of America

ISBN   0-13-284100-2

Prentice-Hall International (UK) Limited, *London*
Prentice-Hall of Australia Pty, Limited, *Sydney*
Prentice-Hall Canada Inc., *Toronto*
Prentice-Hall Hispanoamericana, S.A., *Mexico*
Prentice-Hall of India Private Limited, *New Delhi*
Prentice-Hall of Japan, Inc., *Tokyo*
Simon & Schuster Asia Pte. Ltd., *Singapore*
Editora Prentice-Hall do Brasil, Ltda., *Rio de Janeiro*

CONTENTS

Contents

4

THE SOCIAL CONTEXT OF PUBLIC POLICY   87

5

THE PUBLIC POLICY PROCESS   119

6

INTERNATIONAL DIMENSIONS OF PUBLIC POLICY   150

7

PUBLIC ISSUES MANAGEMENT   180

Contents

8

CORPORATE POLITICAL STRATEGIES 216

FOREWORD

With the rapid growth in recent years of courses in such areas as personnel, organizational behavior, production, decision science, labor relations, and small business management, there has developed an increased need for a viable alternative to the standard 500- or 600-page, casebound textbook. The Essentials of Management Series has been designed to fill that need. The Series consists of brief, survey books covering major content areas within the management discipline.

Each book in the Series provides a concise treatment of the key concepts and issues within a major content area, written in a highly readable style, balancing theory with practical applications, and offering a clarity of presentation that is often missing in standard, full-length textbooks. I have selected authors both for their academic expertise and their ability to identify, organize, and articulate the essential elements of their subject. So, for example, you will find that the books in this Series avoid unnecessary jargon, use a conversational writing style, include extensive examples and interesting illustrations of concepts, and have the focus of a rifle rather than that of an encyclopedic shotgun.

The books in this Series will prove useful to a wide variety of readers. Since each covers the essential body of knowledge in a major area of management, they can be used alone for introductory survey courses in colleges and universities or for management development and in-house educational programs. Additionally, their short format makes them an ideal vehicle to be combined with cases, readings, and/or experiential materials by instructors who desire to mold a course to meet unique objectives. The books in this Series offer the flexibility that is either not feasible or too costly to achieve with a standard textbook.

Stephen P. Robbins
Series Editor

PREFACE

The importance of public policy to business executives can hardly be overestimated. Indeed, it seems fair to say that the economic environment in which business operates is more a function of public policy than it is of traditional free market forces. The aggregate economic conditions that a company faces as far as employment and income levels are concerned are largely determined by the fiscal and monetary policies of government. Specific industries are affected by protectionist measures, environmental regulation, subsidies, and tax policies. Beyond the industrial level, the fate of individual companies is oftentimes in the hands of government when a company is dependent on winning a government contract or has need for a guaranteed loan from the government to continue in business.

The foregoing are merely illustrations of the way in which public policy can affect business organizations. Since public policy is so important, it is necessary for business executives and business students to have some knowledge of what public policy is all about and how it is formulated. Knowledge of how public policy shapes the business environment is important in order to understand the impact specific measures might make on a particular company, industry, or the entire business sector. The public policy process must be understood so business executives can know how and when to appropriately and effectively participate in public policy formulation. To abdicate this role is to leave the fate of business up to government officials, public interest group leaders, and other participants in the public policy process. This hardly seems to be a responsible position for corporate management to take in view of its responsibilities to stockholders, employees, consumers, or the public at large.

Public policy is too important to be left up to government or interest groups alone. Many of the adverse consequences of government regulation formulated in the 1960s and 1970s might have been avoided if business had been more active in its formulation. Business has a responsibility to participate in the public policy process and help solve the nation's economic and social problems. In the words of John Dunlop, former Secretary of Labor and a leading advocate of public policy for business:

> **The absence of effective leadership for the business community on many public policy questions—in consensus building and in dealing with other groups and governments—means that business enterprises forfeit almost entirely to politicians. The rapid expansion of government regulations in recent years and specifically government's penchant for ridged, bureaucratic**

"command and control" regulations, even when ineffective and counter-productive, have arisen in part from a lack of coherence and consensus within the business community about more constructive choices for achieving social purposes.[1]

    This book is designed for use by business executives and students in schools of business and management. It is hoped that the book will find a market in the trade, both for reading by individual executives and in executive development programs. In academia, the book should be useful in a business and society course as well as a traditional business policy course where environmental influences on business policy are considered. It should also be useful for executive development programs sponsored by schools of business and management.

    As the title of the book indicates, the essentials of public policy for management are covered in the various chapters. This second edition contains some major changes from the first edition that will make the book more useful and comprehensive. An entirely new chapter dealing with the international dimensions of public policy has been added because of the development of a world economy. It is thus important for managers and students to have some understanding of public policy in an international context. Since the subject of ethics has become of great interest in the last several years, the relation of ethics to public policy is discussed in Chapter 4. Chapter 7, which deals with public issues management, has been extensively revised with new material and a different organization. All of the other chapters have been updated with current material and reorganized as necessary.

    The evolution of the public policy concept as a new dimension of management is discussed in the first chapter. In Chapter 2, some definitional and conceptual material related to public policy is discussed to provide some intellectual foundations for subsequent material. An historical overview of major developments in public policy and business is presented in Chapter 3. The social context of public policy is next discussed to give the reader an idea of how public issues originate in our society that may result in formal public policy. The process by which public policy is formalized is discussed in Chapter 5, which entails a description of the way in which the federal government operates. Chapter 6 deals with international dimensions of public policy by discussing the international regulatory environment and some public policy areas that are international in nature. The subject of public issues management is discussed and analyzed in Chapter 7 to familiarize the reader with an evolving function within corporations through which management's response to public issues that affect the corporation is formalized. The political strategies that can be adopted for public policy participation is the subject of Chapter 8. These strategies are discussed in a framework that corresponds with the stages of public policy formulation.

    Thanks are due to many people who were influential in the writing of this book. William C. Frederick of the University of Pittsburgh is owed a great debt of personal gratitude for introducing me to the field of business environment and public policy, and serving as my mentor during my years of study at that institution. Lee E. Preston and James E. Post deserve credit for introducing me to the concept of public policy in their book, *Private Management and Public Policy,* which was very influential

[1]John T. Dunlop, "The Concerns: Business and Public Policy," *Harvard Business Review,* vol. 57, no. 6 (November–December 1979), p. 86.

in shaping my thinking. Equally influential was Murray L. Weidenbaum, whom I worked with for three years at the Center for the Study of American Business (CSAB) at Washington University in St. Louis, Missouri. This association made me aware of the impacts public policy makes on business.

My work with the American Assembly of Collegiate Schools of Business, which along with the CSAB sponsored the study of the business environment/public policy field that I conducted, acquainted me with all aspects of the public policy dimension of management. Stephen P. Robbins, the series editor, deserves thanks for reviewing the first and second editions of the book at an early stage of development and making many suggestions for improvement. The people at Prentice Hall with whom I worked, including Alison Reeves and Major Brooks, provided a great deal of assistance and encouragement at every step of the process. Their interest in this project is greatly appreciated. Finally, my wife deserves no end of credit, not only for her understanding and support in writing the book, which took time away from family responsibilities, but also for her help in typing the manuscript.

ESSENTIALS OF
PUBLIC POLICY
FOR
MANAGEMENT

THE EVOLUTION OF PUBLIC POLICY AS A NEW DIMENSION OF MANAGEMENT

⟸ **IDEAS TO BE FOUND** ⟹
IN THIS CHAPTER

- Changes in the social environment of business
- Corporate social responsibility
- Corporate social responsiveness
- The growth of public policy
- Public policy as a new dimension of management

Management education underwent a period of concentrated self-examination in the late 1950s and early 1960s with the publication of two comprehensive studies that were widely discussed throughout the business and academic communities.[1] These reports were followed by a third study which summarized the above reports and offered a series of recommendations for the improvement of management education.[2] Many credit these reports with providing the basic ideas that have given shape to modern management education. They were very influential in changing the content and structure of management education across the country.

Among other things, these reports stressed the importance of including "environmental" courses in the curriculum of business schools and of promoting research into environmental issues and problems. It was clear from the references made to the business environment that these reports were referring not

---

[1]Frank C. Pierson, *The Education of American Businessmen* (New York: McGraw-Hill, 1959); Robert A. Gordon and James E. Howell, *Higher Education for Business* (New York: Columbia University Press, 1959).

[2]Committee for Economic Development, *Educating Tomorrow's Managers* (New York: CED, 1964).

only to the more traditional economic and legal environments, but to the newer concerns with the social and political environments as well. For example, one author stressed the need for "the manager of tomorrow to understand, and be sensitive to, the entire economic, political, and social environment in which we will live and in which his business will operate and be judged."[3]

While not necessarily introducing the idea of the environment to business education and management practitioners, these reports at least reawakened interest in a broad range of environmental influences on business as part of a professional business education. A narrow vocationalism, the reports stressed, that ignored these environmental influences, was not appropriate to prepare managers for the world in which they must exercise their vocation or profession. The importance of the environment to business is best described in the following quote:

> There are two points to stress about the relations between business firms and their environment. One is the fact of mutual interaction. The environment helps to determine the alternatives on the basis of which business decisions are made and also affects the value systems which supply the criteria for choosing among these alternatives. At the same time, business firms, individually and particularly collectively, react upon their environment. It is this fact that makes it so important for businessmen to bring a keen sense of social responsibility to their jobs. More than economic effects ensue from their decisions. Business activity affects government policy in a variety of ways. It helps to determine the conditions of community living; it has been largely responsible for the kind of urban civilization in which we live; it helps to shape the intellectual and moral tone of the times.

> Another important aspect of the interrelations between business and its environment is that these relations are continuously changing, evolving out of the past into a future that can be but vaguely foreseen. Change and uncertainty are the very essence of the businessman's life. It is a truism that the world which today's students will have to manage a generation hence will be much different from the world which they and their teachers know at present. Businessmen clearly have to be equipped to deal with unforseen change, to have some idea of the sources of change in their environment, and, so far as this is possible, to anticipate change.[4]

The last paragraph could not have been more prophetic. The decade of the 1960s was one of sweeping social change that affected business organizations in almost all aspects of their operations. The focus on civil rights for minorities, equal rights for women, protection of the physical environment, safety and health in the workplace, and a broad array of consumer issues has had far-reaching and long-lasting impacts on business organizations and on the manage-

---

[3]Pierson, *Education*, p. 323.
[4]Gordon and Howell, *Higher Education*, p. 65.

ment of these organizations. The long-term effect of this social change is a dramatic change in the "rules of the game" by which business is expected to operate.

CHANGES IN THE SOCIAL ENVIRONMENT OF BUSINESS Although social movements have appeared at various times throughout American history, they seemed to proliferate in the 1960s. The decade began with the civil rights movement based on the dissatisfaction of blacks with their status in American society. Pressures for change had been building for several years, but the dramatic event that precipitated the movement was the refusal of a black woman, Rosa Parks, to move to the rear of a city bus in Birmingham, Alabama, a customary practice in southern states with Jim Crow laws. This refusal led to her arrest and ignited a social movement throughout the South in support of civil rights for blacks. Boycotts of buses and white merchants, and nonviolent demonstrations and marches were used with great success to influence public opinion. The result of this movement was the passage of new federal laws related to civil rights that attempted to provide equal opportunity for blacks and other minorities to pursue their interests in all areas of American society.

Soon after the civil rights movement began to have a major impact on American society, many women began to express dissatisfaction with their lot in society. They complained that the lack of equal opportunity in the workplace—being paid less than men for performing essentially the same job, being denied an opportunity to move into higher-paying jobs in management and the professions, and a host of other problems. They complained about being stereotyped as housewives and mothers, being treated as sex objects, and being treated unfairly when applying for credit. Thus began a feminist movement to pursue equal status for women in American society. The movement also used the tactics of boycotts and demonstrations to influence public opinion, and pressed for legislation and even a constitutional amendment, which was subsequently defeated, to assure equal rights for women in all areas of American life.

The consumer movement resulted from dissatisfaction with the quality of products available on the marketplace, the inadequate response of companies to consumer complaints, the meaninglessness of warranties, the number of accidents related to consumer products, and similar problems. The consumer movement was concerned with a variety of issues that grew out of a technologically sophisticated and complex marketplace coupled with a highly affluent and educated population that had high aspirations and expectations regarding the quality of life it wanted for itself. The dramatic event that sparked the movement was the publication in 1965 of Ralph Nader's *Unsafe at Any Speed*, a book that was critical of the Corvair automobile and indicted the producer, General Motors, for a lack of concern about automobile safety. The response of General Motors to this book catapulted Nader into a leadership position in the consumer movement. The primary tactic used by the consumer movement to pursue its goals was one of working within the political system to pass an enormous amount of consumer legislation.

The ecology movement sprang up almost overnight, helped by books that focused on DDT and other alleged evils that were being perpetuated by business and causing environmental problems. During the latter years of the 1960s, many of the energies that had gone into the civil rights movement were channeled into the environmental movement as the former matured. Public consciousness about pollution of the environment increased rapidly. The result was a major public policy effort to control pollution and correct for the deficiencies of the market system in controlling the amount and types of waste discharged into the environment.

> Fifteen or so years ago, pollution and ecology were two terms rarely found in the lexicon of business. Today environmental survival and pollution abatement are major topics of the times and receive prominent exposure in the literature of business and economics. If any one issue provided the initial sustenance for social responsibility proponents, that issue was the effect of business operations and practices on the physical environment. Probably more words have been written on this subject than on most others of a business and social problems context.[5]

Other social changes that were taking place in the 1960s and 1970s had to do with the growth of entitlement programs (social security, medicare, medicaid, food stamps, etc.) that captured an ever-increasing share of the federal budget. The safety and health consciousness of the population spilled over into a concern about safety and health in the workplace, where a crisis atmosphere was created that led to a comprehensive federal law dealing with occupational safety and health. Concern about the ethical standards of business emerged out of the Watergate experience and the foreign payments controversy.

It is clear that a major social revolution took place during the 1960s and 1970s that had major impacts on business. There was a change of values throughout society evidenced by a concern about the social impacts of business, a change of personal attitudes as business received more criticism, and a change of social organization as more and more interest groups emerged to institutionalize these social concerns.

There are many reasons for this unprecedented amount of social change. The educational level of society increased after World War II, which may have increased the aspirations and expectations of many people for a higher quality of life than they were presently experiencing. Television and other media had an enormous impact on the amount of information flowing throughout society, making people aware of problems and events instantaneously, and influencing

[5]Arthur Elkins and Dennis W. Callaghan, *A Managerial Odyssey: Problems in Business and Its Environment*, 2nd ed. (Reading, Mass.: Addison-Wesley, 1978), p. 173.

public opinion in support of emerging social movements. There was also a general euphoria throughout American society in the 1960s that the great society could be created by eliminating poverty, cleaning up pollution, and solving all our social problems, while providing an ever-increasing standard of living for all citizens.

Perhaps society can also be thought of in the familiar model developed by Abraham Maslow with respect to individual development. During the 1950s, many people became relatively affluent and moved into a middle-class or even upper-class status. We were blessed with new products that made life easier and more interesting. Thus a large part of society may have felt that its basic economic or lower-order needs were satisfied, and thus attention could be turned toward fulfillment of higher order needs such as pollution control, respect for the basic rights of all citizens, increasing the safety and health aspects of the workplace and marketplace, and providing more economic resources for the less fortunate members of society.

CORPORATE SOCIAL RESPONSIBILITY

Given this kind of a social revolution, it is not surprising that the social environment was given increasing attention during the 1960s and 1970s by business corporations and schools of business and management. Although some scholars suggest that the concept of corporate social responsibility may have had its origins in the 1930s, the concept really came into its own during the 1960s as a response to the changing social values of society.[6] Executives began to talk about the social responsibilities of business and develop specific social programs in response to problems of a social, rather than economic, nature. Schools of business and management implemented new courses in business and society or in the social responsibilities of business.

There are many definitions of social responsibility, but in general it means that a private corporation has responsibilities to society that go beyond the production of goods and services at a profit—that a corporation has a broader constituency to serve than that of stockholders alone. Corporations relate to society through more than just the marketplace and serve a wider range of human values than the traditional economic values implied when the corporation is viewed solely as an economic institution. Corporate social responsibility means that corporations have a responsibility to help society solve some of its most pressing social problems (many of which corporations helped to cause) by devoting some of their resources to the solution of these problems.

The concept of social responsibility received increasing attention during the 1960s because of the need for corporations to respond to the changing social environment of business. This change was often described as a change in the

---

[6]See William C. Frederick, "From CSR_1 to CSR_2: The Maturing of Business and Society Thought," Graduate School of Business, University of Pittsburgh, 1978, Working Paper No. 279, p. 1.

terms of the contract between business and society that reflected changing expectations regarding the social performance of business.[7] The old contract between business and society was based on the view that economic growth was the source of all progress, social as well as economic. The engine providing this economic growth was considered to be the drive for profits by competitive private enterprise. The basic mission of business was thus to produce goods and services at a profit, and by doing this, business was making its maximum contribution to society and, in fact, being socially responsible.[8]

The new contract between business and society was based on the view that the single-minded pursuit of economic growth produced some detrimental side effects that imposed social costs on certain segments of society or on society as a whole. The pursuit of economic growth, it was believed, did not necessarily lead automatically to social progress. In many cases it led instead to a deteriorating physical environment, an unsafe workplace, needless exposure to toxic substances on the part of workers and consumers, discrimination against certain groups in society, urban decay, and other social problems. This new contract between business and society involved the reduction of these social costs of business through impressing upon business the idea that it has an obligation to work for social as well as economic betterment. This new contract does not invalidate the old contract—it simply adds new terms or additional clauses to that contract (see Figure 1.1) and includes a responsibility for both economic and social impacts.

> Today it is clear that the terms of the contract between society and business are, in fact, changing in substantial and important ways. Business is being asked to assume broader responsibilities to society than ever before and to serve a wider range of human values. Business enterprises, in effect, are being asked to contribute more to the quality of American life than just supplying quantities of goods and services.[9]

Social responsibility is fundamentally an ethical concept. It involves changing notions of human welfare and emphasizes a concern with the social dimensions of business activity that have a direct connection with the quality of life in society. The concept provides a way for business to concern itself with these social dimensions and pay some attention to its social impacts. The word *responsibility* implies that business organizations have some kind of obligation toward the society in which they function to deal with social problems and contribute more than just economic goods and services.

---

[7]See Melvin Anshen, *Managing the Socially Responsible Corporation* (New York: Macmillan, 1974).

[8]See Milton Friedman, "The Social Responsibility of Business Is to Increase Its Profits," *New York Times Magazine*, Sept. 13, 1970, pp. 122–126.

[9]Committee for Economic Development, *Social Responsibilities of Business Corporations* (New York: CED, 1971), p. 12.

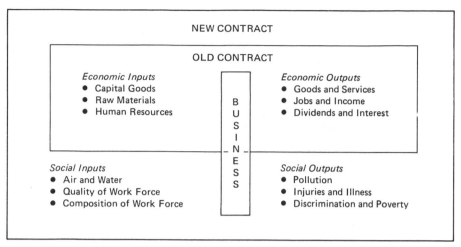

Figure 1.1
The Contract Between Business and Society

Source: Rogene A. Buchholz, *Business Environment and Public Policy: Implications for Management and Strategy Formulation*, 2nd ed. © 1986, p. 24. Reprinted by permission of Prentice Hall, Englewood Cliffs, NJ.

Arguments in Favor of Social Responsibility

The debate about social responsibility reflected many of these ethical or moral dimensions (see Exhibit 1.1). Proponents of the concept argue that if public expectations of business have changed, business has no choice but to accommodate itself to these changes. An institution is allowed to exist only because it performs a useful function in society, and business's charter can be amended or revoked at any time if it fails to live up to society's expectations. Thus if business wants to continue to exist, it must respond to changes in society and do what society demands. If society wants business to respond to social values, it must do so or be threatened with extinction.

Another argument in support of social responsibility is that profit maximization should be seen over a longer time period than in the past. Expenditures to help solve social problems may reduce short-run profits, but it is in the long-run self-interest of business to produce environmental conditions that are favorable for business survival and continued profitability. Business is dependent on the environment for the resources that it uses to fulfill its role in society, thus enlightened self-interest dictates a business concern for social problems. Business cannot hope to remain a viable institution in a deteriorating society.

A third argument is that business will gain a better public image by being socially responsible. If the values of society have indeed changed, a company that is responsive to these changes should be more favorably thought of than one that is not responsive. This would mean more customers, more sales of products, better employees, better stock market performance, and easier ac-

Exhibit 1.1
Arguments in Favor of Social Responsibility

- Keep in tune with public expectations
- Long-run self-interest
- Gain a better public image
- Avoid government regulation
- Balance of responsibility with power
- Business has useful resources
- Social problems can be seen as business opportunities
- Business has contributed to social problems

---

cess to capital markets to raise funds for expansion. Thus a business organization that is seen to be socially responsible will gain a competitive advantage over its rivals that do not have as good a public image.

One of the most powerful arguments for social responsibility is that by being socially responsible business may be able to avoid government regulation. This is based on the belief that social issues or expectations go through some sort of evolutionary sequence. According to this argument, if business does not respond properly to a change in social expectations, the expectations will be picked up by the political system and find their way into legislation that, if passed, will result in regulation to force business to comply or pay penalties in case of violations. As an issue moves through this sequence, the options for business are narrowed to where they become almost nonexistent. Thus the best strategy for business is to get involved with an issue in the early stages of its development, and if business can make a proper response that effectively meets societal expectations, government regulation may be avoided altogether.

Another argument to support the notion of social responsibility relates business power to responsibility. Since business has a large amount of social power in that its activities and decisions affect the environment, consumers, employees, community conditions, and many other areas of society, it has an equal amount of responsibility for these effects. Responsibility is a necessary reciprocal of power, and any imbalance opens the door to irresponsible behavior that may negatively affect the welfare of society. Responsibility arises from power, and if business insists on avoiding its social responsibilities, then some of its power may be gradually taken away by other groups or institutions in society (such as government).[10]

There is also the argument that business has enormous resources that would be useful in solving social problems. Business has managerial talent, expertise in many technical areas, and physical and financial resources, all of which can be very useful in helping to alleviate society's problems. Business is

---

[10]Keith Davis and William C. Frederick, *Business and Society: Management, Public Policy, Ethics*, 5th ed. (New York: McGraw-Hill, 1984), pp. 33–34.

also known for its innovational ability and its concern for efficient use of resources, which are also beneficial assets in the social realm. Thus business ought to be encouraged or perhaps even required to try its hand at solving social problems. The basic idea behind this argument is that if social problems can be privatized, society is likely to benefit from more efficient use of resources to deal with these problems than if they are left entirely to the government.

The idea that social problems can be turned into profitable opportunities is an especially intriguing one for some business executives. A few corporations claim this argument as their justification for social involvement. They built plants in ghetto areas, for example, not necessarily out of a moral sense of doing good, but out of a more practical business sense of exploiting a profit-making opportunity. A lot of wasted talent in these areas can be put to good use in making products. Certain companies might also claim that enough useful products can be recovered from waste materials to make a pollution control program a profitable endeavor.

Finally, there is the moral argument that business has an obligation to help solve social problems because it helped create or at least perpetuate them in the first place. Business causes pollution, it creates unsafe workplaces, it helps perpetuate discrimination through its hiring and promotion practices. Therefore business has a moral responsibility to deal with these negative impacts on society, rather than leaving them for someone else to solve. Many social problems are the direct result of business operations and these are quite properly the social responsibility of business.

Arguments Against Social Responsibility   Despite these supporting arguments, the concept of social responsibility has some serious problems raised by those who do not support the concept wholeheartedly or who simply oppose it on ideological or other grounds (see Exhibit 1.2). One such problem is simply the matter of definition. S. Prakash Sethi has written that social responsibility "has been used in so many different contexts that it has lost all meaning. Devoid of an internal structure and content, it has come to mean all things to all peo-

Exhibit 1.2
Arguments Against Social Responsibility

- Difficult to define the concept
- Lack of accountability
- Increase of business power
- Dilutes responsibility to shareholders
- Lack of skills and incentives to deal with social problems
- Reduces international competitiveness
- Corporations are not moral agents
- Undermines the free enterprise system

ple."[11] This diversity and vagueness has left concerned citizens, business-people, scholars, and public policymakers confused.

This definitional problem exists at both the conceptual and operational levels, but at the latter level it becomes a particularly crucial problem as corporations try to be specific about their social responsibilities. How shall a corporation's resources be allocated to help solve social problems? With what specific problems shall the corporation concern itself? What priorities should be established? What goals or standards of performance should be developed? How much money should be spent? What technology should be employed? What measures are appropriate to determine adequate performance?

There is no market mechanism to answer these questions about resource allocation. The market does not work in allocating resources for the provision of public goods and services. Preferences or desires for public goods and services are not revealed through market behavior, it could be argued, and thus the market offers little or no information to the manager that is useful in making decisions about solving social problems. For most corporations, there is no money to be made in pollution control, affirmative action programs, hiring the disadvantaged, or other social efforts. The measurement of long-run profits or the profits that might result from an improved corporate image proved to be problemmatical.

In the absence of a market mechanism, management could presumably make these operational decisions on their own according to whatever criteria they deem appropriate. However, this raises the accountability problem. Milton Friedman posed a crucial question in this regard: What right do managers of private corporations have to determine public policy for their organizations?[12] Friedman argues that when managers assume the right to make decisions about social investment they are involved in the realm of public decision making without being subject to any of the guidelines or limitations imposed by the market. Nor are they subject to any democratic political process as a check on their decision making. In effect, businesspeople would be imposing taxes on the public by using stockholders', consumers', and employees' money for a public purpose. Furthermore, they would be making the decisions on how these funds should be spent. They would be spending someone else's money for a social interest and exercising governmental (political) power without any definite criteria to follow. This leaves the public with nothing more than businesspeople's claim that their actions are in the public interest—a claim that has no clear meaning and thus cannot be challenged by the public whose interests are at stake. Social responsibility would, therefore, mean whatever managers want it to mean, and represents:

---

[11]S. Prakash Sethi, "Dimensions of Corporate Social Responsibility," *California Management Review*, vol. 17, no. 3 (Spring 1975), p. 58.

[12]Friedman, "Social Responsibility," pp. 122–126.

an invasion into the public domain by managers who are not selected through any public process, are not subject to annual review provided by elections, are not forced to engage in public dialogue with their constituents, are not required to justify the expenditures of corporate funds (involuntary taxes) before a budget committee of the Congress, and need not balance competing interests before coming to their decisions.[13]

Without some kind of accountability a corporation's decisions can be arbitrary. A corporation may make philanthropic grants or hire disadvantaged people and incur extra costs for training, but the corporation, or more precisely its managers, would be deciding what causes are worthy of support and what people should be singled out as disadvantaged and deserving. Since these activities are most likely consistent with their own values, corporate responsibility advocates would probably be satisfied with these corporate actions. But what if corporations tried to defend foreign payments on the grounds that this action was socially responsible behavior in the host country? Would advocates be happy with this action? The point is that corporate power used in this manner is not accountable and is not to be trusted. It is dangerous to assume that corporate managers know what is best for society, yet the social responsibility doctrine encourages nonelected corporate executives to impose their tastes and preferences on the society as a whole.

Related to this view of social responsibility is the argument that if business does take over activities that traditionally have been considered within the domain of other institutions or individuals (such as government or community agencies), it might substantially increase its power and influence over the other members and institutions of our society and become a monolithic institution, being all things to all people. Business would then provide for both our economic well-being and our social well-being. Such a concentration of power in one institution would lead to a breakdown of pluralism and pose a threat to individual freedoms of the American people.[14]

Another argument against corporate social responsibility posed by Milton Friedman is that he believes the sole responsibility of a corporation is to the shareholders. The manager of a corporation, according to Friedman, is only a salaried employee of the owners, and is legally and ethically bound to earn the highest return on their investment while staying within the rules of the game. Thus managers must abide by the principles of profit maximization. They have no legal or moral right to pursue any other objectives, social or otherwise. Business is strictly an economic institution that has the sole responsibility of creating economic wealth.[15]

---

[13]F. A. Hayek, "The Corporation in a Democratic Society," *Management and Corporations, 1975* (New York: McGraw-Hill, 1960), p. 106.

[14]Theodore Levitt, "The Dangers of Social Responsibility," *Harvard Business Review*, vol. 36, no. 5 (September–October 1958), pp. 41–50.

[15]Friedman, "Social Responsibility," pp. 122–126.

Some people question the ability of business to solve social problems. Businesspeople, by and large, have no experience in dealing with such problems. There is no reason to believe they will be any more effective, or even as effective, as other institutions that have more experience and expertise in dealing with these kinds of problems. There is not enough incentive for them to pursue social goals with the same vigor with which they pursue private goals, which would stimulate them to develop the necessary expertise and to gain needed experience.

> Private efforts it is argued, will be more efficient because corporations have demonstrated great efficiency in pursuing private goals. Unfortunately, such efficiency observed in the pursuit of private goals cannot necessarily be transferred to efforts directed toward public or social goals. The organizational structure of the corporation which delivers efficient production of private goods and services cannot be expected to pursue social goals with the same efficiency simply because the incentives for doing so are absent.[16]

Social responsibility must also be looked at in an international context. If business organizations in the United States spend significant sums of money to be socially responsible, this expenditure will increase their costs and undoubtedly be added to the cost of their products. If these firms are competing in an international marketplace with firms from other countries that do not have these social costs added to their products, these foreign firms will enjoy an even greater competitive advantage than they already do because of lower wage scales and other factors. Hence U.S. firms are likely to have lower sales internationally, which will further contribute to our balance of trade problems. The consequences of this reduced competitiveness could be loss of jobs in the United States, lower dividends for stockholders, higher prices for consumers, and other social and economic effects.

Another argument against social responsibility is that it is fundamentally a moral concept, and it is difficult if not impossible for organizations to respond to the moral imperatives inherent in such a concept. People can have moral responsibilities, but organizations cannot. They are structured to attain certain practical objectives and are basically amoral in their operations. A moral concept such as social responsibility does not apply to organizations such as corporations because they are not moral agents that can act for moral reasons.

Finally, it is argued that the concept of social responsibility is a subversive doctrine that would undermine the principles upon which a free enterprise system is based. For managers to be held accountable for the use of corporate resources to solve social problems, people affected by these decisions would have to be represented at some point in the decision-making process. This could mean that consumers, minorities, women, environmentalists, and so on

---

[16]Gerald D. Keim and Roger E. Meiners, "Corporate Social Responsibility: Private Means for Public Wants?" *Policy Review*, no. 5 (Summer 1978), p. 83.

would all have to be represented on the board of directors, for example. Such a diversity of interests means that decision making in the corporation would be political rather than economic in nature. Decisions would reflect the political power of these various interests rather than the single objective of economic profitability.[17] However, the politicalization of decision making in economic organizations mirrors the operation of a socialistic economy, thus social responsibility would subvert the principles of a free enterprise economy.

> The view has been gaining widespread acceptance that corporate officials and labor leaders have a social responsibility that goes beyond serving the interests of their stockholders or their members. This view shows a fundamental misconception of the character and nature of a free economy. In such an economy, there is one and only one social responsibility of business—to use its resources and engage in activities designed to increase its profit so long as it stays within the rules of the game, which is to say, engages in open and free competition, without deception or fraud. . . . Few trends could so thoroughly undermine the very foundations of our free society as the acceptance by corporate officials of a social responsibility other than to make as much money for their stockholders as possible. This is a fundamentally subversive doctrine.[18]

After the smoke began to clear from this debate, it was clear to both proponents and opponents of corporate social responsibility that there were certain key issues that had not, and perhaps could not, be settled. One key issue concerned the operational definition of social responsibility. How shall a corporation's resources be allocated to help solve social problems? With what specific problems shall a given corporation concern itself? What priorities shall be established? Does social responsibility refer to company actions taken to comply with the law or only to those voluntary actions that go beyond legal requirements? What goals or standards of performance are adequate? What measures shall be used to determine if a corporation is socially responsible or socially irresponsible?

The traditional marketplace provided little or no information to the manager that would be useful in making decisions about solving social problems. The concept of social responsibility provided no clearer guidelines for managerial behavior. Given this lack of precision, corporate executives who wanted to be socially responsible were left to follow their own values and interests or some rather vague generalizations about changing social values and new public expectations. What this meant in practice, however, was often difficult to determine.

Another key problem was that the concept of social responsibility did not

---

[17]See Paul MacAvoy, "Economic Efficiency the Priority. LTV: Looking Ahead—Corporate Social Responsibility: Where Does It Begin? Where Does It End?" *The Wall Street Journal*, January 20, 1983, p. 7.

[18]Milton Friedman, *Capitalism and Freedom* (Chicago: University of Chicago Press, 1962), p. 133.

take into account the competitive environment in which corporations function. Many advocates of social responsibility treated the corporation as an isolated entity that had unlimited ability to engage in unilateral social action. But it came to be increasingly recognized that corporations are severely limited in their ability to respond to social problems. If a firm unilaterally engages in social action that increases its costs and prices, it places itself at a competitive disadvantage relative to other firms in the industry that may not be concerned about being socially responsible.

> . . . every business . . . is, in effect, "trapped" in the business system that it has helped to create. It is incapable, as an individual unit, of transcending that system . . . the dream of the socially responsible corporation that, replicated over and over again can transform our society is illusory. . . . Because their aggregate power is not unified, not truly collective, not organized, they [corporations] have no way, even if they wished, of redirecting that power to meet the most pressing needs of society. . . . Such redirection could only occur through the intermediate agency of government rewriting the rules under which all corporations operate.[19]

The debate about social responsibility never took this institutional context of corporations seriously. Concerted action to solve social problems is not feasible in a competitive system unless all competitors pursue roughly the same policy on the same problems. Since collusion among competitors is illegal, the only way such concerted action can occur is when some other institution, such as government, makes all competitors engage in the same activity and pursue the same policy. And, in fact, this is what happened. While the debate about social responsibility was continuing and corporate executives were asking for a definition of their social responsibilities, government was rewriting the rules under which all corporations operate through a vast amount of legislation and regulation pertaining to the physical environment, occupational safety and health, equal opportunity, and consumer concerns.

The last issue that remained unresolved in the debate about social responsibility concerns the moral underpinnings of the notion. The term *responsibility* is fundamentally a moral term that implies an obligation to someone or something. It is clear that business has an economic responsibility to produce goods and services and perform other economic functions for society. These economic responsibilities constitute the primary reason for having a business organization. But why does business have social responsibilities? What are the moral foundations for a concern with the social impacts of business?

The proponents of social responsibility produced no clear and generally accepted moral principle that would impose upon business an obligation to

---

[19]Neil W. Chamberlain, *The Limits of Corporate Responsibility* (New York: Basic Books, 1973), pp. 4, 7.

14

work for social betterment.[20] Ascribing social responsibility to corporations does not necessarily imply that they are moral agents that are then responsible for their social impacts. Various moral strictures were used to try and impose this obligation, such as business survival, enlightened self-interest, responsible use of power, and corporate citizenship, and various arguments were made to try and link moral behavior to business performance. Little was accomplished, however, by way of developing solid and acceptable moral support for the notion of social responsibility. Thus the debate about social responsibility was very moralistic in many of its aspects—a debate that often generated a good deal of heat but very little light in most instances.

CORPORATE SOCIAL RESPONSIVENESS

The intractability of these issues, according to one author, "posed the dreadful possibilities that the debate over corporate social responsibility would continue indefinitely with little prospect of final resolution or that it would simply exhaust itself and collapse as a viable legitimate question."[21] But beginning in the 1970s, a theoretical and conceptual reorientation began to take place regarding corporate responses to the social environment. This new approach was labeled *corporate social responsiveness*, and while initially it appeared that only semantics was involved, it gradually became clear that the shift from responsibility to responsiveness was much more substantive. This shift represented an attempt to escape the unresolved dilemmas that emerged from the social responsibility debate. This new concept of corporate social responsiveness was defined by one author as follows:

> Corporate social responsiveness refers to the capacity of a corporation to respond to social pressures. The literal act of responding, or of achieving a generally responsive posture, to society is the focus of corporate social responsiveness. . . . One searches the organization for mechanisms, procedures, arrangements, and behavioral patterns that, taken collectively, would mark the organization as more or less capable of responding to social pressures. It then becomes evident that organizational design and managerial competence play important roles in how extensively and how well a company responds to social demands and needs.[22]

Thus attention shifted from debate about a moral notion, social responsibility, to a more technical or at least morally neutral term, social responsiveness. Research in corporate social responsiveness reflected this same shift and focused on internal corporate responsiveness to social problems and examined

[20]Frederick, "From CSR₁ to CSR₂," p. 5.
[21]Ibid., p. 5.
[22]Ibid., p. 6.

the ways in which corporations responded to such problems. For example, Ackerman and Bauer[23] developed a conceptual model that outlined three stages of the internal response process of corporations: awareness, commitment, and implementation (see Figure 1.2).

In the first stage, the chief executive officer recognizes a social problem to be important. This awareness is marked by several activities. Initially, the chief executive officer may begin to speak out on the issue at meetings of industry and trade associations, stockholders, and civic groups. He or she may also commit corporate resources to special projects, such as ghetto plants, waste recovery facilities, and training centers. Finally, the CEO perceives the need for an up-to-date company policy, which is then communicated to all managers in the organization. However, responsibility for implementing the policy is assigned as a matter of course to the operating units as part of their customary tasks performed in running the business. Although this approach fails to provoke acceptable action or achievement with respect to the problem in most cases, the major outcome of this phase is at least a sense of enriched purpose and an increased awareness of social problems.[24]

The key event heralding the beginning of phase two is the appointment of a staff specialist who reports to the chief executive officer or one of his or her senior staff. The staff specialist coordinates the corporation's activities in response to a social problem, helps the chief executive officer perform public duties, and ensures that the corporation's response to the problem is implemented throughout the organization. The specialist begins to gather more systematic information on the company's activities relating to the problem and matches this data with his or her assessment of environmental demands. This is the beginning of an internal data system and a systematic manner of assessing and interpreting the environment to management. The specialist also mediates between operating divisions and external organizations, including government agencies that are pressuring the corporation.[25]

Eventually, however, it is discovered that the appointment of a staff specialist still fails to elicit the corporate response envisaged in corporate policy. The staff specialist's attempts to force action on the corporation are alien to the decentralized mode of decision making within most corporate organizations. He or she becomes overburdened with moderating conflict within the organization and crisis-by-crisis involvement. However, at least a good deal of technical and administrative learning is accomplished in this phase.[26]

In the third phase, top management sees the organizational rigidities to be more serious than previously acknowledged. They cannot be waved away with a

[23]Robert W. Ackerman and Raymond A. Bauer, *Corporate Social Responsiveness* (Reston, Va.: Reston Publishing Co., 1976).

[24] Robert W. Ackerman, "How Companies Respond to Social Demands," *Harvard Business Review*, vol. 51, no. 4 (July–August 1973), p. 92.

[25]Ibid., pp. 92–93.

[26]Ibid., p. 93.

Organizational Level	Phase 1	Phase 2	Phase 3
Chief Executive	Issue: Policy problem Action: Write and communicate policy Outcome: Enriched purpose, increased awareness	Obtain knowledge Add staff specialists	Obtain organizational commitment Change performance expectations
Staff Specialists		Issue: Technical problem Action: Design data system and interpret environment Outcome: Technical and administrative learning	Provoke response from operating units Apply data system to performance measurement
Division Management			Issue: Management problem Action: Commit resources and modify procedures Outcome: Increased responsiveness

* Phase 1—social concerns exist but are not specifically directed at the corporation.
* Phase 2—broad implications for the corporation become clear but enforcement is weak or even nonexistent.
* Phase 3—expectations for corporate action become more specific and sanctions (governmental or otherwise) become plausible threats.

Figure 1.2

Ackerman/Bauer Model of Corporate Responsiveness Phases of Organizational Involvement

Source: From R. Ackerman and R. Bauer. *Corporate Social Responsiveness: The Modern Dilemma* (Reston, Va.: Reston Publishing Co., 1976), p. 128. Reprinted with permission of Reston Publishing Co., Inc., a Prentice-Hall Co., 1480 Sunset Hills Rd., Reston Va. 22090.

policy statement nor can they be overcome with a staff specialist. Instead, the whole organizational apparatus has to become involved. In this phase, the CEO attempts to make the achievement of a social policy objective a goal for all managers in the organization by institutionalizing the policy. This attempt involves modifying procedures of the company that are related to setting objectives, reward systems, performance measurement, and similar procedures.[27]

This initial research by Ackerman and Bauer triggered other models of the corporate response process. For example, S. Prakash Sethi also developed a three stage model that defined corporate behavior as social obligation, social responsibility, and social responsiveness.[28] In the first stage, social obligation, the corporation seeks legitimacy by meeting legal and economic criteria only. The corporation believes it is accountable only to its stockholders and strongly resists any regulation of its activities. In the second stage, social responsibility, the corporation searches for legitimacy by recognizing the limited relevance of meeting only legal and economic criteria, and accepts a broader set of criteria for measuring corporate performance that includes a social dimension. Management considers groups other than stockholders that might be affected by its actions and is willing to work with these outside groups for good environmental legislation. In the third stage, social responsiveness, the corporation accepts its role as defined by the social system, and recognizes that this role is subject to change over time. Furthermore, it is willing to account for its actions to other groups, even those not directly affected by its actions, and assists legislative bodies in developing better legislation. Thus business becomes an active supporter as well as promoter of environmental and social concerns.

From these examples, it can be seen that corporate social responsiveness deals with how corporations respond to social problems. Attempts were made to identify key variables within the organization that related to its responsiveness and to discover structural changes that would enable a corporation to respond to social pressures more effectively. The important questions in this research were not moral, related to whether a corporation should respond to a social problem out of a sense of responsibility, but were more pragmatic and action-oriented, dealing with the ability of a corporation to respond and what changes were necessary to enable it to respond more effectively.

One of the advantages of the social responsiveness philosophy is its managerial orientation. The concept ignores the philosophical debate about responsibility and obligation and focuses on the problems and prospects of making corporations more socially responsive. One of the reasons for research into corporate response patterns is to discover those responses that have proven to be most effective in dealing with social problems.

The approach also lends itself to more rigorous analytical research in examining specific techniques, such as environmental scanning or the social

[27]Ibid., pp. 93–95.
[28]Sethi, "Dimensions," pp. 58–64.

18

audit, to improve the response process. Such research can also discover how management can best institutionalize social policy throughout the organization. One can investigate which organizational structures are most appropriate, what role top management can play in enabling corporations to respond to social problems, what changes in the reward structure improve the corporation's response to social problems, what role the public affairs departments should play in the response process, and how social policy can be best formulated for the organization as a whole.

Given these advantages, however, the concept of corporate social responsiveness still faces the same key problems that plague the concept of social responsibility. The concept of social responsiveness does not clarify how corporate resources shall be allocated for the solution of social problems. Companies respond to different problems in different ways and to varying degrees. But there is no clear idea as to which pattern of responsiveness will produce the greatest amount of social betterment. The philosophy of responsiveness does not help the company decide what problems to get involved in and what priorities to establish. In the final analysis, it provides no better guidance to management than does social responsibility on the best strategies or policies to be adopted to produce social betterment. The concept seems to suggest that management, by determining the degree of social responsiveness and the pressure it will respond to, decides the meaning of social responsiveness and what social goods and services shall be produced.[29]

The concept of social responsiveness does not take the institutional context of business any more seriously than did social responsibility. Research has not dealt very thoroughly with the impact government regulation was making on the corporation and how the corporation was responding to this change in the political environment. Individual institutions were again treated as rather isolated entities that could choose a response pattern irrespective of the institutional context in which that corporation operated. There was not enough concern with business-government relations and the role government played in the social response process.

Finally, although the question of an underlying moral principle or theory is ignored in research dealing with corporate social responsiveness in favor of more action-oriented concerns, this turns out to be a dubious advantage. Social pressures are assumed to exist and it is believed that business must respond to them. This places business in a passive role of simply responding to social change rather than trying to influence the direction and magnitude of change. The concept of social responsiveness provides no moral reason for business to get involved in social problems. It contains no explicit ethical or moral theory and advocates no specific set of moral principles for business to follow in making social responses.[30]

[29]Frederick, "From CSR$_1$ to CSR$_2$," pp. 12–13.
[30]Ibid., pp. 14–16.

THE GROWTH OF PUBLIC POLICY

In the mid-1970s, academics and businesspeople began to realize that a fundamental change was taking place in the political environment of business—government was engaged in shaping business behavior and making business respond to a wide array of social problems by passing an unprecedented amount of legislation and writing new regulations pertaining to these problems. The political system responded to the social revolution of the 1960s by enacting over one hundred new laws regulating business activity. Many new regulatory agencies were created or new responsibilities were assigned to old agencies. These agencies issued thousands of rules and procedural requirements that affected business decisions and operations.

This regulatory role of government continued to expand until the 1980 election of Ronald Reagan. The new type of social regulation, as it came to be called, affected virtually every department of functional area within the corporation and every level of management. This growth of regulation was referred to as a second managerial revolution. Decision-making power and control over the corporation shifted from the managers of corporations to a vast cadre of government regulators who were influencing—and in many cases controlling—managerial decisions in the typical business corporation.[31] The types of decisions that became increasingly subject to government influence and control were basic operational decisions such as what line of business to go into, where products could be made, how they could be marketed, what products could be produced, and other such decisions.[32]

During the late 1970s, more and more attention was paid to the changing political environment of business. Books were written that provided a comprehensive overview of the impacts government regulation was making on business.[33] Studies were completed that attempted to measure the costs of social regulation to the private sector.[34] This activity drew attention to the political environment of business and indicated that this environment, largely hostile to business, was giving rise to legislation and regulation that interfered with the ability of business to perform its basic economic mission. Social regulation was costly, it had negative impacts on productivity, it contributed to inflation, and it diverted management attention from the basic task of running the business. Largely because of this activity, a national debate on regulation was initiated that culminated in 1980 by an administration that promised to reduce the regulatory burden on business.

[31]Murray L. Weidenbaum, *Business, Government and the Public* (Englewood Cliffs, N.J.: Prentice-Hall, 1977), p. 285.

[32]Murray L. Weidenbaum, *The Future of Business Regulation*(New York: AMACOM, 1979), p. 34.

[33]Ibid.

[34]See Murray L. Weidenbaum and Robert DeFina, *The Cost of Federal Regulation of Economic Activity* (Washington, D.C.: American Enterprise Institute, 1978); Arthur Anderson, *Cost of Government Regulation* (New York: The Business Roundtable, 1979).

The theoretical and conceptual foundations for this public policy approach were laid a few years earlier by Preston and Post who attempted to define the functions of organizational management within the specific context of public policy.[35] They stated that public policy is, along with the market mechanism, the source of guidelines and criteria for managerial behavior. The public policy process is the means by which society as a whole articulates its goals and objectives, and directs and stimulates individuals and organizations to contribute to and cooperate with them. Appropriate guidelines for managerial behavior are to be found in the larger society, not in the personal vision of managers or in the special interest of groups. Thus a business organization should analyze and evaluate pressures and stimuli coming from public policy in the same way it analyzes and evaluates market experience and opportunity.

Thus began a serious concern with public policy as a new dimension of management. Many business leaders have since recognized the importance of public policy to business and are advocating that business managers become more active in the political process and work more closely with government and other groups to help shape public policy. The motivation for this concern with public policy is clear. If the rules of the game for business are being rewritten through the public policy process and business is being forced to respond to social values through complying with laws and regulations, then business has a significant interest in learning more about the public policy process and becoming involved in helping to write the rules by which it is going to have to live. These rules should not be left solely up to public interest groups, congressional representatives and staff, or agency employees.

Business has since come to adopt a more sophisticated approach to public policy—an approach that has been called the *proactive stance*. This term means that rather than fighting change, which often proved to be a losing battle, or simply accommodating itself to change, business attempts to influence change by becoming involved in the public policy process. Thus business attempts to influence public opinion with respect to specific social issues or with regard to social issues of concern to society, and it can attempt to influence the legislative and regulatory process with regard to specific laws and regulations.

Academia has responded to this public policy focus by putting more public policy content into its old business and society or business and government courses. New courses have been instituted that focus explicitly on the public policy process, government regulation of business or public issues management. Efforts have been made to integrate public policy issues and political activities into strategic planning concepts and techniques. Research has focused on regulatory reform, political action committees, advocacy advertising, executive liability, lobbying activities, and environmental forecasting and strategic planning.

[35]Lee E. Preston and James E. Post, *Private Management and Public Policy* (Englewood Cliffs, N.J.: Prentice-Hall, 1975).

The public policy focus has some distinct advantages over the corporate social responsibility and corporate social responsiveness concepts discussed earlier. For the most part, there is no question about the nature and extent of management's social responsibilities. Once regulations are approved, these responsibilities are spelled out in excruciating detail. The government gets involved in specifying technology that can be employed, publishing labeling requirements, developing safety standards for products, specifying safety equipment, and hundreds of other such management responsibilities. Where questions arise about the legality or feasibility of regulations, the court system is available to resolve these disputes. Management is thus told in great detail what social problems to be concerned with and to what extent it has to respond.

Obviously, the public policy focus treats business in its institutional context and advocates that managers learn more about government and the public policy process so managers can appropriately influence the process. Government is recognized as the appropriate body to formalize and formulate public policy for the society as a whole. Some form of response by government to most social issues is believed to be inevitable, and no amount of corporate reform along the lines of corporate social responsibility or corporate social responsiveness is going to eliminate some form of government involvement. Government has a legitimate right to formulate public policy for corporations in response to changing public expectations.

> Society can choose to allocate its resources any way it wants and on the basis of any criteria it deems relevant. If society wants to enhance the quality of air and water, it can choose to allocate resources for the production of these goods and put constraints on business in the form of standards. . . . These nonmarket decisions are made by those who participate in the public policy process and represent their views of what is best for themselves and society as a whole. . . . It is up to the body politic to determine which market outcomes are and are not appropriate. If market outcomes are not to be taken as normative, a form of regulation which requires public participation is the only alternative. The social responsibility of business is not operational and certainly not to be trusted. When business acts contrary to the normal pressures of the marketplace, only public policy can replace the dictates of the market.[36]

There is also, at least on the surface, no need for a moral underpinning for a business obligation to produce social betterment. Society makes decisions about the allocation of resources through the public policy process based on its notions about social betterment. The result is legislation and regulation that directly impinges on business behavior. Business, then, has a moral obligation to obey the law as a good citizen. Failure to do so subjects business and its

[36]Rogene A. Buchholz, "An Alternative to Social Responsibility," *MSU Business Topics* (Summer 1977), pp. 12–16. Reprinted by permission of the publisher, Graduate School of Business Administration, Michigan State University.

executives to all sorts of penalties. The social responsibility of business is thus to follow the directives of society at large as expressed in and through the public policy process.

PUBLIC POLICY AS A NEW DIMENSION OF MANAGEMENT

Throughout most of its history, the corporation has been viewed solely as an economic institution with only economic responsibilities. These responsibilities include producing goods and services to meet consumer needs, providing employment for much of the nation's work force, paying dividends to shareholders, and making provision for future growth. If these economic responsibilities were fulfilled, business was considered to have discharged its obligations to society and made its maximum contribution to society's wealth.

As briefly described in this chapter, the last twenty-five years have seen a dramatic change in the environment in which business operates. The economic functions of business are no longer as dominant as they traditionally have been and must be seen in relation to the social and political roles business has been asked to assume. The business institution has been reshaped to meet these new responsibilities as the government, through the public policy process, has defined new roles for business to perform in society.

This changing role of business in society has, of course, made an impact on the managerial task within corporations. Managers have had to incorporate social and political concerns into their decision making. These concerns have become a part of routine business operations in many corporations as managers spend more and more of their time dealing with public policy matters.

This new dimension of management was foreseen some years ago by Walter G. Held, former director of Advanced Management Programs for the Brookings Institution.[37] Writing in the *Columbia Journal of World Business*, Held stated that management theory at that time revealed a striking penchant toward introspection with relatively little attention being paid to the world in which business was challenged to survive and grow. That external world involved a changing relationship between business and government. Many of the major problems confronting a business executive, Held asserted, were becoming less business and more societal in one of another of their aspects, and increasingly, societal problems were becoming governmental in nature.

Thus, in addition to technical, administrative, and human relations skills, the manager of a modern corporation must also learn and develop skills that are relevant to the public policy dimension of the manager's task. Research is needed, Held said, to define more precisely the nature of these skills and the proficiency required in them. At a minimum the manager must be "sensitized

---

[37]Walter G. Held, "Executive Skills: The Repertoire Needs Enlarging," *Columbia Journal of World Business*, vol. 2, no. 2 (March–April 1967), pp. 81–87.

to the importance of public policy, the processes by which it is made, and the factors that are relevant to public policy issues and their impact on business."[38]

More recently, Henry Tombari, assistant professor of Management Sciences at the California State University at Hayward, has described the role of management in modern society as "politico-economic" in nature. Such a role requires management to become involved in the public policy process as well as the market process. Management must reshape the nation's primary economic institution, the corporation, into one that is politico-economic and fits with society's values and its political system.[39]

Fran Steckmest, former public affairs consultant for Shell Oil Company, calls an executive who is skilled in the public policy process a "public policy corporate executive."[40] This type of executive deals effectively with the public policy dimension of business as an integral factor in managing the corporation. The public policy corporate executive recognizes that the day of the cloistered executive has passed and has the knowledge, skills, experience, and attitudes for this new role. Steckmest describes the qualifications that are needed to operate effectively in the public policy arena as follows:

Knowledge: A basic understanding of the U.S. social, economic, and political systems, including history, structure, institutions, and processes; an understanding of current and emerging social, economic, and political issues impacting corporations and society; familiarity with the principles and techniques for public policy analysis; and an understanding of basic attitudes and viewpoints of the leadership of significant institutions and interest groups.

Skill: Ability to apply the foregoing knowledge in planning, day-to-day decision-making, and particularly in communicating effectively under the varying circumstances required in the public policy process; e.g., person-to-person, small meetings, speeches, legislative testimony, and press, television and radio interviews.

Experience: Participation in the public policy process; e.g., analysis of public policy issues and formulation of corporate positions; explaining public issues and positions by speeches, legislative testimony and TV/radio appearances; and interaction with counterparts in government, the media, academia, unions and public interest groups. Participation in the political process; e.g., activity on behalf of a political party or advocacy group; election campaign work, or service as an elected or appointed official.

Attitude: Personal commitment to sustain and improve the U.S. system of political democracy and capitalist economy. Also, as William S. Sneath,

[38]Ibid., p. 85.

[39]Henry A. Tombari, "The New Role of Business Management," *The Collegiate Forum* (Fall 1979), p. 12.

[40]F. W. Steckmest, "Career Development of the Public Policy Corporate Executive," *Public Affairs Review* (1981), pp. 71–87.

Chairman of the Union Carbide Corporation advises: "Corporate participation in the public policy process requires conduct which engenders credibility and trust; recognition that there is no perfect public policy; and understanding that the process works by balancing interests and the corporate goal must be to strengthen—not dominate—the system."[41]

Underscoring the need for this type of executive, Steckmest goes on to say:

> [CEO's] who do not recognize the social and political role of the corporation or are reluctant to play their role in public affairs . . . forfeit their opportunity to influence or cope more effectively with the business environment. . . . The result . . . is increased isolation of the CEO from public contact, decreased sensitivity to changing public attitudes, and misinterpretation or over-reaction to new issues—too late to change the course of the now-mature issue, but with ample time to inflict page one damage on the corporation's reputation, largely by presenting a corporate image of insensitivity or inflexibility concerning the issue.[42]

These words apply not only to the chief executive officer, but to all managers whose job is affected in one way or another by public policy. According to Murray Weidenbaum, former chairman of the Council of Economic Advisors, public policy, because of its impact on business and management, is no longer a spectator sport for business.[43]

SELECTED REFERENCES

ACKERMAN, ROBERT W. *The Social Challenge to Business.* Cambridge, Mass.: Harvard University Press, 1975.

ARAM, JOHN D. *Managing Business and Public Policy: Concepts, Issues and Cases,* 2nd ed. Boston: Ballinger, 1986.

————, and RAYMOND BAUER. *Corporate Social Responsiveness: The Modern Dilemma.* Reston, Va.: Reston Publishing Co., 1976.

BOWEN, HOWARD R. *Social Responsibilities of Businessmen.* New York: Harper & Row, 1953.

CAVANAGH, GERALD F. *American Business Values,* 2nd ed. Englewood Cliffs, N.J.: Prentice-Hall, 1984.

CHAMBERLAIN, NEIL. W. *Remaking American Values: Challenge to a Business Society.* New York: Basic Books, 1977.

[41]Ibid., p. 75.
[42]Ibid., p. 74.
[43]See Murray Weidenbaum, "Public Policy: No Longer a Spectator Sport for Business," *Journal of Business Strategy,* vol. 1, no. 1 (Summer 1980).

_____. *The Limits of Corporate Responsibility.* New York: Basic Boosk, 1973.

DAVIS, KEITH, and WILLIAM C. FREDERICK. *Business and Society: Management, Public Policy, Ethics,* 5th ed. New York: McGraw-Hill, 1984.

EELLS, RICHARD, and CLARENCE WALTON. *Conceptual Foundations of Business.* Homewood, Ill.: Richard D. Irwin, 1961.

FRIEDMAN, MILTON. *Capitalism and Freedom.* Chicago: University of Chicago Press, 1962.

HYSOM, JOHN L. and WILLIAM J. BOLCE. *Business and Its Environment.* St. Paul, Minn. West, 1983.

KLEIN, THOMAS A. *Social Costs and Benefits of Business.* Englewood Cliffs, N.J.: Prentice-Hall, 1977.

LUTHANS, FRED, RICHARD M. HODGETTS, and KENNETH R. THOMPSON. *Social Issues in Business: Strategic and Public Policy Perspectives,* 4th ed. New York: Macmillan, 1984.

MADDEN, CARL H. *Clash of Culture: Management in an Age of Changing Values.* Washington, D.C.: National Planning Association, 1972.

McGUIRE, JOSEPH W. *Business and Society.* New York: McGraw-Hill, 1963.

PRESTON, LEE E., and JAMES E. POST. *Private Management and Public Policy.* Englewood Cliffs, N.J.: Prentice-Hall, 1975.

RESEARCH AND POLICY COMMITTEE OF THE COMMITTEE FOR ECONOMIC DEVELOPMENT. *Social Responsibilities of Business Corporations.* New York: Committee for Economic Development, 1971.

SAWYER, GEORGE C. *Business and Its Environment: Managing Social Impact.* Englewood Cliffs, N.J.: Prentice-Hall, 1985.

STARLING, GROVER. *The Changing Environment of Business,* 3rd ed. Boston: PWS-Kent, 1988.

STEINER, GEORGE A., and JOHN F. STEINER. *Business, Government, and Society: A Managerial Perspective,* 5th ed. New York: Random House, 1988.

STURDIVANT, FREDERICK W. *Business and Society: A Managerial Approach,* 3rd ed. Homewood, Ill.: Richard D. Irwin, 1985.

TOMBARI, HENRY A. *Business and Society: Strategies for the Environment and Public Policy.* New York: Dryden, 1984.

CONCEPTUAL FOUNDATIONS
OF PUBLIC POLICY

═══ **IDEAS TO BE FOUND** ═══
IN THIS CHAPTER

- Definition of public policy
- Elements of the market system
- Elements of public policy
- The role of public policy

The business institution has been reshaped and the managerial role has been affected by many public policy measures designed to accomplish both economic and noneconomic goals of society. Particularly over the last two decades, public policy has become an important determinant of corporate behavior as market outcomes have been increasingly altered through the public policy process.

Business functions in two major social processes through which decisions are made about the allocation of corporate resources. These are the market system and the public policy process. Both processes are necessary to encompass the broad range of decisions that a society needs to make about the corporation. The market mechanism and public policy are both sources of guidelines and criteria for managerial behavior.[1]

Business has not had to concern itself throughout most of its history with the public policy process. It could assume with some confidence that the basic value system of American society was economic and thus whatever public policies resulted were generally supportive of business interests. There are excep-

---

[1]Lee E. Preston and James E. Post, *Private Management and Public Policy: The Principle of Public Responsibility* (Englewood Cliffs, N.J.: Prentice-Hall, 1975), pp. 12–13.

tions to this, of course, but throughout most of U.S. history public policy has by and large been designed to promote business rather than interfere with its functioning.

People believed in the market mechanism to allocate resources and were willing to abide by most of its outcomes. If some people in society become extremely wealthy and others remained desperately poor, so be it—equality of wealth and income was not a goal of the market system or of society as a whole, for that matter. If polluted air and water resulted from the production process, so be it—air and water were considered to be free goods available to business management for the disposal of waste material. If some workers worked in unsafe conditions, so be it—they were free to quit and take a job elsewhere if they did not believe they were being adequately compensated.

With the social changes U.S. society has experienced over the past few decades, business can no longer assume that public policy will be supportive of its interests. In fact, most of the social responsibilities of business that are now public policy measures interfere with normal business operations and result in nonproductive investments from a strictly economic point of view. Public policy measures directed toward pollution control, safety and health, and the like interfere with the ability of business to fulfill its basic economic mission.

Thus it is important for management to have a conceptual understanding of public policy and how the public policy process differs from the market system as a resource allocator. The public policy process responds to different values or at least responds to values in a different manner from the market, and these differences are important to understand how public policy impacts business. Management also needs to understand the role that public policy plays in a market-oriented society. This chapter will provide some of these important conceptual foundations, which will serve as a theoretical underpinning for the chapters that follow, particularly those that deal with more practical considerations.

DEFINITION OF PUBLIC POLICY   There are many concepts related to public policy that need at least a working definition to provide a framework from which to discuss more practical and action-oriented concerns. A definition of the term *public policy* is in order. One way to define the term is simply to say that public policy is policy made by a public body, such as government, that is representative of the interests of the larger society. Government, as stated in Chapter 1, is the legitimate institution to make public policy. Whatever policy it formulates in the form of legislation, regulation, executive orders, or court decisions is public policy. Such a definition, however, is too simple—it does not do justice to the complexity of government or society and is unnecessarily restrictive.

Anderson, Brady, and Bullock state that a useful definition of public policy will indicate that public policy is a pattern of governmental activity on some topic or matter that has a purpose or goal. Public policy is purposeful, goal-oriented behavior rather than random or chance behavior.[2] This definition does not make the mistake of equating decision making with policy or confusing the stated goal of action with what is actually done. Public policy consists of *courses* of action, according to these authors, rather than separate discrete decisions or actions performed by government officials. Furthermore, public policy refers to what governments actually do, not to stated or intended goals of action. With these criteria in mind, the authors offer the following as their definition of public policy.

> A goal directed or purposeful course of action followed by an actor or set of actors in an attempt to deal with a public problem. This definition focuses on what is done, as distinct from what is intended, and it distinguishes policy from decisions. Public policies are developed by governmental institutions and officials through the political process (or politics). They are distinct from other kinds of policies because they result from the actions of legitimate authorities in a political system.[3]

Theodore J. Lowi defines public policy as a government's expressed intention, which is sometimes called its purpose or mission. Lowi further points out that a public policy is usually backed by a sanction, which is a reward or punishment to encourage obedience to the policy. Governments have many different sanctions or techniques of control to assure that their policies are followed.[4] Thomas R. Dye defines public policy as whatever governments choose to do or not to do. Dye argues that public policy must include all actions of government and not just stated intentions of either government or government officials. He also points out that public policy must include what government chooses not to do, as government inaction with respect to particular issues can have as great an impact on society as government action.[5]

Preston and Post offer a much different definition of public policy. First of all, they refer to policy as principles that guide action. They stress the idea of generality, by referring to principles rather than specific rules, programs, practices, or the actions themselves, and also emphasize activity or behavior as opposed to passive adherence.[6] Public policy, then, refers to the principles that guide action relating to society as a whole. These principles may be made explicit in law and other formal acts of governmental bodies, but Preston and Post are quick to point out that a narrow and legalistic interpretation of the term public policy should be avoided. Policies can be implemented without formal

[2]James E. Anderson, David W. Brady, and Charles Bullock III, *Public Policy and Politics in America* (North Scituate, Mass.: Duxbury Press, 1978), pp. 4–5.

[3]Ibid., p. 5.

[4]Theodore J. Lowi, *Incomplete Conquest: Governing America*, 2nd ed. (New York: Holt, Rinehart and Winston, 1981), p. 423.

[5]Thomas R. Dye, *Understanding Public Policy*, 3rd ed. (Englewood Cliffs, N.J.: Prentice-Hall, 1978), p. 3.

[6]Preston and Post, *Private Management*, p. 11.

articulation of individual actions and decisions. These are called *implicit policies* by Preston and Post.[7]

The first few definitions are unnecessarily restrictive. Government need not engage in a formal action for public policy to be put into effect. A good example is the debate that took place concerning South Africa. Before the U.S. government took any specific actions regarding economic sanctions, various religious and secular groups in society applied pressure by divesting themselves of stock they held in companies that were doing business in South Africa and did their best to persuade companies with facilities in the country to leave. Many companies responded to these pressures and changed their policies in doing business with or in South Africa without needing the sanctions of formal public policy to motivate them.

The Preston and Post definition, however, confuses principles and action. Principles can guide action, but the principles themselves are not necessarily the policy. More appropriately, policy refers to a specific course of action with respect to a problem, but not to the principles that guide the action. Current monetary policy is a specific course of action taken by the Federal Reserve Board to either tighten or loosen the money supply. The principles that guide this action are derived from some kind of theory, either monetarist or otherwise, but these principles do not constitute the policy itself. Public policy involves choices related to the allocation of scarce resources to achieve goals and objectives, and public policy makers must make choices among contending allocations of scarce resources. These choices represent courses of action taken with respect to particular problems.

Thus public policy is a specific course of action taken collectively by society or by a legitimate representative of society, addressing a specific problem of public concern, that reflects the interests of society or particular segments of society. This definition emphasizes a course of action rather than principles. It does not restrict such action to government, it refers to the collective nature of such action, and does not claim that each and every public policy represents the interests of society as a whole. Enough interests have to be represented, however, so that the policy is supported and can be implemented effectively.

The specific course of action that is eventually taken with respect to a problem is decided through the *public policy process*. This term refers to the various processes by which public policy is formed. There is no single process by which public policy is made in our country.[8] It is made by means of a complex, subtle, and not always formal process. Many agents who do not show up on any formal organization chart of government nevertheless influence the outcome of the public policy process.[9]

[7]Ibid.

[8]Anderson, Brady, and Bullock, *Public Policy*, p. 6.

[9]B. Guy Peters, *American Public Policy: Promise and Performance*, 2nd ed. (Chatham, N.J.: Chatham House, 1986), p. vii.

The policy of our country concerning South Africa was formed through a process involving public opinion, interest groups, institutions, demonstrations, the media, and a host of other actors. When public policy is formalized by government, there still is no single process. Public policy can be made through legislation passed by Congress, regulations issued in the Federal Register, executive orders issued by the President, or decisions handed down by the Supreme Court. The process of making public policy begins in society as problems and issues are defined. These issues may find their way into formal institutions for some policy decisions and then return to the society again for implementation.[10]

The *public policy agenda* is that collection of topics and issues with respect to which public policy may be formulated.[11] There are many problems and concerns that various people in society would like to be acted on, but only those that are important enough to receive serious attention from policymakers comprise the public policy agenda. Such an agenda does not exist in concrete form, but is found in the collective judgment of society, actions and concerns of interest groups, legislation introduced into Congress, cases being considered by the Supreme Court, and similar activities. The manner in which problems in our society get on the public policy agenda will be a subject of later discussion.

With these working definitions of some essential concepts in mind, we can turn to other conceptual considerations. Preston and Post state that the scope of managerial responsibility and the goals that management is to serve are determined through both the public policy process and the market mechanism.[12] Both public policy and the market mechanism are processes through which members of society make decisions about the allocation of resources for the provision of goods and services. These processes are quite different in concept and operation. In order to have a thorough understanding of public policy, it is necessary to compare and contrast these two methods of allocating resources.

ELEMENTS OF THE MARKET SYSTEM   The market system could be discussed as a holistic concept, as is done in most literature. But it seems that our purposes would better be served by breaking the concept of the market down into various conceptual elements that make up the whole, comparing and contrasting these elements with similar elements in the public policy process. This allows for some interesting comparisons to be made between the working of the market system and the public policy process. Table 2.1 lists the elements of both processes that will be discussed.

---

[10]Ibid.

[11]Preston and Post, *Private Management*, p. 11.

[12]Ibid., p. 13.

Table 2.1
Conceptual Elements of the Market System and the Public Policy Process

Market System	Public Policy Process
Exchange Process	Political Process
Private Goods and Services	Public Goods and Services
Economic Value System	Diverse Value System
Self-Interest	Public Interest
The Invisible Hand	The Visible Hand
Economic Roles	Political Roles
(Producers-Consumers-Investors-Employees)	(Politicians-Citizens-Public Interest Groups)
Consumer Sovereignty	Citizen Sovereignty
Profits as Reward	Power as Reward
Business as the Major Institution	Government as the Major Institution
Operating Principles: efficiency, productivity, growth	Operating Principles: justice, equity, fairness

Source: Rogene A. Buchholz, *Business Environment and Public Policy: Implications for Management and Strategy Formulation,* 2nd ed. © 1986, p. 71. Reprinted by permission of Prentice Hall, Englewood Cliffs, NJ.

The Exchange Process At the heart of a market system is an exchange process where goods and services are traded between the parties to a particular transaction. In a strictly barter type of situation where money is not used, goods and services are exchanged directly for other goods and services. Where money is present, it serves as an intermediate store of value in that goods and services are exchanged for money and then the same money can be used to purchase other goods and services immediately or some time in the future. Money has little or no value in and of itself, but it is valued for what it represents and what it can purchase. The use of money greatly facilitates exchange over a barter type of economy.

Thus, in the market system, all kinds of exchanges between people and institutions are continually taking place. People exchange their labor for wages and salaries, and in turn exchange this money for goods in a retail establishment. Investors exchange money for new stock or bond issues in a corporation which exchanges this money for purchases of raw materials or new plant and equipment. Farmers exchange their produce for money which may be used to buy new farm machinery or seed for the next planting.

Decisions as to whether or not to exchange one thing for another are made by individuals and institutions acting in their own self-interest, based on the particular value they attach to the entities being exchanged. People decide whether the item they want is of sufficient value to warrant the sacrifice of something they already have that is of value to them. Exchanges will not normally take place unless there is an increase of value to both parties of the exchange. The exchange process is not normally a zero-sum game.

Based on these individual decisions in the market, then, resources are allocated according to the preferences of individuals for one kind of merchandise over another, one job over another, the stock of one corporation over another. Thus the values assigned to particular goods and services and the resulting decisions concerning allocation of resources for the production and distribution of these goods and services are made through an exchange process.

Private Goods and Services   The nature of the goods and services that are exchanged is a second element of the market system. These goods and services are private in the sense they can be purchased and used by individual persons or institutions. They become the private property of the persons who attain them and do not have to be shared with anyone. The goods and services exchanged in the market are thus *divisible* into individual units and can be totally consumed and enjoyed by the people or institutions who obtain the property rights to them.

Thus one can buy a house, car, or piece of furniture, and these items become private property to enjoy and use entirely in one's own self-interest. People can also contract for or purchase services and have a legal right to expect that the services will be provided. The legal system supports this concept of property rights and enables people to enforce these rights if necessary to protect their property from unwanted encroachment by others. This social arrangement provides a degree of security for people regarding their own property and forces them, in turn, to respect the property rights of others. Thus property rights can be assigned to the goods and services traded in the market because of their divisibility into individual units that can be privately enjoyed and consumed.

Common Economic Value System   The values of all these entities that are exchanged in the market system are able to be expressed in common units that form an underlying economic value system. The worth of an individual's labor, the worth of a particular product or service, the worth of a share of stock can all be expressed in economic terms. This is not to suggest that the fundamental value of everything is economic in nature. One person might value a particular piece of residential property because of the view it commands of the surrounding countryside, thus making the aesthetic value of the property of primary concern. Another person might desire a particular art object because of its religious or historical value. However, in order for exchange to take place where money is involved, these other values eventually have to be translated into economic values.

This economic value system thus serves as a common denomination in that the worth of everything can be expressed in a common unit of exchange, such as dollars and cents. The terms on which an object can be acquired in the marketplace reflect the collective subjective evaluations of the worth of that object to many different people. This facilitates the exchange process and makes it possible for individuals to assess trade-offs more easily than if such a common denominator were not available. People can make an informal benefit-cost analysis when making a decision in the marketplace by comparing the benefits a good or service will provide them with the costs involved in acquiring the product or service. For example, people enter a store with money they have earned. They assess the price of the goods available by comparing the benefits these goods will provide to the real costs (the effort involved in earning the money) of attaining them. Since both sides of this benefit-cost equation are expressed in the same units, this assessment can be made rather easily.

This common value system allows a society to allocate its resources according to the collective preferences of its members. All the diverse values that people hold in relation to private goods and services are aggregated through the market system into a collective demand schedule. If a particular product is not valued very highly by great numbers of people, aggregate demand for that product will not be very high. Its price will have to be low in order for it to be sold, if it can be sold at all, and not many resources will be used for its production. If a particular job is valued very highly by society and the people who can perform the job are scarce relative to demand, the wage or salary paid to perform the job will have to be high to attract people to perform the job. Resources are thus allocated according to the values of society as expressed through the exchange process. Resources will go where the price, wage and salary, or return on investment are highest, all other things being equal. Thus resources are allocated to their most productive use where they can be combined to produce the greatest wealth for society in comparison with other alternatives.

Self-Interest

In a market economy, people are free to use their property, choose their occupation, and strive for economic gain in any way they choose—subject, of course, to limitations that may be necessary to protect the right of all people to do the same thing. Society may also place limitations on the use of property and choice of occupation because of moral standards. The selling of drugs, for example, is illegal, as are many other uses of property for purposes that are not seen as contributing to the welfare or wealth of society.

The pursuit of self-interest is assumed to be a universal principle of human behavior, with a powerful advantage, as far as motivation is concerned, over other forms of human behavior. The pursuit of one's own interest is believed to elicit far more energy and creativity from human beings than would the pursuit of someone else's interests, especially under coercive conditions. Not only is it difficult to determine what the interests of other people are, it is also difficult to find a way to sustain a high level of motivation if much of the effort one expends goes for the benefit of other people.

The definition of self-interest in a market economy is not provided by government for all its citizens but is determined by each individual participating in the exchange process. If the self-interest of an individual were defined by someone else, the concept would have no meaning. Thus self-interest is an individual concept. Yet, within a market system, the definition of self-interest is not completely arbitrary, depending on the whims of each individual. The existence of a common underlying economic value system makes the definition of self-interest take on a certain economic rationality.

If one is engaged in some aspect of the productive process, economic rationality dictates that self-interest consists of maximizing one's return on his or her investment. Entrepreneurs are expected to maximize profits, investors to maximize their returns in the stock market, and sellers of labor are expected to obtain the most advantageous terms for themselves. Consumers are expected to maximize the satisfaction to themselves through their purchases of goods and services on the marketplace. If one were to seek the lowest return on investment or the least satisfaction from goods and services, this would be viewed as irrational behavior under normal circumstances.

The Invisible Hand

Resources are allocated in a market system by an invisible hand, a mythological concept to be sure, but one that is a crucial element of a market system. There is no supreme authority in government such as a planning commission that makes decisions for the society as a whole about what goods and services get produced and in what quantities, and allocates resources accordingly. These decisions are made by the individuals who participate in the marketplace and express their preferences as based on their self-interest. These preferences are aggregated by the market, and, if strong enough relative to particular goods and services, elicit a response from the productive mechanism of society to supply the goods and services desired.

The invisible hand consists of the forces of supply and demand that result from the aggregation of individual decisions by producers and consumers in the marketplace. Resources are allocated to their most productive use as defined by these individuals collectively. According to Adam Smith, society as a whole benefits more from this kind of a resource allocation process than if someone were to consciously try and determine the best interests of society. Pursuit of one's own selfish ends, without outside interference, is believed to result in the greatest good for the greatest number of people.

> As every individual, therefore, endeavours as much as he can both to em-
> ploy his capital in the support of domestic industry, and so to direct that
> industry that its produce may be of the greatest value; every individual
> necessarily labours to render the annual revenue of the society as great as
> he can. He generally, indeed, neither intends to promote the public inter-
> est, nor knows how much he is promoting it. By preferring the support of
> domestic to that of foreign industry, he intends only his own security; and
> by directing that industry in such a manner as its produce may be of the
> greatest value, he intends only his own gain, and he is in this, as in many
> other cases, led by an invisible hand to promote an end which was no part of

his intention. Nor is it always the worse for the society that it was no part of it. By pursuing his own interest he frequently promotes that of the society more effectually than when he really intends to promote it.[13]

Economic Roles

The marketplace requires certain roles to be performed in order for it to function. All of these roles have an economic character to them. People can be producers who turn raw materials into goods that sell on the market, consumers who buy these goods and services for their use, investors who provide capital for the producers, or employees who work for producers and receive wages or salaries in exchange for their contributions to the production process. All of these roles are vital to the functioning of a market system. They are called economic roles because people are pursuing their economic self-interest in performing them. There are other important roles to be performed in society, of course, but economic roles are dominant in a society organized around free market principles.

Consumer Sovereignty

The most important economic role in a market system is performed by the consumer. At least in theory, consumers, through their choices in the marketplace, guide the productive apparatus of society and collectively decide what goods and services get produced and in what quantities. When there is enough demand for a product, resources will be allocated for its production. If there is not enough demand, the product will not be produced and resources will go elsewhere.

Consumer sovereignty is not to be confused with consumer choice. In any society, consumers always have a choice to purchase or not to purchase the products available in the marketplace. Consumer choice exists in a totally planned economy. Consumer sovereignty implies that the range of products with which consumers are confronted is also a function of their decisions, and not the decisions of a central planning authority. Thus consumers are ultimately sovereign over the entire system.

There are those who would argue that consumer sovereignty in today's marketplace is a fiction—that consumers are manipulated by advertising, packaging, promotional devices, and other sales techniques to buy a particular product. Sometimes this manipulation is said to be so subtle that the consumer is unaware of the factors influencing his or her decision. Thus the demand function itself has come under control of corporations and consumer sovereignty is a myth. Producers are sovereign over the system, and consumers are made to respond to the producers decisions about what to produce.[14]

[13]Adam Smith, *The Wealth of Nations* (New York: Modern Library, 1937), p. 423.

[14]See, for example, John Kenneth Galbraith, *The New Industrial State* (Boston: Houghton Mifflin, 1967).

Although there may be some truth to these views, they do not constitute the whole truth. It is hard to believe that consumers are totally manipulated by these techniques. They still have to make choices among competing products, and the producers selling these products are all trying to manipulate the consumer. In the final analysis, the individual consumer is still responsible for his or her decision. Undoubtedly many factors besides the particular sales techniques employed by a company influence the purchase decision. In the absence of a central authority making production decisions for the entire society, it is safe to assume that some degree of consumer sovereignty exists. As long as there are competing products or acceptable substitutes, some products may not sell well enough to justify continued production. They disappear from the marketplace, not because producers desire to remove them, but because consumers have decided not to buy them in sufficient quantitites.

Profits as Reward

The reason products disappear when they do not sell is because there is no profit to be made. Profits are the lifeblood of a business organization, and without profits a business organization normally cannot survive. Profits are a reward to the business organization or entrepreneur for the risks that have been taken in producing a good or service for the market. If the management of a business organization guesses wrong and produces something people do not want and cannot be persuaded to buy, they will find that the market is a stern taskmaster. No rewards will be received for this effort, and the product will be removed from the market.

Profits are also a reward for combining resources efficiently to be able to meet or beat the competition in producing a product for which there is a demand. Some entrepreneurs may be able to pay lower wages, employ a more efficient technology, or have some other competitive advantage. A lower price can be charged and high-cost producers are driven from the market. This effort is rewarded with increased profits as society benefits from having its resources used more efficiently.

Business as the Major Institution

The major institutional actor in the market system is the business organization that is driven by the profit motive to produce goods and services to meet consumer demand. This is not to suggest that business is the only institution that is producing something useful for society. Hospitals provide medical services and governments produce a wide range of goods and services for citizens. But these other institutions are not driven by the profit motive as is business and cannot offer the full range of goods and services that business can when functioning in a market economy. The business organization is the primary productive institution in a market economy, and most of the decisions about the allocation of society's resources for the production of private goods and services are made within the walls of the business institution.[15]

Operating Principles   The primary operating principles that are used to measure performance in a market system are concepts such as efficiency, productivity, and growth. There are quantitative measures for these concepts, and although they may be imprecise in many respects, these measures at least provide some idea as to how well the market system is functioning. If economic growth is declining or negative, for example, the economy is judged to be functioning poorly, and policy measures are taken to try and correct this deficiency. These principles are thus crucial to the operation of a market system. Good performances along these dimensions of efficiency, productivity, and growth help a great deal to make market outcomes acceptable to society.

ELEMENTS OF PUBLIC POLICY   The public policy process can be broken down into comparable elements to facilitate discussion and comprehension of the concept. Such a procedure will enable a comparison with the market system to be made element by element, rather than trying to compare the two complex concepts as a whole. This procedure should introduce more precision into the discussion, a most worthy goal when dealing with such comprehensive intellectual abstractions.

Political Process   Instead of an exchange process, values are assigned to particular entities in the public policy process and decisions are made about allocation or resources through a political process. The political process is a complex amalgam of power and influence that involves many actors pursuing different interests who try to persuade and influence others in order to achieve their objectives. Politics has often been called the art of the possible, meaning a balancing of interests is necessary to resolve conflicts in order to arrive at a common course of action. People usually have to be willing to give up something in order to reach agreement among all the members of a group. The usual outcome of the political process reflects the principle that no one gets everything he or she wants and yet everyone has to get something in order to satisfy themselves that the

[15]At first glance, it might seem that such an active role for business conflicts with the principles of consumer sovereignty described earlier. If productive institutions are guided by consumers as they make choices in the marketplace, management decisions could be seen as merely responses to the choices made by consumers. But business organizations are not merely passive entities in the market system, and real decisions are made in these organizations about whether or not to meet consumer demand, what technology to employ, and so on, that take consumer preferences into account along with many other factors. Thus the principle of consumer sovereignty does not mean business is simply a passive respondent.

objective is worth pursuing. Thus compromise and negotiation are necessary skills to participate effectively in the political process.

The function of a political process is to organize individual effort to achieve some kind of collective goal or objective that individuals or private groups find it difficult, if not impossible, to achieve by themselves. People participate in the exchange process because they believe they can achieve their individual objectives better by making some kind of trade, but the parties to the exchange do not have to share objectives or agree on a course of action. Let's say some people in a community want to build a road, which no one person in the community can or would want to build alone. To get the road built, enough people in the total community have to agree they want a road and are willing to contribute the necessary resources. But even after this decision is made, these people are going to have different ideas as to what kind of road should be built, where it should be located, and other related matters. These differences have to be resolved through the political process in order for the road to be constructed.

The task of the political system is to manage such conflicts by (1) establishing rules of the game for participants in the system, (2) arranging compromises and balancing interests of the various participants, (3) enacting compromises in the form of public policy measures, and (4) enforcing these public policies.[16] The outcome of the political process is not usually under the control of a single individual or group as is the outcome of an exchange process. The outcome of the political process depends on how much power and influence one has, how skillful one is at compromising and negotiating, and the variety and strength of other interests involved. Decisions can be made by vote (where the majority rule) by building a consensus, or by exercising raw power and coercing other members of a group to agree with your course of action. Outcomes are highly uncertain, in most instances, and contain many surprises.

The outcome of the exchange process is much more certain, as people usually know that their decisions are directly connected to the outcome. If people choose to part with a sum of money, they only do so because they know they will receive a product or service they want in return. Producers sell their products for a specific sum of money, not for some promise to pay an unspecified amount. The value of goods and services, as well as money, changes over time. But at the discrete moment of exchange, people usually have a pretty good idea of what they are getting.

In the political process, especially if it involves a representative democracy, people are not always certain what they are getting. They may vote for a candidate they believe will support the issues they favor and who seems to share similar values. But elected public officials may not carry out their campaign promises, and even if they do, their vote may count for nothing in the final outcome if few others voted the same way on the issues.

People pursue their own interests through the political process based on

---

[16]Dye, *Understanding Public Policy*, p. 23.

the values they hold relative to the objectives being sought collectively. But these values cannot be expressed directly or precisely, particularly in a representative democracy. Individual preferences are rarely matched because of the need for compromise, and the outcome is highly uncertain because of the complex interactions that take place between all the parties to a transaction. Yet resources for the attainment of public policy objectives are allocated through the political process that combines individual preferences into common objectives and courses of action.

Public Goods and Services

Public policy decisions have to be made through a political process because of the nature of the goods and services that are provided. These goods and services can appropriately be referred to as public goods and services (see box), as distinguished from the private goods and services described in the market system.

Public goods and services are *indivisible* in the sense that the quantity produced cannot be divided into individual units to be purchased by people according to their individual preferences. One cannot, for example, buy a piece of clean air to carry around and breathe wherever one goes. Nor can one buy a share of national defense over which one would have control. This indivisibility gives these goods their public character because if people are to have public goods and services at all, they must enjoy roughly the same amount.[17] No one owns these goods and services individually—they are collectively owned and private property rights do not apply. Thus there is nothing to be exchanged and decisions about these goods and services cannot be made through the exchange process.

The concept of public goods and services needs further explanation. The literature about this subject usually refers to national defense as the best example of a public good—something tangible provided by government for all its citizens that cannot be provided by the citizens for themselves.

Pollution is generally considered to be an example of an externality, defined as either a beneficial or detrimental (pollution is detrimental) effect on a third party (homeowner who lives close to a polluting factory) who is not involved in the transaction between the principals (customer and producer) who caused the pollution because of their activities in the marketplace. Yet the results of pollution control (clean air and water) can also be called a public good as they are entities with beneficial physical characteristics for human health that are widely shared in different amounts by people in society.

Something like equal opportunity might be called a social value in

---

[17]John Rawls, *A Theory of Justice* (Cambridge, Mass.: Harvard University Press, 1971), p. 266.

that it is a particular goal of our society that is important for many of its members because of their individual values or ethical sensibilities. Yet if these values are widely shared or an important part of a society's heritage, policies designed to promote equal opportunity also produce a public good in that it is good for society to implement its basic values.

Thus the concept of public goods and services as used here is an all-inclusive concept that refers to all these various outcomes of the public policy process. This broader use also includes the maintenance of competition when this is a basic value of a society and maintenance of economic stability that makes it possible for people to find employment and maintain or improve their material standard of living.

Source: Rogene A. Buchholz, *Business Environment and Public Policy: Implications for Management and Strategy Formulation*, 2nd ed., © 1986, p. 78. Reprinted by permission of Prentice Hall, Englewood Cliffs, NJ.

One might argue, however, that even though public goods and services have these characteristics, they could still be provided through the market system rather than the public policy process. For example, suppose the market offered a consumer the following choice: two automobiles in a dealer's showroom are identical in all respects, even as to gas mileage. The only difference is that one car has pollution control equipment to reduce emissions of pollutants from the exhaust whereas the other car has no such equipment. The car with the pollution control equipment sells for $500 more than the other.

If a person values clean air, it could be argued that he or she would choose the more expensive car to reduce air pollution. However, such a decision would be totally irrational from a strictly self-interest point of view. The impact that one car out of all the millions on the road will have on air pollution is infinitesimal. Hence there is no relationship in this kind of a decision between costs and benefits. In effect one would be getting nothing for one's money unless many other people made the same decision. Such actions, however, assume a common value for clean air that does not exist. Thus the market never offers consumers this kind of choice. Automobile manufacturers know that pollution control equipment will not sell in the absence of federally mandated standards.

There is another side to the coin, however. If enough people in a given area did buy the more expensive car so that the air was significantly cleaner, there would be a powerful incentive for others to be free riders. Again, the impact of any one car would not alter the character of the air over a region. One would be tempted to buy the polluting car for a cheaper price and be a free rider by enjoying the same amount of clear air as everyone else and not paying a cent for its provision.

Because of these characteristics of human behavior and the nature of public goods and services, the market system will not work to provide these goods and services for a society that wants them. When goods are indivisible among large numbers of people, the individual consumer's actions as expressed in the market will not lead to the provision of these goods.[18] Society must register its desire for public goods and services through the political process because the bilateral exchanges facilitated by the market are insufficiently inclusive.[19] Only through the political process can compromises be reached that will resolve the value conflicts that are inevitable in relation to public goods and services.

Diverse Value System   Value conflicts are more pronounced in the public policy process because of the existence of a diverse value system. There is no underlying value system into which other values can be translated. No common denominator exists by which to assess trade-offs and make decisions about resource allocation to attain some common economic objective, such as improving one's material standard of living or increasing the nation's gross national product.

What is the overall objective, for example, of clean air and water, equal opportunity, occupational safety and health, and similar public goods and services? One could say that all these goods and services are meant to improve the quality of life for all members of society. If this is the objective, how can benefits be assessed in relation to costs, and trade-offs analyzed?

The costs of pollution control equipment, for example, can be determined in economic terms. This equipment should be beneficial to health by reducing the amount of harmful pollutants people have to breathe and improving the ascetic dimension by making the air smell better. Safety may also be enhanced through an improvement of visibility for aircraft. The difficulty lies in translating all these diverse benefits into economic terms so that a direct comparison with costs can be made.

What is the price tag for the lives saved by avoiding future diseases that may be caused by pollution? What is the economic value of having three more years added on to one's life span because of living in a cleaner environment? What is the value of reducing the probability that children will be born with abnormalities because of reduction of toxic substances in the environment? What is the value of perserving one's hearing by reducing the noise emitted by machinery in the workplace? What is the appropriate value of being able to see the mountains from one's house?

The difficulty of expressing all these intangibles in economic terms so that people's preferences are matched should be apparent. But in spite of these difficulties, insurance agents, legal experts, scientists, and agency administrators routinely assign values to human life, ranging from a few dollars to many millions of dollars, depending on the methods used to calculate these values.

[18]Gerald Sirkin, *The Visible Hand: The Fundamentals of Economic Planning* (New York: McGraw-Hill, 1968), p. 45.

[19]James Buchanan, *The Demand and Supply of Public Goods* (Chicago: Rand McNally, 1968), p. 8.

One of the most precise ways of calculating the value of a human life it to break down the body into its chemical elements. Some experts have determined that the value of a human life on this basis is about $8.37, which has increased $1.09 in six years because of inflation.[20] Obviously, such a method is not acceptable for most public policy purposes, and other methods have been used or proposed by policymakers.

- An early approach to placing a value on an individual's life was called the foregone earnings method. This is an idea based upon the discounted cash flow technique. It calculates the present value of estimated future earnings that are foregone due to premature death. In addition, estimated medical costs and other associated expenses are often included.
- A newer method has arisen that is termed "willingness to pay." The value of life is estimated from questions people are asked about how much they would be willing to pay to reduce the probability of their death by a certain small amount. Results of these studies yield values anywhere between $50,000 and $8 million per life saved.
- A third method is based on the analysis of wage premiums for dangerous jobs or hazardous occupations. For example, if a group of workers is paid a wage increment of $3 million for jobs that have two deaths per year above the expected frequency, they have valued each life at $1.5 million. Studies of this type have yielded values between $300,000 and $3.5 million.[21]

The diversity of economic valuation that results from these techniques is not surprising. People are going to place vastly different values on their lives. Some people may believe they are worth any economic expenditure no matter how great. Others may feel their lives are relatively worthless. People's valuation of their lives will also change with age and other circumstances. Such diversity renders the use of analytical techniques such as those described above highly questionable.

When people are making individual choices about private goods and services, a diverse value system presents no problems. They are forced to translate these diverse values into economic terms and make choices accordingly. But making choices about public goods and services is another matter. There seems to be no way to force a translation of the diversity into a common value system that is acceptable, realistic, and appropriate. Should more money be spent on reducing the emissions from coke ovens than on improving highway safety? How much money should be spent on cleaning up existing dumpsites for hazardous wastes? For these kinds of public policy questions, the political process seems to be a reasonable way to aggregate the diversity of people's values to make a decision when there is no common value system to use for more rational calculations.

[20]William R. Greer, "Pondering the Value of a Human Life," *The New York Times*, August 16, 1975, p. 16.

[21]John D. Aram, *Managing Business and Public Policy* (Boston: Pitman, 1983), pp. 229–230.

The Public Interest   The universal motivating principle in the
public policy process is the public inter-
est rather than self-interest. This principle is invoked by those who make
decisions about public policy. Elected public officials often claim to be acting in
the interests of the nation as a whole or of their state or congressional district.
Public interest groups also claim to be devoted to the general or national
welfare. These claims make a certain degree of sense. When politicians have to
make a decision about the provision of some public good or service, they cannot
claim to be acting in the self-interest of everyone in their constituency. When
goods and services are indivisible across large numbers of people, it is impossible for individual preferences to be matched. Nor can public policy makers
claim to be acting in their own self-interest; such a claim is not politically
acceptable. Some more general principle such as the public interest has to be
invoked to justify the action.

The definition of the public interest, however, is problematical. The term
can have at least four meanings.[22] The public interest can refer to the aggregation, weighing, and balancing of a number of special interests. In this view the
public interest results through the free and open competition of interested
parties who have to compromise their differences to arrive at a common course
of action. The public interest is the sum total of all the private interests in the
community that are balanced for the common good. This definition allows for a
diversity of interests.

The public interest can also refer to a common or universal interest that all
or at least most of the members of a society share. A decision is in the public
interest if it serves the ends of the whole public rather than those of some sector
of the public, if it incorporates all of the interests and concepts of value that are
generally accepted in our society. Such a definition assumes a great deal of
commonality as to basic wants and needs of the people who comprise a society.

There is also an idealist perspective as to the meaning of the public
interest. Such a definition judges alternative courses of action in relation to
some absolute standard of value, that in many cases exists independently of the
preferences of individual citizens. The public interest is more than the sum of
private interests; it is something distinct and apart from basic needs and wants
of human beings. Such a definition has a transcendent character and refers to
such abstractions as "intelligent goodwill" or "elevated aspirations" or "the ultimate reality" that human beings should strive to attain. The difficulty with this
definition is finding someone with a God-like character who can define these
abstractions in an acceptable manner.

Another definition of the public interest focuses on the process by which
decisions are made rather than the specification of some ideal outcome. This

[22]See Douglas G. Hartle, *Public Policy Decision Making and Regulation* (Montreal, Canada: The
Institute for Research on Public Policy, 1979), pp. 213–218.

definition involves the acceptance of some process, such as majority rule, to resolve differences among people. If the rules of the game have been strictly followed, which in a democratic setting means that interested parties have had ample opportunity to express their views, then the outcome of the process has to be in the public interest by definition.

These definitions all have their problems, making an acceptable definition as difficult to arrive at as a specific public policy itself. Most public policies undoubtedly reflect all of these definitions in some manner. Before leaving this subject, one additional caveat must be mentioned. Those in a position of power and influence can never really escape their own self-interest and legitimately claim to be acting solely in the public interest or general good of society, however it is defined. Politicians want to get reelected and will vote for those goods and services they believe have an appeal to the majority of their constituency. Public interest groups want to extend their power and influence in society, and might be more appropriately called special interest groups. Thus the definition of the public interest can never be entirely divorced from the self-interest of those who are doing the defining.[23]

The Visible Hand

Whatever definition of the public interest is invoked, resources are allocated in the public policy process by a visible hand. That visible hand is the group of decision makers in the public policy process who have been most active and influential in arriving at a common course of action. They are the ones who consciously allocate resources for the production of public goods and services they believe the public wants—those goods and services they believe serve the public interest. If they make the wrong decisions and do not adequately serve the public interest, however it may be defined, they can be held accountable and removed from their position of power and influence.

Something of a supply and demand process occurs here in that if enough citizens demand something, at least in a democratic society, the system will eventually respond. But the decisions about resource allocation are visible in that certain people in the public policy process—elected public officials, government bureaucrats, and public interest groups—can be held accountable for these decisions if they are not in the public interest and thus not acceptable throughout the entire society. The market system does not fix responsibility so precisely, as decisions about resource allocation are made by thousands of people participating in the marketplace. The concept of the invisible hand is thus appropriate for a market system but not for the public policy process.

[23]There is a school of thought called *public choice theory* that looks at government decision makers as rational, self-interested people who are just like the rest of us, and view issues from their own perspective and act in light of the personal incentives. While voters, politicians, and bureaucrats may desire to reflect the "public interest" and often advocate it in support of their decisions, this desire is only one incentive among many with which they are faced and is likely to be outweighed by more powerful incentives related to self-interest of one sort or another.

Political Roles People play diffferent roles in the public policy process than they do in the market system. These roles, of course, have a political character. Elected public officials are directly involved in the public policy process, but they are few in number relative to the total population. The same can be said of other government workers, such as those who serve on congressional staffs or regulatory agencies and have a real influence on public policy outcomes. These are the key decision makers in the public policy process and they have the most visible impact on the outcome of the public policy process.

The average person simply plays the role of citizen by voting for a representative of his or her choice, contributing money to a campaign, writing to elected public officials about particular issues, and similar measures. At the extreme, this role could involve driving one's tractor to Washington, D.C. and clogging the city streets in protest of certain governmental actions. Joining large social movements such as the civil rights movement is another way for the average person to exercise political influence. Widespread support for issues such as this has an effect on the voting of elected public officials. Finally, people can join public interest groups or support them with contributions and fulfill a political role in this fashion. Most citizens, however, are those who elect others to engage in the business of governing in the public interest and go about their daily tasks with a minimum of political participation.

Citizen Sovereignty Citizens are supposedly sovereign over the public policy process as consumers are supposedly sovereign over the market system. The vote is the ultimate power that citizens have in a democratic system. Public officials can be voted out of office if they do not perform as the majority of citizens in their constituency would like. The citizens can then vote someone else into office whom they believe will make decisions about allocation of resources for production of public goods and services that are more consistent with the citizens' preferences. In the interim period between votes, citizens can express their preferences and try to influence the outcome of the public policy process either individually, through contact with public officials, or collectively, through interest groups.

There are two problems with this notion of citizen sovereignty that need to be mentioned. One concerns the idea of manipulation that was mentioned in connection with consumer sovereignty. Candidates for elected public office are advertised and packaged as if they are products, and in recent years, television advertising has been used more and more in political campaigns. Are citizens being manipulated by these promotional techniques, causing them to vote for an image created on television rather than for an individual whom they have little or no chance to know? Has citizen sovereignty been rendered obsolete by the packaging of candidates to appeal to the prejudices of people with little consideration given to the merits of issues important to the election?

Another problem with citizen sovereignty is the bad reputation the average citizen has regarding participation in the political process. Voter turnouts are often very low in many elections. A number of those who do vote probably know little about the candidates and the issues that are at stake in the election. Many people are not interested in public issues, particularly those that do not affect them directly. Taking an interest means spending time on political concerns that might be more profitably devoted to the family or to leisure activities. Many citizens do not derive primary satisfaction from political participation and, unlike the marketplace, they do not have to participate to fulfill their basic needs and wants. The cost of participation in public affairs seems greater than the return. People who do not participate thus sacrifice their sovereignty and power to the minority—those individuals in the society who do have a strong interest in political life and choose to actively participate in the formulation of public policy for the society as a whole.[24]

Power as Reward   The reward for a public official or candidate for office is the attainment of power and influence in the public policy process. If an incumbent has done a good job in office—assessed citizen preferences correctly and been able to supply the public goods and services the citizens of his or her constituency want—he or she will most likely be reelected and retain the power they acquired. If there is enough dissatisfaction with the incumbent, and a newcomer comes along who appears to be more responsive to citizen preferences and makes promises that people believe, that new person may be elected to office and granted the power that goes with the office.

The elected public official seeking power can be compared with the entrepreneur seeking profits. Although power is not as quantifiable a concept as profit, it is no less a powerful motivator for those who want to be in positions of influence. Power accrues to people who make correct decisions, who are skillful at compromise and negotiation, and who can persuade people that they can be trusted with power and will use it in the public interest so that the society as a whole benefits. Power is the lifeblood of politicians. Without it they will wither and die and eventually fade away into oblivion.

Government as the Major   The major institutional force operative in
Institution   the public policy process is government, primarily the federal government and to a lesser extent state and local government. Other institutions are also active in the public policy process. For example, business has always been and will continue to be an institutional force in the public policy process. Public interest groups are another institutional force that can be quite influential. As stated

[24]Aaron Wildavsky, *Speaking Truth to Power: The Art and Craft of Policy Analysis* (Boston: Little, Brown, 1979), pp. 253–254.

previously, not all public policies need to involve formal government action to be effective.

But government is the principal institution involved in formulating public policy that shapes the behavior of business organizations. Many policies do not become public policies until they are adopted, implemented, and enforced by some governmental institution. Government lends legitimacy to policies by making them legal obligations that command the loyalty of citizens. Government policies extend to all people in a society, whereas the policies of other groups or organizations, such as business, reach only a segment of society. Government also monopolizes the legitimate use of force in seeing to it that public policies are followed by those who are affected. Only government can legitimately imprison violators of its policies.[25]

Government acts as a promoter of business through tariff protection, subsidies, tax credits, and tax breaks. In some situations, government becomes a guarantor of business survival. It regulates business in four aspects: competitive behavior, industry regulation, social regulation, and labor-management relations. Government is a buyer of goods and services from private business. In this capacity it can promote such public policy goals as equal opportunity through the terms of the contract it makes with private business. It manages the economy through the use of fiscal and monetary policies. In all of these activities government is engaged in formulating and implementing public policy that shapes and guides business behavior. Most of the decisions about the allocation of resources for the production of public goods and services are made by government, which has a legitimate right to formulate public policy for the society as a whole.

Operating Principles

The operating principles of the public policy process are concepts like justice, equity, and fairness. These concepts are often invoked to justify the decisions made in the public policy process about resource allocation. Although efficiency is certainly a consideration in many public policy measures, it will in many cases be sacrificed in the interests of justice, equity, and fairness. Government moves forward by a complex process of compromise and negotiation and divides authority and applies checks and balances to limit power that would never make sense for private business organizations.

There are no quantitative measures for these concepts of justice, equity, and fairness, but nonetheless, society has some idea as to how well the public policy process is performing along these lines. If certain courses of action are seen as grossly unfair to enough people in society, pressures will mount to change the policies. These principles are important to the operation of the public policy process and make the outcomes acceptable to society. For instance, if justice has been served by a policy, an outcome will be accepted even though it may entail great sacrifice on the part of the citizens affected.

---

[25]Dye, *Understanding Public Policy*, p. 20.

THE ROLE OF PUBLIC POLICY The Preston-Post view of public policy and the market system holds that both of these processes are the source of guidelines for managerial behavior. However, they do not have the same legitimacy in U.S. society when it comes to allocating resources efficiently and productively. Since government is the major institution involved in the public policy process, our attitudes toward public policy are all tied up with government. Our ideology holds that government is a necessary evil to provide for the national defense and other necessary items that cannot be provided in any other manner. Many believe that the best government is the government that governs least, and that government is inefficient and cannot be trusted to allocate society's resources to their best uses.

We thus have no positive theory of government because we believe our society is basically a market-oriented society. The market can be trusted to allocate resources efficiently, and government interference should be kept to a minimum. Government exists to help the private sector do its job better; government does not have the same kind of legitimacy as does the private sector for many resource allocation decisions.

Given this kind of ideology, then, what role does public policy play in society? Why is public policy important in dealing with certain public problems at various times in our history? Perhaps this role can be best understood by describing a framework of social change called the *mythic/epic cycle of social change* and applying this to a market-oriented society. This theory or model grows out of the post-Enlightenment critical study of the history of religions.[26] As the name suggests, this theory consists of two major cycles. The mythic cycle addresses itself to the problem of maintaining a shared sense of meaning and continuity in a society. The epic cycle deals with radical change from essentially one society to another.

According to this theory, societies maintain a shared sense of meaning and a particular vision of reality through myth. *Myth* is that collection of shared stories that mediate ultimate reality to a given society, and is, therefore, directed toward psyche, internal reality, personal transformation, and process. Societies usually do everything they can to keep myths alive to preserve themselves and maintain continuity for as long as possible. Societies undergo radical change, however, through the process of an epic struggle of a cultural hero. *Epic* focuses on history, human relationships, and events. Together these cycles provide a model for a society in equilibrium and a society undergoing radical change.[27]

[26]See Owen Barfield, *Poetic Diction: A Study in Meaning* (New York: McGraw-Hill, 1964); Joseph Campbell, *The Hero with a Thousand Faces*, 2nd ed. (Princeton, N.J.: Princeton University Press, 1971); Edward F. Edinger, *Ego and Archetype* (Baltimore, Md.: Penguin Books, 1974); Mircea Eliade, *Patterns in Comparative Religion* (New York: Sheed & Ward, 1958); and Claude Levi-Strauss, *Structural Anthropology*, translated by Claire Jacobson and Brooke Grundfest Schoepf (New York: Basic Books, 1963).

[27]Ken Koehbeck, "The Mythic/Epic Cycle and the Creation of Social Meaning." Unpublished paper (St. Louis, Mo.: Washington University, 1979), p. 3.

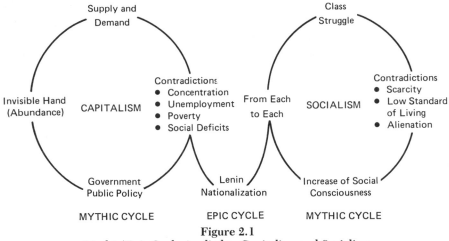

Figure 2.1
Mythic/Epic Cycle Applied to Capitalism and Socialism

Source: Rogene A. Buchholz, *Business Environment and Public Policy: Implications for Management and Strategy Formulation*, 2nd ed., © 1986, p. 85. Reprinted by permission of Prentice Hall, Englewood Cliffs, NJ.

Applied to a capitalistic system (see Figure 2.1), the primal mythical reality is Adam Smith's notion of the invisible hand, a mythical view of reality regarding how a society provides itself with material goods and services. The invisible hand is a secularized version of God, who promises abundance to his people. If the invisible hand is left alone to do its work (laissez faire) and competition prevails, everyone's cup will run over with wealth and riches. People can pursue their own self-interest and society as a whole will benefit. Thus stories of free enterprise and entrepreneurship are all part of this primal reality.

This primal reality is eventually differentiated into a more scientific concept that provides a structural view of the way the system works. This view was provided by the mechanistic concept of supply and demand, that these forces are in effect the invisible hand and allocate resources to the appropriate places and provide full employment for all the members of society willing and able to work. Economic theories were thus developed to describe the workings of a market system in scientific terms so we could understand it better and prescribe policy changes.

Eventually, however, contradictions appear that challenge the primal view of reality. The competitive free-enterprise system, left to its own devices, tends toward oligopoly or even monopoly. Thus imperfections of competition appear. Unemployment also appears, particularly during recessions or depressions, which cannot be blamed on the people themselves. Many are not able to share in the abundance a capitalistic society produces and live out the Horatio

50

Alger story. Instead they remain hopelessly rooted in poverty. Social deficits appear in the form of pollution or toxic wastes not disposed of properly.

These contradictions require some sort of mediation if the primal vision of reality on which society rests is to be maintained. In our society, the government becomes the primary mediator to deal with these contradictions through public policy measures, to enable the system to continue functioning. The mythic cycle is profoundly conservative, and as long as adequate mediating terms can be found the society will remain stable. Change will have occurred, of course, but it will not be perceived as such because the change has been incorporated into the original mythic structure.

If these contradictions cannot be successfully mediated or reconciled, however, the epic cycle starts and the old order begins to break apart. The people who are affected by the contradictions express their alienation and oppression in what has been called a lament—a legal petition to the powers governing the universe to intervene. Eventually, a hero appears who delivers the people from their alienation and despair and becomes the leader of the new social order. That order then proceeds to maintain itself through the mythic cycle.[28]

Something like this must have happened in Czarist Russia during the Bolshevik revolution. The contradictions of the capitalistic system could not be reconciled in that country. Eventually a hero appeared (Lenin) who promised to deliver the oppressed people from their despair by abolishing the institutions of a capitalistic society (private property) and founding a new order based on a vision of reality appropriated from Marxist theory. This change involved an overthrow of old myths and the establishment of new ones to support the new order that emerged.

The primal vision of reality in this order is the myth "to each according to his need, from each according to his ability." The differentiating principle to describe how the system works is the notion of a class struggle. Contradictions that appear include scarcity and a lower standard of living when compared with many nations of the world. Perhaps the most basic contradiction of all is the alienation of workers from the bureaucracy that runs the society and the formation of labor unions to promote workers' rights in a society that is supposed to be the workers' paradise. These contradictions are successfully mediated by increasing the social consciousness of the people through purges or other coercive means and propaganda.

Ordinarily, then, societies operate in the mythic mode. Only when the underlying vision of reality on which the social order rests breaks down because of unreconciled contradictions does true epic appear. The epic cycle always deals with radical social change. Usually the outcome of an epic cycle is the establishment of a new social order. Should this not happen, people can face

[28]Ibid., p. 4.

generations of oppression and anarchy. One destroys old myths and gods only at the risk that no new ones may appear to give life meaning and order.

Clearly the time frame for this model is unpredictable. The process of mythic stability can go on for generations, even thousands of years, without serious disruption. Even when the alienation stage is reached, the epic cycle may not take place for generations, or the hero figure essential to triggering rapid and radical social change may appear overnight and the revolution be accomplished in a matter of hours. The model gives no basis for estimating the time parameters for any stage or movement.[29]

Thus public policy plays the role of mediator in our society, resolving contradictions that appear from time to time between the way the system is supposed to function and the way it is actually performing. If these contradictions can be resolved to the satisfaction of enough members in the society, radical change will be prevented and society will remain essentially stable as far as its basic institutions and mode of operation is concerned. The self-understanding of that society will be preserved and most people will still believe in the same myths and ideologies.

SELECTED REFERENCES

ANDERSON, JAMES E. *Public Policy-Making*, 2nd ed. New York: Holt, Rinehart & Winston, 1979.

BUCHANAN, JAMES. *The Demand and Supply of Public Goods*. Chicago: Rand McNally, 1968.

CARTER, LIEF H. *Administrative Law and Politics*. Boston: Little, Brown, 1983.

DUNN, WILLIAM N. *Public Policy Analysis: An Introduction*. Englewood Cliffs, N.J.: Prentice-Hall, 1981.

DYE, THOMAS R. *Understanding Public Policy*, 3rd ed. Englewood Cliffs, N.J.: Prentice-Hall, 1978.

GALBRAITH, JOHN KENNETH. *Economics and the Public Purpose*. Boston: Houghton Mifflin, 1967.

————. *The New Industrial State*. Boston: Houghton Mifflin, 1967.

HARTLE, DOUGLAS G. *Public Policy Decision Making and Regulation*. Montreal: The Institute for Research on Public Policy, 1979.

LINEBERRY, ROBERT L. *American Public Policy*. New York: Harper & Row, 1978.

OLSON, MANCUR. *The Logic of Collective Action*. Cambridge, Mass.: Harvard University Press, 1977.

[29]Ibid., p. 7.

PAUL, ELLEN F., and PHILIP C. RUSSO, JR. *Public Policy: Issues, Analysis, and Ideology.* Chatham, N.J.: Chatham House Publishers, 1982.

PERETZ, PAUL, ED. *The Politics of American Economic Policy Making.* Armonk, N.Y.: M. E. Sharpe, 1987.

PETERS, B. GUY. *American Public Policy: Promise and Performance,* 2nd ed. Chatham, N.J.: Chatham House, 1986.

PRESTON, LEE E., and JAMES E. POST. *Private Management and Public Policy.* Englewood Cliffs, N.J.: Prentice-Hall, 1975.

RAWLS, JOHN. *A Theory of Justice.* Cambridge, Mass.: Harvard University Press, 1971.

SIRKIN, GERALD. *The Visible Hand: The Fundamentals of Economic Planning,* New York: McGraw-Hill, 1968.

SMITH, ADAM. *The Wealth of Nations.* New York: Modern Library, 1937.

STARLING, GROVER. *The Politics and Economics of Public Policy: An Introductory Analysis with Cases.* Homewood, Ill.: Dorsey, 1979.

WILDAVSKY, AARON. *Speaking Truth to Power: The Art and Craft of Policy Analysis.* Boston: Little Brown, 1979.

HISTORICAL DEVELOPMENTS
IN PUBLIC POLICY

◄═══ IDEAS TO BE FOUND ═══►
IN THIS CHAPTER

- The rise of modern industrial society
- The Great Depression
- The post-industrial society

History provides some clear examples of the role public policy plays in society. There are clearly identifiable periods in U.S. history when major problems appeared in the system that were resolved through public policy measures. During those times, the market was not trusted because people either believed it could not respond effectively to the problems society was experiencing or because they were not willing to accept the outcomes that would result if the market were left alone to work things out according to its own dictates. Thus public policy arises out of deficiencies in the market system, either real or perceived, that appear from time to time in our history. The market cannot always resolve problems that threaten a society's basic self-understanding.

> Once the historical dimension is added, evil men and motivations vanish, and we see our economic controls for what they are; living social artifacts. They do not constitute any kind of system. They are a nonsystem. They are not designed to be a system. . . . Economic planning is not why the controls were created, and it is not what people who work in the attendant bureaucracy do. From the ICC and the Sherman Act down to the latest federal regulatory agency, our federal controls were created to cope with, or

else to finesse, specific problems arising from everyday economic life at specific points in time.[1]

Dealing with these periods of major problems or contradictions in our society will aid in understanding the role public policy plays in mediating these contradictions, the issues that give rise to public policy measures, and the way public policy affects the economy and business. The public policies to be discussed in this chapter are still the major areas of public policy with which business has to be concerned. These public policies and the problems they address are by no means historical artifacts but are ongoing policies that continue to shape business behavior.

THE RISE OF MODERN INDUSTRIAL SOCIETY

The American economy grew rapidly during the period between the founding of the nation and the beginning of the Civil War. Between 1790 and 1840, the population rose from 3.9 million to 17.1 million, and the total volume of goods produced and distributed increased enormously.[2] Inventions such as the cotton gin helped to establish whole new industries, like the textile industry. Iron making dominated the metal-working industries. Other important industrial products during the period included leather, lumber, spirits and malt liquors, animal and vegetable oil, copper and brass, carriages of all kinds, and gunpowder.[3]

In spite of this growth, however, the size and nature of business enterprises in all these industries changed little. According to Alfred Chandler, the business enterprises producing and distributing these goods continued to be traditional single-unit enterprises managed by the owners and employing fewer than fifty workers.[4] Thus the economy was comprised of many small businesses in competition with each other. There was little institutional innovation to create larger organizations.

The major constraint on the size of business organizations was the availability of energy to business. Again according to Chandler, as long as production depended on traditional sources of energy, such as people, animals, and wind power, there was little incentive for businesses to create large organizations. Such sources of energy could not generate a large enough volume of output in production and number of transactions in distribution to require the creation of

[1]Jonathan R. T. Hughes, *The Governmental Habit: Economic Controls from Colonial Times to the Present* (New York: Basic Books, 1977), p. 7.

[2]Robert R. Russel, *A History of the American Economic System* (New York: Appleton-Century-Crofts, 1964), p. 113.

[3]Alex Groner, *The American Heritage History of American Business and Industry* (New York: American Heritage Publishing Co., 1972), pp. 68–70.

[4]Alfred Chandler, *The Visible Hand: The Managerial Revolution in American Business* (Cambridge, Mass.: Belknap Press, 1977), p. 14.

large business organizations. The low speed of production and slow movement of goods meant that the maximum daily activity at each point of production and distribution could be easily handled by small personally owned and managed enterprises.[5]

The major development during this period as far as industrial growth was concerned was the building of an infrastructure—the web of transportation, communication, and basic industries essential to advanced forms of industry and trade. Between 1783 and 1801, more than 300 business corporations were chartered by the states to build roads, bridges, canals, and water systems. The corporate form of organization was used primarily for these "public utility" purposes.

Roads such as the Philadelphia-Lancaster turnpike were built. Rivers such as the Hudson, Delaware, and Susquehanna became important for transporting goods. Canals such as the Erie, which linked Albany and Buffalo, were built. By 1840, more than 400 railroad companies were operating almost 3,000 miles of track—more than the total mileage in all of Europe. Finally, the communications industry flourished with the invention of the telegraph and the use of other forms of communication, such as newspapers and books.[6] The development of this infrastructure was crucial for further economic growth and was supported by public policy through land grants to railroads, the use of the corporate form of organization, and similar measures.

After the Civil War, the United States experienced an unprecedented period of economic growth. Per capita wealth and income increased dramatically. There was scarcely a millionaire in the country in 1790; in 1850 there were twenty-five millionaires in New York City alone, eighteen in Boston, and another nine in Philadelphia. People in most parts of the country were generally experiencing rising standards of living with respect to food, housing, clothing, health care, and education.[7]

The United States was rapidly changing into an industrial society as more factories were built and more and more people took jobs in the industrial sector. The agricultural sector declined since fewer people were needed to support the rest of the population. One definition of an industrialized country is a country in which 50 percent or more of the occupied males are engaged in nonagricultural pursuits. The United States achieved this distinction in about 1880.[8]

There were a number of reasons for this rapid growth. First, the existence of an effective transportation system meant that finished goods and raw materials could be moved around the country fairly easily. Factories could be located where labor was available and built large enough to take advantage of economies of scale. Second, changes in agriculture made it possible for a smaller and

[5]Ibid., p. 17.

[6]Groner, *American Heritage History*, pp. 83–106.

[7]Russel, *American Economic System*, p. 277.

[8]See Russel, *American Economic System*, pp. 338–39; Groner, *American Heritage History*, p. 157.

smaller proportion of the population to feed the rest of the country. This released millions of workers to take jobs in the newly developing industries and other occupations.

A third reason was the development of a cheap source of energy to support economic growth. The opening of the anthracite coal fields in eastern Pennsylvania removed the technological constraint that Chandler claims kept business enterprises small for many years. Cheap coal provided heat for large-scale production in foundries, became the source of steam power for railroad locomotives, and became an efficient fuel for generating steam power to drive machines in factories. Coal allowed new technologies to be developed that speeded up production of goods and services and led to the rise of the modern business enterprise.[9]

The fourth factor in this growth was the emergence of a group of entrepreneurs who were able to build large-scale business enterprises to take advantage of these potentials. There were people like Commodore Vanderbilt, Jay Gould, Daniel Drew, and Jim Fisk in railroads; Andrew Carnegie in steel; Charles Pillsbury in flour milling; John D. Rockefeller in oil; and John Pierpont Morgan in banking and the steel industry. Although historians either condemn these people as robber barons or praise them as captains of industry, it seems clear that they and others like them understood the potentials of the changes taking place around them, took up the challenge, and created huge industrial enterprises that formed the foundations of our modern business system. They recognized the strength of the new foundations of business and successfully put capital and resources to work to make large business enterprises possible. They were an important ingredient in the United States becoming an industrial society. The productive use of the capital they were able to accumulate created unprecedented economic growth for the country.[10]

Thus the modern business enterprise was born in response to a number of changes taking place in U.S. society. The corporate form of organization increasingly began to be used to make these enterprises even larger, as it allowed more capital to be accumulated and spread the risk across large numbers of stockholders. These large enterprises enabled mass production techniques to be used, which permitted a relatively small working force to produce an ever-increasing output. Machinery was placed and operated in such a way that several stages of production were integrated and synchronized technologically and organizationally within a single industrial establishment.[11]

The growth of these large individual enterprises, however, posed a threat to the competitive structure of the economy. They had unprecedented economic power and took steps to eliminate competitors and gain an even larger share of the market. The various organizational innovations of the late nine-

[9]Chandler, *The Visible Hand*, pp. 75–78.
[10]Groner, *American Heritage History*, pp. 155–182, 193–224.
[11]Chandler, *The Visible Hand*, pp. 240–241.

teenth century were eventually seen to have anticompetitive effects on the economy and society. As competition between businesses became more severe, some of these businesses tried different industrial arrangements to reduce or at least control this competition. Some of these innovations are briefly discussed below.

> **Gentlemen's Agreement:** An informal unwritten contract among competitors in an industry to set uniform prices for their products or to divide territories so as not to compete in the same geographic markets.
>
> **Pool:** A more formal arrangement by all competitors in a given industry regarding standardized prices and operations. Decisions in a pool were governed by votes, which were allocated to pool members on the basis of market share.
>
> **Trust:** An actual change of ownership for a given company. Stockholders of many competing firms turned their shares (and voting rights) over to "trustees" who became directors of one large supercorporation. This large corporation then issued trust certificates back to the original stockholders.
>
> **Holding Company:** An arrangement supported by state laws that allowed companies to hold stock in other companies. Several competitors would each buy stock in a firm whose only apparent function was to set policy for the owning companies.

The use of these devices and the elimination of competition led to a high degree of concentration in some industries. Table 3.1 shows the percentage of output produced by the dominant firm in some key industries at the turn of the century. The years between 1897 and 1904 saw a great surge of business combinations and concentration in certain industries. There were 318 industrial combinations in this period that included 5,300 plants with a combined capitalization of more than $7 billion. More than 1,000 different railroad lines were consolidated into six major systems that controlled almost $10 billion in capital. The trust device was particularly useful for combinations, and the trusts that

Table 3.1
Concentration in Selected Industries

International Harvester	1900	85% of harvesting machines
National Biscuit	1902	70% of biscuit output
American Can	1901	90% of industry output
Corn Products	1902	80% of industry capacity
U.S. Leather	1902	60% of leather output
Distillers Securities	1902	60% of whiskey output
International Paper	1902	60% of all newsprint
American Sugar Refining	1900	100% of refined sugar

Source: Adapted from Robert R. Russel, *A History of the American Economic System* (New York: Appleton-Century Crofts, 1964), p. 277.

were created in petroleum, cottonseed oil, linseed oil, sugar, whiskey, and lead processing came to dominate their industries for decades.[12]

There are some advantages to a concentrated industrial structure. The existence of a national market to be served by large enterprises gave them a cost advantage because of the potential volume they could produce. The combination of several small companies into a large enterprise increased production because of better coordination and planning resulting in increased efficiency. Firms had greater stability with assured sources of supply and controlled markets.

There were also many disadvantages to this industrial structure. Competition was reduced as small firms were driven out of business because of inefficiency or the predatory pricing practices of large enterprises. Competition itself was often ruthless and cutthroat as firms sometimes cut prices below cost to drive competitors out of business. Collusion between firms was not uncommon. The economic power of large firms gave them the power to dictate the terms of trade to smaller groups—such as farmers, independent groups, and wholesalers—and transcend market forces.

The contradiction that thus appeared during this period of history was that the competitive market system was destroying itself through concentration and predatory competitive practices. Such developments awakened the fear Americans have always had of concentrations of power, whether political or economic. The U.S. democratic system was based on a system of checks and balances to prevent the accumulation of power by any one branch of government, but it began to appear that there was no comparable system of checks and balances in an unregulated market economy.

Regardless of the historical reasons behind the development of large enterprises, there is a certain logic behind the competitive process that would lead one to expect this kind of outcome. Competition, followed to its logical conclusion, means that some person or organization will eventually win out over all the others. The reason for engaging in competition is to win as big as possible. Furthermore, if the competitive system is completely unregulated, competitive behavior will sink to the lowest common denominator. If one competitor uses unfair methods of competition (such as predatory pricing) and these methods win a larger share of the market, that competitor has an unfair advantage over its competition. In the absence of rules to prevent anti-competitive behavior, other competitors will have to adopt the same behavior in order to survive.

The sports world can be looked to as an example of the competitive process in action. Rules have been passed to outlaw unfair methods of competition such as spitballs or holding by offensive linemen. These rules change as society and the competitive process changes. But in baseball or football, there is an end to the season, and one team emerges a winner over all the others and is crowned World Series or Super Bowl Champion.

[12]Groner, *American Heritage History*, pp. 197–200.

The same is not true of the economy. The season can never end, and if one business or group of businesses begins to look like a big winner over others in the industry, the competitive process is threatened. The market system does not automatically insure that competition will continue indefinitely or that competition will be fairly conducted. In the late nineteenth century, it appeared that the outcome of a completely unregulated competitive process was controlled by one or a few firms in most industries. Such a result produced a fundamental contradiction into the heart of the society's self-understanding and brought pressures on government to resolve this contradiction.

Eventually the government took action against these large industrial combinations with specific public policy measures. Two forms of government regulation were born during the late 1800s—regulation of a specific industry and regulation of competitive behavior. The former was begun in 1887 with the creation of the Interstate Commerce Commission (ICC) to regulate the railroads. The authority of this commission was later extended to other forms of transportation and other agencies were created to regulate communications, the airlines, and other industries. Regulation of competitive behavior began with the Sherman Antitrust Act of 1890, which made restraints of trade and attempts to monopolize an industry illegal. The antitrust area was extended in 1914 with the passage of the Federal Trade Commission Act to outlaw unfair methods of competition, and the Clayton Antitrust Act which focused on specific anticompetitive behaviors.

Antitrust Legislation

There are three theories to explain the motivation behind antitrust legislation. The first is the standard theory found in most American history textbooks, which holds that these measures were the result of a strong populist movement led by the farmers and other groups who were fearful of the power of these big business combinations. These groups apparently believed that the huge industrial combinations that were created were nothing more than the result of a few industrial leaders' greed and lust for power. The problem was that as these people accumulated more and more capital, they began to dictate the terms of trade to the rest of society rather than being subject to the pressures of competition. Something had to be done to break up these combinations and restore more competition in the economy. The government responded to these desires and passed the necessary legislation, supported by the executive branch under President Theodore Roosevelt, who became known as "the trust-buster." This was a case of the little guys against the big guys, with the little guys having the government on their side to restore a balance of power.[13]

The second theory was developed by a group of revisionist historians in

[13]Russel, *American Economic System*, pp. 363–370.

the 1960s who rewrote certain periods of American history.[14] This theory holds that certain key business leaders themselves realized that not only their profits but their very existence might be challenged by cut-throat competition and other evils of a completely unregulated competitive system. The various anti-competitive arrangements that business leaders worked out among themselves were voluntary attempts to gain control over this situation and develop a more rational and stable system. But these voluntary attempts failed for one reason or another. Thus some business leaders came to believe that perhaps political means might succeed where voluntary means had failed, and actively supported government regulation. If government could stabilize the system by establishing certain rules of competition and enforcing them uniformly, corporations would be able to function in a predictable and secure environment, permitting reasonable profits to be earned over the long run.

The third theory holds that competition disappeared not because of the lust for power of a few business leaders but because of the technological possibilities inherent in large-scale enterprise. The efficiency of the production and distribution system could be increased dramatically when all the stages of production and distribution, from mining of raw materials to delivery of a finished product to the consumer, could be combined in a single business enterprise under the direction of a single management. Thus administrative coordination of these various stages became more efficient and more profitable than market coordination.[15]

Society also benefited from these large enterprises in that more goods were produced at lower prices than would otherwise be possible. But because of the growth of these large "integrated" enterprises, the visible hand of the management of these enterprises replaced the invisible hand of market forces. This happened when and where new technology and expanded markets permitted a historically unprecedented high volume and speed of materials through the process of production and distribution. These enterprises grew into powerful institutions and came to dominate major sectors of the economy, and the managers of these enterprises became the most influential group of economic decision makers. But it was not good to allow such power to go completely unregulated. Competition as a regulator was disappearing and the government had to assume the role through antitrust legislation.

The Sherman Act was the first piece of antitrust legislation. The most important parts of the Sherman Act are Sections 1 and 2 (see box). Section 1 attacks the act of combining or conspiring to restrain trade and focuses on methods of competition or firm behavior. This section seems to make illegal every formal agreement among firms aimed at curbing independent action in

[14]See Gabriel Kolko, *The Triumph of Conservatism* (New York: Free Press, 1963); Paul Conkin, *The New Deal* (New York: Thomas Y. Crowell, 1967); Ellis W. Hawley, *The New Deal and the Problem of Monopoly* (Princeton, N.J.: Princeton University Press, 1966).

[15]Chandler, *The Visible Hand*, p. 8.

the market. Section 2 enjoins market structures where seller concentration is so high that it could be called a monopoly.

SHERMAN ACT OF 1890

Sec. 1. Every contract, combination in the form of trust or otherwise, or conspiracy in restraint of trade or commerce among the several States, or with foreign nations, is hereby declared to be illegal. Every person who shall make any such contract or engage in any such combination or conspiracy, shall be deemed guilty of a misdemeanor, and, on conviction thereof, shall be punished by fine not exceeding five thousand dollars, or by imprisonment not exceeding one year, or by both said punishments, in the discretion of the court.

Sec. 2. Every person who shall monopolize, or attempt to monopolize, or combine or conspire with any other person or persons, to monopolize any part of this trade or commerce among the several States, or with foreign nations, shall be deemed guilty of a misdemeanor, and, on conviction thereof, shall be punished by fine not exceeding five thousand dollars, or by imprisonment not exceeding one year, or by both said punishments, in the discretion of the court.

The Clayton Act attacks a series of business policies insofar as they could substantially lessen competition or tend to create a monopoly. The language of the Sherman Act was quite broad, leaving a good deal of uncertainty as to what specific practices were in restraint of trade and thus illegal. The Clayton Act was passed to correct this deficiency by being more specific and barring price discrimination (later supplemented by the Robinson-Patman Act), tying arrangements, and exclusive dealing arrangements. It also contained a section that was designed to slow down the merger movement by forbidding mergers that substantially lessen competition or tend to create a monopoly (later strengthened by the Celler-Kefauver Amendments).

The Federal Trade Commission Act of 1914 created the Federal Trade Commission, which was empowered to protect consumers against all "unfair methods of competition in or affecting commerce." It was left up to the commission itself to decide what methods of competition were unfair. In 1938, the Wheeler-Lea Act amended this section to read "unfair or deceptive acts or practices in commerce," thereby empowering the FTC to pursue trade practices deemed unlawful whether or not competition was affected.

The purpose of these antitrust laws is to limit the economic power of large corporations that can control markets by reducing competition through concentration. The role of government is to maintain something called a "workable competition" on the theory that resources are allocated more efficiently and prices are lower in a competitive system than one dominated by large corporations.

The problem with antitrust laws is their application. Society vacillates when it comes to acceptance of the large corporation. This was evident immediately after the antitrust laws were passed, when the courts remained pro-business for several years. In 1895, for example, the Supreme Court ruled that American Sugar Refining was not a monopoly in restraint of trade and therefore not in violation of the Sherman Act. A year earlier, the court had issued an injunction against the union in the Pullman strike on the basis that it was a conspiracy in restraint of interstate commerce. In the Danbury Hatters case of 1908, the striking union was declared financially liable for damages resulting from a boycott. The Justice Department lost seven of the first eight cases it brought under the Sherman Act. Finally, in 1911, two trusts (Standard Oil and American Tobacco) were found guilty of violating the Sherman Act and were ordered to dissolve into several separate firms.[16]

The same ambiguity is evident in more recent years. In the 1970s, the "bigness is bad" philosophy seemed to prevail. Cases were filed against IBM and AT&T, bills were introduced into Congress to limit conglomerate mergers, and the antitrust agencies attacked oligopoly itself through the infamous cereal case (FTC v. Kellogg et al.) and theories about shared monopolies. In the early 1980s, the IBM and the cereal cases were dropped, and mergers were allowed between U.S. Steel and Marathon Oil, and DuPont and Conoco, for example, signaling a much softer line on antitrust litigation.

There are obvious benefits to large-scale production, distribution, and organization. Economies of scale, more efficient coordination, and increased research and development expenditures on the part of large organizations are not figments of the imagination. But empirical research has not been able to establish conclusively the superiority of either a competitive or concentrated system on dimensions like pricing or innovations that are of importance to society. The antitrust laws maintain an allegiance to the ideals of competition and institutionalize our fear of large concentrations of power. Yet their application is flexible to allow the benefits of concentrated industries to be exploited when society deems appropriate.

Industry Regulation

This type of regulation is the oldest, beginning with the Interstate Commerce Commission (ICC) of 1887, which was established to provide continuous surveillance of private railroad activity across the country. Although some states had practiced such regulation before the federal government, the inability of the states to regulate railroads effectively led to the passage of this act, which set the pattern for additional regulatory commissions of this type. The ICC was an

[16]Groner, *American Heritage History*, pp. 214–215.

innovation because it represented a new location of power in the federal system, and served as a prototype for regulation by independent commission as federal regulatory powers were expanded into other areas of industry and commerce. Thus followed the Federal Power Commission, the Civil Aeronautics Board, and the Federal Communications Commission, all examples of industry regulation.

One reason for this type of regulation is the belief that certain natural monopolies exist where economies of scale in an industry are so great that the largest firm would have the lowest costs and thus drive its competitors out of the market. Since competition cannot act as a regulator in this situation, the government must perform this function to regulate these industries in the public interest.

Another reason for industry regulation is that an agency may be needed to allocate limited space, as in the case of the airlines and broadcasters. The threat of predatory practices or destructive competition is often used to justify regulation of the transportation industry. Regulation may be needed, it is often argued, to provide service to areas that would be ignored by the market. An example is the provision of railroad and airline service to small towns and cities. Finally, some argue that regulation is needed to prevent fraud and deception in the sale of securities.

Thus utilities are regulated at the federal level by the Federal Energy Regulatory Commission (FERC), whose purpose is to regulate interstate aspects of the electric power and natural gas industries. This agency, associated with the new Department of Energy (DOE), succeeded the Federal Power Commission (FPC) in 1977. Where federal regulation of utilities does not apply, state regulatory commissions have been created.

The Federal Communications Commission (FCC) regulates domestic and foreign communications by radio, television, wire, cable, and telephone. The Civil Aeronautics Board (CAB) promotes and regulates the civil air transport industry. Surface transportation, including trucks, railroads, buses, oil pipelines, inland waterway and coastal shippers, and express companies are regulated by the Interstate Commerce Commission (ICC). The Securities and Exchange Commission (SEC) regulates the securities and financial markets to protect the public against malpractice.

This type of regulation focuses on a specific industry and is concerned about its economic well-being. The major concerns of agencies such as the ICC is with rates, routes, and the obligation to serve. Decisions about these economic matters are primarily made through adjudicatory procedures where interested parties present their arguments. After a lengthy process of review, the agency reaches a decision, which may be appealed in the courts.

Although the original impetus for regulation may have come from consumers who believed they needed protection, the so-called capture theory suggests that these agencies eventually become a captive of the industry they are supposed to regulate. This happens because of the unique expertise possessed by members of the industry or because of job enticements for regulators who leave government employment. The public or consumer interest is often viewed as subordinate because the agency comes to focus on the needs and concerns of the industry it is regulating. Many view regulated companies as nothing more than a government-supported cartel that earns higher profits and charges higher prices than would be the case if competition prevailed.

Pressures for reform of industry regulation began to build. Finally, in 1978, Congress passed a deregulation bill aimed at air passenger service, which allowed airlines to offer new services without CAB approval and granted them a great degree of freedom to raise and lower their fares. The CAB itself went out of existence and those activities that were still necessary to continue were transferred to other agencies. Companies in the railroad industry were given the right to charge as little or as much as they pleased for hauling fresh fruits and vegetables instead of following FCC-approved rates. Similar pressures mounted to deregulate some aspects of the trucking industry and abolish some of the FCC's control over commercial radio broadcasting.

THE GREAT DEPRESSION   After 1900, the modern multiunit industrial enterprise became a standard for managing the production and distribution of goods in the United States. By 1917, most U.S. industries had acquired their modern structure. Companies like United States Steel, Standard Oil, General Electric, and Westinghouse were founded. For the rest of the century, large industrial structures such as these continued to cluster in much the same industrial groups, and the same enterprises continued to be the leaders in the concentrated industries in these groups.[17]

Whole new industries were founded during the early years of the twentieth century, including the automobile industry.[18] One leading entrepreneur in the early years of this period was Henry Ford. He brought together concepts of mass production, interchangeable parts, and central assembly with great effectiveness. The production process Ford put together enabled him to produce a cheap form of mass transportation by keeping costs low enough to price his product for the lowest or largest possible mass market (see box). In 1909, Ford built 10,660 cars. By 1919, there were 6.7 million cars on the road; by 1929, 27 million. The phenomenal growth of the auto industry stimulated road construction and commercial construction, led to the formation of many new auto dealerships, and tremendously benefited the rubber and steel industries.[19]

[17]Chandler, *The Visible Hand*, p. 345.

[18]Ibid., pp. 455–468.

[19]Groner, *American Heritage History*, pp. 218–220, 275–278; "America in 1929: The Prosperity Illusion," *Business Week*, September 3, 1979, p. 6.

In 1916, Ford announced a price cut from $440 to $360 on the basic Model T automobile. The stockholders brought suit against the company, claiming that Ford was unjustified in giving their money away in this fashion. Ford's defense was that the company was clearing $2 to $2.5 million a month, which is all any firm ought to make in his opinion. The court, however, held for the stockholders, ruling that it was not within the lawful powers of a corporation to conduct a company's affairs for the merely incidental benefit of shareholders and for the primary purpose of benefiting others.

Sources: Copyright © 1972 American Heritage Publishing Company, Inc. Reprinted by permission from *The American Heritage History of American Business and Industry* by Alex Groner.

The period from World War I to the Depression was one of unprecedented prosperity. Many people became millionaires, the stock market soared, and production increased dramatically. There were many reasons for this burst of growth. The United States emerged from World War I economically and physically undamaged, giving it an advantage in world markets. Mass production methods became widely applied in many industries, increasing production of goods and services. Several major new products, such as automobiles and electric power, created or stimulated many new jobs and markets. Installment buying became popular and, coupled with the widespread use of advertising and sales techniques, stimulated consumption of these new products. Finally there were enormous profits to be made in stock market speculation, and low margin requirements made it possible for many people to participate (see box).[20]

Then came the crash. It was very difficult for those who did not live through this period of our history to grasp the full impact of the Depression. Statistics such as those in Table 3.2 tell only part of the story. Unemployment soared to almost 25 percent of the labor force—over 12 million people out of 52 million workers in a nation of 122 million. Breadlines, clusters of tarpaper shacks called "Hoovervilles," and gray armies of job hunters became symbols of the period. Consumption spending slid by one-fifth and investment collapsed entirely. Waves of panic struck the banking system from late 1930 through 1933, forcing more than 9,000 banks with deposits of $7 billion to close their doors. More than nine million savings accounts were lost, and thousands of businesses went bankrupt because they could not take their money out of the bank.[21] Panic selling hit the stock market and paper fortunes were lost overnight when the crash began.

[20]"America in 1929: The Prosperity Illusion," *Business Week*, September 3, 1979, pp. 6–10.
[21]"A Debate That Rages On: Why Did It Happen?" *Business Week*, September 3, 1979, p. 12.

Table 3.2
Key Statistics of the Depression of the 1930's

Index	1929	1931
Gross National Product (billions)[a]		
Current dollars	103.1	58.0
Farm income	12.0	5.3
Corporate profits	9.8	−3.0
Industrial production (1935–1939 = 100)[b]	110.0	57.0
Durable goods production (1934–1939 = 100)[b]	132.0	41.0
Steel production as percent capacity[c]	—	20.0
New private construction activity ($ billion)[d]	8.3	1.7
Automobile sales (millions of cars)[e]	5.4	1.3
Industrial stock prices (average dollars per share)[f]	311.0	65.0
Unemployment (millions)[g]	1.5	12.1
Percent of labor force	3.2	23.6
Farm products, wholesale price index (1957–1959 = 100)[g]	64.0	20.0

[a]U.S. Department of Commerce
[b]Federal Reserve Board
[c]American Iron and Steel Institute
[d]U.S. Bureau of the Census
[e]Automobile Manufacturers Association
[f]Dow Jones
[g]U.S. Bureau of Labor Statistics
Source: George A. Steiner, *Business and Society* (New York: Random House, 1971), p. 59.

Between March 3, 1928 and Sept. 3, 1929, American Can went from 77 to 181⅞, AT&T from 179½ to 335⅝, Anaconda Copper from 54½ to 162, Electric Bond & Share from 89¾ to 203⅝, General Motors from 139¾ to 181⅞, and Westinghouse from 91⅝ to 313. The New York Stock Exchange soared from 236 million shares in 1923 to more than 1 billion in 1929. Five million share days became commonplace.

Source: "America in 1929: The Prosperity Illusion," *Business Week*, September 3, 1979, p. 9. Quoted with permission.

There is a great deal of debate over the cause of such a drastic change in the fortunes of the country, but the following seem to emerge as some of the major causes. First, the soaring stock market was more the result of speculation than increases in real physical wealth. Low margin requirements encouraged such speculation. People borrowed heavily to buy stocks and participate in the rise of the market. When the psychology of the market changed and investors sensed it had reached a peak, they began selling to get their profits and run. Panic quickly set in and the whole speculative structure collapsed rapidly.

Second, the prosperity of the late 1920s was not shared by the agricultural sector. Farm purchasing power steadily deteriorated throughout the period, aggravated by the inelastic demand for farm products. Coupled with this was a bad and worsening inequality in the distribution of income. Most of the money in the 1920s went to those who were already wealthy rather than to workers with lower incomes. Smaller proportions of total income went toward wages and salaries. Much of the money that was received by the wealthy was reinvested in new productive facilities, causing an overextension of factory capacity. Workers simply could not buy all that the economy was producing.

Then the Smoot-Hawley tariff was passed, which further aggravated the situation. It was a very restrictive tariff structure that caused other countries to pass retaliatory tariffs of their own. This action curbed our exports to foreign countries just at the time such markets were badly needed. With the decline of both domestic and foreign markets, business investment was curtailed and layoffs of workers were increased.

Finally, the Federal Reserve System adopted a restrictive monetary policy during the late 1920s, which some scholars believe was the major cause of the Depression.[22] This action cut off credit to business and resulted in lagging business investment through the end of the period just before the crash.

The real causes of the Depression are many and complex, however, the long-term effects are quite clear. New areas of public policy were created. Franklin Delano Roosevelt won the election of 1932 promising a New Deal for the American people. This New Deal consisted of a series of public policy measures (see Table 3.3) that were unprecedented in U.S. history. The federal government assumed responsibility for stimulating business activity out of an economic depression and for correcting abuses in the economic machinery of the nation. It sought to relieve businesses, farmers, workers, homeowners, consumers, investors, and other groups from the distresses brought on by the adverse economic situation. In the famous 100 days that followed Roosevelt's swearing in, the president asked for, and Congress speedily granted, an un-precedented list of emergency legislation that plunged the federal government deeply and unalterably into the affairs of society and the economy. During Roosevelt's first two years, ninety-three major pieces of legislation were passed that directly affected banking, business, agriculture, labor, and social welfare. This flow of legislation set the stage for the role government would be playing a generation later and dramatically increased the importance of public policy to the society as a whole and business in particular.[23]

Whether all these public policy measures really pulled the economy out of the Depression is again a matter of debate. The record, as shown in Table 3.4, is spotty. Unemployment never recovered its 1929 low, and gross national product in 1939 had barely recovered its 1929 high. Some historians believe that there

[22]See Milton Friedman and Anna J. Schwartz, *A Monetary History of the United States* (Princeton, N.J.: Princeton University Press, 1963).

[23]"Interventionist Government Came to Stay," *Business Week*, September 3, 1979, p. 39.

Table 3.3
Public Policy Measures of the New Deal Period

Year	Measure	Explanation
1932	Emergency Banking Relief Act	Reopened banks under government supervision
1932	Civilian Conservation Corps	First federal effort to deal with unemployment (youth) through direct public works
1932	Federal Emergency Relief Act	Required Washington to fund state-run welfare programs
1932	Reconstruction Finance Corporation	First use of government credit to aid troubled private companies
1933	Agricultural Adjustment Act	First system of agricultural price and production supports
1933	Tennessee Valley Authority Act	First direct government involvement in energy production and marketing
1933	Glass-Steagall Banking Act	Created bank deposit insurance Divorced commercial and investment banking Prohibited interest on checking accounts
1933	National Industrial Recovery Act	First major attempt to plan and regulate the entire economy through the use of industry and trade associations and codes of competition. First act to allow collective bargaining and wage and hour regulation. Portions were declared unconstitutional.
1934	National Housing Act	Provided for federal mortgage insurance and for regulation of housing standards
1935	Wagner Act	Promoted collective bargaining and prohibited unfair labor practice by employers
1935	Social Security Act	Created a system of social insurance and a national retirement system
1938	Agricultural Adjustment Act	Extended price supports, instituted payments, and launched wide federal management of agriculture
1938	Fair Labor Standards Act	Provided for minimum wage, 40-hour week, overtime, and control of child labor

Source: Rogene A. Buchholz, *Business Environment and Public Policy: Implications for Management and Strategy Formulation,* 2nd ed., © 1986, p. 100. Reprinted by permission of Prentice Hall, Englewood Cliffs, NJ.

were three parts to the Depression that in effect lasted until World War II. These were: (1) the long, nearly uninterrupted decline for 3½ years to the low point of March 1933; (2) a gradual upturn for another 3½ years until August of 1937; and (3) a final plunge and ascent leading to the war production period.[24]

In the late 1930s, President Roosevelt became disappointed with the performance of the economy and turned on business. He called for an investigation of economic concentration, forming a Temporary National Economic Committee to do the investigation, declaring that free enterprise was ceasing to be

[24]Groner, *American Heritage History,* p. 302.

Table 3.4
Employment and Production 1929–1942

Year	Unemploy- ment as a Percentage of the Labor Force[a]	Gross National Product per Capita in Dollars[b]	Year	Unemploy- ment as a Percentage of the Labor Force	Gross National Product per Capita in Dollars
1929	3.1%	$696	1936	12.7%	$ 650
1930	8.7	619	1937	9.7	682
1931	15.8	563	1938	13.2	647
1932	23.5	478	1939	12.3	702
1933	24.7	485	1940	10.1	760
1934	20.7	537	1941	7.6	903
1935	17.6	561	1942	4.4	1,024

[a]People on work relief and people in the armed forces are counted as employed.
[b]Dollars all of the same purchasing power.
Source: Robert R. Russel, *A History of the American Economic System* (New York: Appleton-Century-Crofts, 1964), p. 564. Reprinted with permission.

free enterprise. Parallel with this development was the efforts of Thurman Arnold, the Assistant Attorney General, to enforce the antitrust laws more vigorously.[25] These efforts became more or less academic with the advent of the war years, which called on the nation's productive capacity as never before, and ended concern about the Depression for some time.

Contradictions appeared during this period of history. Unemployment threw millions of people out of work and widespread poverty existed in a nation that only a few years before had believed that poverty would be eliminated and prosperity would be unending. Perhaps the most basic contradiction of all was intellectual—the challenge that the Depression posed to the classical, mechanistic view of the market. The classical view of the market was that it was self-correcting—that with the onset of employment, wages and prices would fall, demand would begin to increase, companies would respond by expanding output and hiring more workers, and these workers would then begin to buy more products. An upward spiral would be set in motion that would eventually pull the economy out of the Depression. Government intervention was not necessary and, in fact, would only interfere with the automatic mechanisms of the market system[26]

The Depression was such a shock to the self-confidence of the nation and the distress it caused was so widespread that people came to fear that self-correction would not happen in time to do any good. They were not willing to sit around in their Hoovervilles starving to death waiting for the market to

[25]Ibid.
[26]"The Scars Still Mark Economic Policy," *Business Week*, September 3, 1979, p. 22.

correct itself. People, including business leaders, wanted action, and they wanted it immediately. The Roosevelt administration promised action.

The government, through public policy, thus stepped in again to mediate these contradictions in the market system. Many believe that Roosevelt, instead of being the enemy of the free market, actually saved the system, and prevented an epic cycle from gaining headway that could have taken the country into some form of socialism. In any event, three new areas of public policy came out of this historical period: the policy process known as *economic management* where government attempts to manage the economy and even out the business cycle, the area of *labor-management relations* where government supported the right of collective bargaining, and the beginnings of a *welfare state* based on a philosophy of entitlements.

Economic Management The public policy measures that came out of the early part of the New Deal were part of a social welfare program designed to help victims of the Depression. The idea that public works programs, for example, should be designed to stimulate the economy through deficit spending had not yet taken root. The immediate problem was to relieve the widespread distress the Depression had caused. Only later did economic theories develop to support the notion of an ongoing government involvement to even out the business cycle through countercyclical spending.[27]

These new theoretical developments came primarily from John Maynard Keynes and his followers in the form of what has since been called Keynesian economics. Keynes pointed out that classical theory was wrong on two counts: in the real world prices and wages did not fall as expected, because of rigidities built into the system; and a reduction in wages of sufficient magnitude to enable business to begin hiring lowers a worker's income drastically and therefore reduces even further the total demand for goods in the economy. The fundamental problem, according to Keynes, was this deficiency in demand, especially the demand for investment goods by business, which kept the economy at low levels of output and employment. Thus if no one else could spend money, government should, thereby priming the pump by putting money back into the economy to stimulate demand for goods and services.[28]

Eventually, these notions took root, culminating in the Employment Act of 1946, in which government was given the responsibility of managing the economy on an ongoing basis rather than simply to stimulate it in crisis situations like a depression. As World War II drew to a close, there was a great deal of concern that a new period of inflation would ensue because people had earned and saved a good deal of money during the war. Many goods and

[27]Ibid.
[28]Ibid.

services had not been generally available. After the war, it was believed there would be a tremendous jump in demand as people took this money and moved into the marketplace. The productive facilities would not be able to keep up with this surge in demand, resulting in too much money in the economy chasing after too few goods—a classic cause of inflation. It was feared this high inflation would eventually lead to another serious downturn in the economy.

To prevent this from happening, the government was given the responsibility of managing the money supply through fiscal and monetary policies. Government was to even out business cycles by pumping money into the economy when necessary, dampening demand by raising taxes, stimulating investment, becoming the employer of last resort, and using other measures designed to maintain a stable economic environment in which business and the society at large could prosper. The idea that the market was self-regulating in this regard was rejected. It was believed that a completely unregulated market system was excessively prone to waves of overinvestment and excess capacity, deficient spending and underemployment of resources. Such "boom and bust" periods as had been experienced throughout much of American history were simply unacceptable. Management of the economy by government to promote stability of employment and purchasing power became a matter of public policy. Rather than trusting the market and succumbing to the ups and downs of normal cyclical behavior, government took on the responsibility of keeping inflation and unemployment under control and creating the conditions for continuing economic prosperity.

Labor-Management Relations   Another area of public policy that resulted from the Depression was labor-management relations. The ordeal of the working class in those years ignited a militance that swept the country and revolutionized the industrial relations system. This militancy forced the federal government to intervene in labor-management relations and to adopt a national labor policy designed to protect the rights of workers to unionize. Out of this intervention came a revived labor movement, the development of collective bargaining as it is known today, and the end of management's unilateral control of the workplace.[29]

Workers found that the market system, particularly during periods of recession and depression when jobs were not readily available, was unable to deal with problems they were experiencing in the workplace—long hours, poor working conditions, low wages, and arbitrary hiring and firing practices. They began to form unions to counter the power of management with organized labor. Before the Depression, management held an overwhelming advantage over the unions. The courts upheld the right of employers to do just about anything to prevent unionism. Companies could fire workers for joining unions, force them to sign a pledge not to join a union as a condition of employment,

---

[29]"The Ruins Gave Rise to Big Labor," *Business Week*, September 3, 1979, p. 26.

require them to belong to company unions, and spy on them to stop unionization before it got started. The attempt to form unions without government help was not very successful, and before the Depression, the workers' interest in unionism was declining.[30]

The National Industrial Recovery Act rekindled this interest. The NIRA authorized businesses to form trade associations to regulate production, and a few union leaders insisted that the bill also gave employees the right to organize and bargain collectively. With the support of public policy and with job security at the forefront of workers' minds because of the Depression, labor leaders found it easier to organize segments of the labor force. When the NIRA was found unconstitutional in 1935, a more comprehensive labor relations law called the Wagner Act was passed. The Wagner Act not only extended the right to organize and bargain collectively to workers, it also proscribed employer actions that interfered with that right, and established the National Labor Relations Board as the enforcement mechanism. After World War II, two additional laws were passed to amend certain provisions of the Wagner Act: the Taft Hartley Act of 1947 and the Landrum-Griffin Act of 1959. Thus were created the rules that govern labor-management relations today.[31]

The Welfare State   The Depression was also responsible for the beginning of another series of public policy measures that can be grouped loosely under the title of welfare. The initial public policies of the New Deal era, as stated previously, were designed to alleviate distress. Many people were the victims of circumstances beyond their control. They were willing and able to work but there simply were no jobs available. Society conceded that the unemployed were not necessarily to blame for their situation and was willing to have government accept responsibility for helping such victims. People were not allowed to starve while waiting for the market to correct itself and make jobs available again.

So began a philosophy of entitlements, in which people believe they have rights to a good job, decent food, clothing, and shelter. The government has a responsibility to guarantee these rights. This philosophy has led to a whole series of measures—such as social security, aid to families with dependent children, medicare and medicaid, and food stamps—designed to help people whose basic needs have not been met, for one reason or another, by the market system.[32]

The largest growth of these entitlement programs took place in the 1960s and 1970s as the nation mounted an effort to eliminate poverty and assure every citizen some guaranteed minimum level of medical care, food, and income. Aid to families with dependent children and medicaid programs, for example, grew

[30]Ibid.
[31]Ibid., pp. 27–28.
[32]"A Watershed In American Attitudes," *Business Week*, September 3, 1979, pp. 46–50.

515 percent and 905 percent respectively in the 1967–77 period. Overall payment to individuals of this sort grew at an average annual rate of 15.3 percent during fiscal years 1966–79 compared with much lower rates for earlier periods. These payments steadily increased as a percent of GNP throughout most of this period. In 1981, 43 percent of the federal budget went to direct payments for individuals.

The motivation for this growth of entitlement programs came from an egalitarian movement in our society. These programs became a means of promoting equality, instead of simply a means to relieve the distresses of certain unfortunate groups. The egalitarian movement was primarily composed of blacks and other minorities, women, welfare workers, and leaders of new unions of government employees.[33] The goal of this movement was to promote an equality of result rather than opportunity, by transferring money from the upper-income levels of society to the lower levels through a series of cash-income assistance programs, such as social security, and in-kind assistance programs, such as medicare and medicaid, that provide basic services to needy people.

The growth of these programs and the egalitarian movement sparked a lively debate in our country. Critics were concerned about the further growth of government these programs demanded. The drive for equality of results contributes to strengthening centralized bureaucratic power because government must allocate outcomes.[34] Others raised questions about the tradeoffs between equality and efficiency. In pursuing equality, society would forego any opportunity to use material resources or rewards as incentives to production. Thus any insistence on carving the pie into equal slices would shrink the size of the pie for everyone.[35] Egalitarians thus posed a threat to the business system.

> Egalitarianism is a vital counter-force to the traditional business philosophy for several reasons: (1) It has a great appeal to the masses, for it promises them their "rights" to a higher life style and greater positions of power; (2) The egalitarian thrust has necessitated (and will continue to demand) the strengthening of centralized power in order to reduce the privileges of the "haves" and the transfer of some of their largess to the "have nots"; (3) It is directly antithetical to the managerial ideology, for it tends to create a society wherein there are smaller numbers of winners and losers, and thereby reduces the capitalistic incentives, which, of course, depend upon the presence, and desirability, of inequalities; and finally, (4) Egalitarianism

[33]John Cobbs, "Egalitarianism: Threat to a Free Market," *Business Week*, December 1, 1975, pp. 62–65; John Cobbs, "Egalitarianism: Mechanisms for Redistributing Income," *Business Week*, December 8, 1975, pp. 86–90; and John Cobbs, "Egalitarianism: The Corporation as Villain," *Business Week*, December 15, 1975, pp. 86–88.

[34]See Dow Votaw, "The New Equality: Bureaucracy's Trojan Horse, *California Management Review*, vol. XX, no. 4 (Summer 1978), pp. 5–17.

[35]Arthur M. Okun, *Equality and Efficiency: The Big Tradeoff* (Washington, D.C.: The Brookings Institution, 1975).

confuses the notion of "progress," for its emphasis is on distribution rather than on production.[36]

The growth of many of these entitlement programs was finally slowed beginning in 1981 with the Reagan administration. Programs such as food stamps, aid to families with dependent children, and student loans were cut significantly. Other programs, such as social security, were not immediately cut for political reasons. These budget cuts, which disproportionately affected lower-income groups, coupled with income tax cuts, which disproportionately benefited upper-income groups, reversed or at least halted the further development of an egalitarian trend in our society. If these changes prove to be long lasting, 1981 could prove to be another watershed year in this area of public policy.

**THE POSTINDUSTRIAL
SOCIETY**

The postwar period, at least until the Arab oil embargo in 1974, was yet another period of prosperity for the United States. By later standards, inflation was very low throughout most of this period. Unemployment was also low, and there were only minor recessions until that of 1974–75. Cities and suburbs grew, people became wealthier, and more and more goods and services were produced until the gross national product topped the trillion-dollar mark. People were overwhelmed with new products, new services, and new inventions to make their lives easier. As more and more people moved into the middle class and came to own homes, buy cars, and acquire all the other amenities, our society became referred to as a *postindustrial society.*[37]

A postindustrial society generally has three characteristics, and the United States had all three of them. The first is the affluence that becomes widespread throughout much of the population. The second is a service-based economy, one in which most of the labor force is engaged in service industries, such as banking or insurance. The third characteristic is a knowledge-based society, one in which people become better and better educated and in which education is crucial to getting and keeping a good job. Unskilled jobs decline as society becomes more technologically sophisticated, demanding more highly skilled people.

If Maslow's hierarchy of needs concept is applied to a society, it seems that throughout the 1950s and early 1960s U.S. society fulfilled its basic economic needs. It could then move up the ladder to the next level and devote attention

[36]Joseph W. McGuire, "Today's Business Climate," *Business and Its Changing Environment,* George A. Steiner, ed. (Los Angeles: UCLA Graduate School of Management, 1978), p. 10. Quoted with permission.

[37]Daniel Bell, *The Coming of Post-Industrial Society: A Venture in Social Forecasting* (New York: Basic Books, 1973).

and resources to solving some of society's social problems. This it did, first in the civil rights movement, when an attempt was made to assure civil rights to blacks and other minorities who had been treated as second-class citizens throughout our history. Soon after this movement peaked, the feminist movement developed to press for women's rights in all areas of American life, from equal job opportunities to equal treatment in the armed services. Then came a serious concern with pollution—air and water pollution at first, then noise and visual pollution, and later toxic substances and hazardous waste disposal. Soon after that came a war on poverty, which sought to eliminate poverty in American society. Then came a new wave of consumerism, touched off by Ralph Nader, which dealt with product safety and quality, warranties, truth in advertising, packaging, and other aspects of the marketplace. At the end of the decade, a new concern about safety and health in the workplace surfaced. And, finally, ethical concerns, initially triggered by illegal campaign contributions in this country and foreign payments in other countries, came in for a great deal of attention.

Thus society experienced one social movement after another in the middle and late 1960s—movements that changed the face of the country and altered fundamental values that had guided this country for years. Out of this change in values new public policy measures arose. These measures have become of increasing concern to business because many of them have interfered with the basic economic mission of business.

In the mid-1970s, U.S. society experienced what was the worst recession since the Great Depression—an economic shock brought on primarily by the Arab oil embargo. Although the country survived that recession, double-digit inflation, soaring energy costs, relatively high levels of unemployment, and declining real income for many people became the order of the day for several years. These factors, many of which seemed out of our control, confronted American society with a whole new set of challenges as it entered the 1980s. These challenges were taken up by the Reagan administration.

The initial challenge was inflation, which erodes incomes and destroys confidence in the future. Throughout the 1950s and 1960s, there were many years when inflation averaged only 1 percent for the entire year. During the late 1970s, the country was fortunate if inflation could be held to a 1 percent level for a month. One important reason behind this high inflation was that the price of oil, which is so basic to our economy, was not under our control. Members of the Organization of Petroleum Exporting Countries (OPEC) were bent on a policy of continued increases throughout the late 1970s to try and maintain the value of their dollar holdings and increase the value of their oil in the ground.

The huge buildup of private sector indebtedness presented a major obstacle to the Federal Reserve System's efforts to control inflation. As long as credit was available, attempts to control the money supply had little effect on demand. People were motivated to buy now before inflation became worse. Business had also been amassing debt with a view to paying it off at some future time in inflation-cheapened dollars. Workers sought a hedge against inflation with higher wage demands that were unchecked by government guidelines. Yet at the same time, the productivity of American industry was declining. Much of the economy was indexed to inflation. Social security benefits rose automatically with increases in consumer prices. The same is true of wages that had a cost of living adjustment (COLA) as part of the contract. Add to these forces the increases in government spending, particularly for entitlement programs, and the additional cost burdens imposed on private business because of social regulation. Government spending was also indexed in a way, because inflation allowed the government to take in more money from taxpayers because of bracket creep. Thus inflation had built up such momentum that it was hard to wring out of the economy.

The Reagan administration declared inflation as public enemy number one and promised to get the economic situation under control. This administration instituted the largest income tax cut in history, cut federal spending—particularly with regard to entitlement programs—continued the tight monetary policy of the Carter administration, and mounted an effort to cut back on government regulation of business.

Inflation indeed was brought under control, and came down to 5–6 percent, which was still high by historic standards, but a great relief from the double-digit levels of previous years. But the cost of accomplishing this reduction was tremendous. We entered a new recessionary period in 1981 that proved to be worse than the one experienced only a few years previously. Unemployment shot up into the double digits and bankruptcies reached record levels. Interest rates stayed in the double digits to choke off any kind of a recovery, and only began to come down in mid-1982 because the economy continued to deteriorate so badly the demand for credit on the part of business and consumers dried up. Thus economic conditions steadily worsened, and no one seemed to have any answers to the economic problems.

However, interest rate declines in mid-1982 sparked a stock market rally of unprecedented proportions. These declines also promoted a revival of economic growth as industries, such as housing and automobiles, picked up steam. The unemployment rate fell out of the double-digit range to remain fixed at around 7 percent for several years, leading many economists to redefine an acceptable rate of unemployment. The economy quickly turned around and continued to roll along at a decent rate of growth for several years. A further stimulus to growth and the stock and bond markets was provided by oil price declines that began in late 1985 and continued into 1986. This decline was triggered by the inability of OPEC to agree on production quotas that would keep oil prices high, and a consequent glut of oil on world markets.

Oil prices fell from a high of around $30 per barrel to less than $10 dollars per barrel on world markets. Although this fall hurt the oil-producing states in the United States, it helped most industries through lower oil prices and was a great benefit to the consumer. Gasoline prices fell dramatically and resulted in the lowest inflation rates in years. Interest rates continued to decline as well, as mortgage rates fell to their lowest levels since the 1970s, which continued to fuel the stock market rise during the first quarter of 1986. More new jobs were created, and although economic growth was not spectacular, it at least continued in the positive range and there was no serious talk of a recession.

Despite all this good economic news, however, there continued to be several ominous threats to continued growth and prosperity. The federal budget deficit ballooned during these years to unprecedented levels, reaching a high of $220.7 billion in 1986. Although the deficit dropped to about $150 billion in each of the next two years, government spending continued at record high levels, as the total federal budget submitted for fiscal year 1988 reached the trillion dollar level for the first time in history. There seemed to be no way in which government spending could be brought under control. The second problem was the trade deficit that grew to a record $169.8 billion in 1986, even though the dollar had fallen sharply against some of the major world's currencies. The last surplus the United States enjoyed in its merchandise trade balance was in 1975, and since that time the trade deficit has continued to grow, making the United States the world's largest debtor nation.

These deficits kept a lid on economic growth and posed a serious problem for future generations. The huge federal deficit continued to put upward pressure on interest rates and the trade deficit exported jobs and income overseas. Consumer debt continued to grow as well, and at the end of 1986, Americans were $170 billion in debt. The average amount owed by families increased from $33,300 in 1985 to $40,500 in 1986—an increase of nearly 22 percent. These kinds of deficits provided ample evidence that the entire country, both private and public sectors, was living beyond its means, and that someday there would be a day of reckoning.

Many thought this day of reckoning had arrived in October of 1987 when the stock market crashed. On October 19, 1987, the Dow plunged 508 points, or an incredible 22.6 percent, almost double the 12.8 percent loss in the 1929 crash. Some $500 billion in paper value, equal to the gross national product of France, vanished. Volume on the New York Stock Exchange topped 600 million shares, almost double the all-time record. While the Dow immediately regained some of that loss, by the end of the week, the Dow had lost 28.3 percent or some $870 billion in value from its high of 2722 reached in August 1987.

A recession seemed to be in the cards, as a loss of that magnitude would have to affect spending and investment decisions, and cause a loss of confidence in the economy. But a recession never happened. The economy continued to grow, eventually setting a record for length of a peace-time expansion. The stock market plunge was seen to be largely the result of overspeculation, particularly in options and futures markets, that was exacerbated by program trading. The real economy remained relatively unaffected. The stock market itself eventually recovered, erasing the 508 point loss on January 24, 1989, when it soared 38.04 points to close at 2256.43, a post-crash high.

Table 3.5
Employment Growth Rates in Selected Industries

Economic Sector	Average Annual Rate of Change		Percent of Total Employed 1986
	1970–80	1980–86	
Service Industries	3.2	2.4	66.6%
Transportation and public utilities	1.3	.3	4.7
Wholesale trade	2.8	1.4	5.1
Retail trade	3.1	2.9	16.0
Finance, insurance, and real estate	3.5	3.4	5.6
Personal services	− .9	3.4	1.0
Business services	6.3	7.5	4.3
Amusement and recreation services	5.0	0.1	0.0
Health services	5.8	3.7	5.9
Legal services	7.8	7.0	0.7
Educational services	1.9	3.9	1.3
Agriculture	− .2	− .8	2.9
Production Industries	.8	− .6	22.1
Mining	5.1	−4.4	0.7
Construction	1.9	2.0	4.4
Manufacturing	.5	−1.1	17.0

Source: U.S. Department of Commerce, Table 631, *Statistical Abstract of the United States, 1988,* 108th ed. (Washington, D.C.: U.S. Government Printing Office, 1987), p. 380.

The trend toward services is clear, as an examination of the growth rates in service and production industries from 1970–1986 in the United States shows (see Table 3.5). This trend accelerated throughout the economic recovery that began in mid-1982 with the decline in interest rates. The goods-producing sector's share of total payroll employment steadily declined throughout the recovery period. In 1984, job growth in the service sector accounted for a little more than four-fifths of all new jobs created, while representing just under 75 percent of all non-farm employment. Between 1982 and 1984, services accounted for 5.2 million of the 7.4 million increase in non-farm jobs.[38] Of the 1.2 million jobs created in 1986, services alone accounted for just under 1 million.[39]

The implications of this change for employment in the United States were believed to be significant. The ability of the goods producing sector in developed countries to produce employment was said to be eroding because of: (1) continued migration of labor-intensive industries to less developed countries where wage-rates are lower, (2) increased automation of those industries remaining in developed countries, and (3) decreasing growth of demand for material

[38]"Business Outlook," *Business Week*, March 25, 1985, p. 22.

[39]"Business Outlook," *Business Week*, February 23, 1987, p. 40.

goods in developed countries as the market becomes saturated and values change.[40]

Because of this transformation, it was argued, society must change its focus and priorities. Major investments and efforts of both the public and private sectors must be directed toward increasing the amount, variety, and quality of services provided. The bulk of employment will have to come from nongoods-producing industries as opportunities to increase employment lie in the service industries. Unless developed countries learn how to provide services as efficiently and effectively as they have historically provided goods, unemployment, underemployment, and a host of other social problems are bound to increase.[41]

The contradictions that appeared in the postindustrial period were every bit as serious as in earlier periods. The social movements that appeared in the 1960s brought into question the article of faith related to economic growth—that economic growth was an unmixed blessing and the supreme objective of the country. It had been believed that economic growth was the source of all progress, social as well as economic. The engine of growth was the drive for profits by competitive private enterprise, which applied new technologies as rapidly as possible to foster economic growth. Business was thought to be solely an economic institution, and in pursuing economic objectives, business was making its maximum contribution to society.

But the civil rights movement and ecology movements, for example, pointed out that economic growth was a mixed blessing—that there were some serious social deficits in the form of discrimination and pollution that were not being treated adequately by the continual pursuit of an ever-increasing gross national product. Discrimination was not being eliminated by the market system, as something called *systemic discrimination* was built into the personnel practices of our economic institutions. The market system provided no means of controlling pollution—there were no incentives to reduce pollution or dispose of toxic wastes properly to mitigate the environmental effects of new technology. These problems had to be given more direct attention in order to improve the *quality of life* for all citizens (a term that came to be increasingly used as a supplement or replacement of economic growth as an overall objective for the nation).

Another contradiction had to do with resource shortages. The Arab oil embargo and subsequent price increases not only made us aware of our dependency on foreign sources of supply. It also confronted us with the possibility of facing real limits to economic growth, a subject that had been discussed previously but now confronted the nation as a reality rather than an academic exercise. The United States has used up a good many of its basic resources to the point where it is dependent on foreign sources for many of its raw materials.

[40]Russell L. Ackoff, Paul Broholm, and Roberta Snow, *Revitalizing Western Economies* (San Francisco: Jossey-Bass, 1984), p. xiv.
[41]Ibid.

But even these foreign sources are finite. Thus the future holds a great deal of uncertainty about the cost and availability of raw materials crucial to the continued survival and operation of a sophisticated and technological society.

Questions began to be raised about the ability of a market system to allocate resources that are in short supply in an effective and acceptable manner. Does a market system that encourages exploitation of resources rather than conservation provide for future generations? Does the market system distribute pain and suffering fairly when critical resources become scarce? Is it right, for example, that those at the low end of the income scale should suffer more than others? Does not everyone have a basic right to be warm in winter and have enough gasoline for normal driving? Does the market system provide adequate incentives for the development of alternative sources of supply when the technologies are complex and expensive, and the lead times are lengthy before a private business can expect a return on investment?

Yet a third contradiction appeared in the deterioration of some of our basic industries. Industries like steel and the automobile industry needed billions of dollars to retool and invest in new technologies to become competitive in world markets. Yet the market system did not seem to be providing the capital needs of these industries or allocating enough capital resources in their direction. The incentives were lacking, and thus these industries continued to deteriorate. The continued growth of services meant that our economy was becoming skewed toward lower-paying jobs in service industries with serious implications for standards of living and continued economic growth.

Social Regulation

The social deficits that were of concern in the 1960s were the subject of government action. Again the market proved unable to respond to these problems and meet the social needs of society. A new area of public policy ensued with the passage of much legislation directed at these problems and the creation of a new form of regulation called *social regulation*. Congress passed all kinds of social legislation related to environmental cleanup, consumer concerns, and other social issues, outdoing the New Deal Congress of Franklin D. Roosevelt. Goverment also created new regulatory agencies, such as the Environmental Protection Agency (EPA), the Equal Employment Opportunity Commission (EEOC), the Consumer Product Safety Commission (CPSC), and the Occupational Safety and Health Administration (OSHA), and gave expanded powers to such existing agencies as the Food and Drug Administration (FDA). This new type of regulation affects every industry in the country rather than a particular industry, as was the old style of regulation patterned after the Interstate Commerce Commission model. These regulatory agencies set and enforce standards, in the case of pollution control and job safety and health, for example, which all companies are expected to meet. Every company is thus left in the same competitive position and at the same time social goods and services are supposedly provided to the society.

Thus business was forced to internalize the so-called social costs of production, and respond to social problems. Business was asked to consider and mitigate the social effects of its economic decisions. The new style of social regulation concerns itself with the conditions under which goods and services are produced and the physical characteristics of products rather than rates, routes, and the obligation to serve, as did the old style of industry regulation. Social regulatory agencies are concerned with noneconomic matters and sometimes pay little or no attention to an industry's basic mission of providing goods and services to the country. They become involved with many detailed facets of the production process, interfering with the traditional prerogatives of management. For example, OSHA sometimes specifies precise engineering controls that must be adopted. The CPSC mandates specific product characteristics it believes will protect consumers from injury.[42]

One reason for this type of regulation is related to the nature of today's workplace and marketplace. It is often argued that when goods and technology are complex and their effects largely unknown, consumers are incapable of making intelligent judgments. Workers may not know the risks they face on various jobs or may not be able to acquire the necessary information. Expert judgment is needed in these areas to protect consumers and workers from unnecessary risks that they cannot assess for themselves.[43]

Another reason for this type of regulation is the existence of situations where the actions of a firm have a harmful effect on others. The cost of external diseconomies, such as air and water pollution cannot be voluntarily assumed by firms unless a government agency exists to enforce standards equally across all firms in an industry. Voluntary assumption by some firms would place them at a competitive disadvantage; regulation is needed to make all companies meet the same standard, leaving them in the same competitive position.[44]

Agencies dealing with social regulation include OSHA, whose purpose is to enforce worker safety and health regulations. The EEOC enforces the antidiscriminatory provisions of the Civil Rights Act and other related laws that have recently come under its jurisdiction. The CPSC was created to protect the public from unreasonable risks of injury associated with consumer products. Protection and enhancement of the physical environment is the responsibility of the EPA. The Bureau of Consumer Protection in the Federal Trade Commission (FTC) deals with false or deceptive advertising of consumer products. The purpose of the FDA is to protect the public against impure and unsafe food, drugs, and cosmetics, and to regulate hazards associated with medical devices and radiation. Finally, the National Highway Traffic Safety Administration (NHTSA) sets standards for motor vehicle safety and fuel economy.

[42]William Lilley III and James C. Miller III, "The New Social Regulation," *The Public Interest*, no. 47 (Spring 1977), p. 53.

[43]Robert E. Healy, ed., *Federal Regulatory Directory 1979–80* (Washington, D.C.: Congressional Quarterly, Inc., 1979), p. 5.

[44]Ibid.

National Economic Planning   This area of public planning is not yet developed, but it certainly is in the discussion stage. Two bills were introduced into Congress to set up a planning mechanism and establish national objectives.[45] The Carter administration attempted to develop a comprehensive energy plan, which consisted of a series of rewards and penalties for consumers and business organizations to adopt behaviors consistent with the goal of energy independence. Some economists advocate a national materials policy to assure the country adequate sources of supply for critical resources. The government attempted to promote the development of synthetic fuel. A massive effort was launched involving billions of dollars to provide incentives for private corporations to invest in research and development for synfuel. There has been much talk about the reindustrialization of America, which most often means the government should directly promote capital formation for modernization of plants and equipment in our basic industries.

Thus the debate has begun as to whether formal economic planning is a proper role for government in mediating the contradictions introduced by resource shortages and the deindustrialization of the United States. This debate intensified during the presidential campaign of 1984, particularly during the Democratic primary. Various kinds of national planning or industrial policy were talked about, including (1) government aid to high-technology industries in order to speed up the transition to a high-tech society and take advantage of our competitive edge in world markets; (2) help for basic industries, such as steel, that are vital to our competitive position in the world and our economic independence; (3) government help for people to retrain and relocate if necessary to find new jobs and cope with the transition to a new kind of postindustrial society; and (4) some kind of a bail-out agency to provide money for failing companies to help them make the necessary adjustments to survive in a changing economy.

One argument for national planning is simply that if government management of aggregate demand has had such success for most of the period since World War II, more such planning on an even more comprehensive basis must be better. Others argue that the difficulties we have experienced since 1974 with high inflation and unemployment make planning a necessity. We have moved into an era of resource shortages, it is said, where the market can no longer allocate resources to their best uses. The market must be supplemented by national economic planning to allocate these scarce resources in a fair and just manner so all members of society can maintain a decent quality of life.

Others point to the success corporations have had with planning and argue that government should be using some of the techniques that corporations have developed to set goals, objectives, and strategies for all its agencies.

---

[45]The Humphrey-Javits bill introduced into the first session of the 94th Congress (S. 1795) and the Humphrey-Hawkins bill introduced into the House (H.R. 50) and Senate (S. 50) in March 1976.

"Our government suffers from the absence of (1) an overall sense of direction, (2) well-defined national goals and objectives, (3) an integrated strategy for achieving such goals and objectives, and (4) a process for answering difficult 'what if?' questions that cut across department lines within the government."[46] The answer is a comprehensive planning system that would solve the problems of energy, national defense, environment, and other concerns of this scope.

Another argument in favor of planning is that business itself would benefit from it; our present haphazard approach to problems like inflation and unemployment does not create an environment in which business can function effectively. A more coordinated and planned response to problems would create a more stable environment for business and help it to gain credibility.[47] Finally, the planning exercise, some argue, would itself be beneficial. There has been a tendency for the nation to charge off after a variety of social and economic goals, all of them desirable but not necessarily compatible with one another. Planning might introduce some realism and discipline to this process.

The arguments against planning are many and formidable. Some fear that this role would inevitably result in more government control over business and eventually produce such a concentration of economic and political power in the hands of the federal government as to threaten our pluralistic system. Such a role involves a further shift in power to government bureaucrats and gives them greater control over the daily lives of citizens.

Another argument against planning is that the sheer size and complexity of the socioeconomic system is simply beyond the capability of people and machines to coordinate effectively. Too many variables and too many decisions would have to be made centrally to take into account all the various interests of society. Critics of planning need only point to the efforts of the Department of Energy to allocate energy resources, and the dislocations and problems these efforts caused.

Finally, the comparison of government planning with planning by business is questioned. There is a fundamental difference, some point out, between the two processes. Business planning is based on the assumption that the ultimate decisions as to the allocation of society's resources are made by individual consumers. Thus business planning is geared to the corporate purpose of attempting to persuade consumers to buy the firm's goods or services. If the company's planning is wrong, it will suffer the consequences.

Government, on the other hand, will determine through a planning process what is in the best interests of society as a whole. If the public does not respond accordingly, the government can use its power to achieve the results it desires. This power includes promotion, procurement, regulation, ownership,

---

[46]Thomas H. Naylor, "The U.S. Needs Strategic Planning," *Business Week*, December 17, 1979, p. 18.

[47]Robert Lekachman, "A Cure for Corporate Neurosis," *Saturday Review*, January 21, 1978, pp. 30–34.

taxation, and other roles it plays in the economy. Unlike a private organization, government may not only plan, it can also command. Whereas a business firm can set goals only for itself, government can establish goals for society as a whole and see that they are followed through some form of government control.[48]

The crucial questions in this discussion concern the allocation of resources, particularly capital resources. Can the market be trusted to allocate resources that are in short supply in a fair and just manner or does public policy need to supplement or even replace the market in some circumstances? In a time of economic and social change, are the adjustments required too great for some businesses and groups of people so that they need help from the government to make the transition? Does the market allocate the burdens of change in an equitable manner or are public policy measures needed to distribute these burdens throughout society? Is public policy necessary to save some of our basic industries for reasons of national security even though they may not be economically profitable when compared with similar industries in other countries? These kinds of questions are basic to the debate about industrial policy or national economic planning. Again, market outcomes are being questioned with respect to goals and objectives that are important to the society as a whole.

There were several periods in U.S. history where new areas of public policy developed in response to contradictions that developed in the market system. These periods are summarized in Table 3.6 in case the reader has

Table 3.6
Major Periods of Public Policy

Historical Period	Contradictions	Public Policy
Rise of modern industrial society	Destruction of competition	Industry regulation Antitrust legislation
The Great Depression	Widespread unemployment and poverty Market not self-correcting.	Economic Management Collective bargaining Welfare system
Postindustrial society	Social deficits Resource shortages Deindustrialization	Social regulation National economic planning

become confused by all the detail in this chapter. Without successful mediation, these contradictions may indeed have developed sufficient pressures to result in a radical transformation of American society. Thus public policy plays a crucial role in responding to values that are not able to be incorporated into the normal workings of a market system.

[48]Murray L. Weidenbaum and Linda Rockwood, "Corporate Planning versus Government Planning," *The Public Interest*, no. 46 (Winter 1977), pp. 59–72.

SELECTED REFERENCES

ALLEN, FREDERICK LEWIS. *The Lords of Creation.* New York: Harper & Row, 1935.

CHANDLER, ALFRED. *The Visible Hand: The Managerial Revolution in American Business.* Cambridge, Mass.: Belknap Press, 1977.

CHANDLER, ALFRED D., and RICHARD S. TEDLOW. *The Coming of Managerial Capitalism: A Casebook on the History of American Economic Institutions.* Homewood, Ill.: Richard D. Irwin, 1985.

CHANDLER, LESTER V. *America's Greatest Depression, 1929–1941.* New York: Harper & Row, 1942.

COCKRAN, THOMAS C., and WILLIAM MILLER. *The Age of Enterprise.* New York: Harper & Row, 1942.

DEGLER, CARL N. *The New Deal.* Chicago: Quadrangle Books, 1970.

GALBRAITH, JOHN KENNETH. *The Great Crash—1929,* 3rd ed. Boston: Houghton Mifflin, 1972.

GOLAMBOS, LOUIS, and JOSEPH PRATT. *The Rise of the Corporate Commonwealth.* New York: Basic Books, 1988.

GRAHAM, OTIS L. *The New Deal: The Critical Issue.* Boston: Little, Brown, 1971.

GREENBERG, EDWARD S. *Capitalism and the American Political Ideal.* Armonk, N.Y.: M. E. Sharpe, 1985.

GRONER, ALEX. *The American Heritage History of American Business and Industry.* New York: American Heritage Publishing Co., 1972.

HACKER, LOUIS M. *The Triumph of American Capitalism.* New York: Simon & Schuster, 1940.

HEILBRONER, ROBERT L. *Beyond Boom and Crash.* New York: Norton, 1978.

JOSEPHSON, MATTHEW. *The Robber Barons.* New York: Harcourt Brace Jovanovich, 1934.

MORISON, SAMUEL E., and HENRY S. COMMAGER. *Growth of the American Republic.* Oxford: Oxford University Press, 1937.

NORTON, HUGH STANTON. *The Employment Act and the Council of Economic Advisers, 1946–1976.* Columbia: University of South Carolina Press, 1977.

RUSSEL, ROBERT R. *A History of the American Economic System.* New York: Appleton-Century Crofts, 1964.

SCHACTMAN, TOM. *The Day America Crashed.* New York: Putnam, 1979.

THE ƧOCIAL CONTEXT
OF PUBLIC POLICY

⟸ IDEAS TO BE FOUND ⟹
IN THIS CHAPTER

- Values
- Ethics
- Social-political structure

How do new areas of public policy, such as those discussed in the last chapter, get started? What can explain the emergence of new issues that were previously unimportant?. What elements combine to cause social change at various times in our history as a nation? How do issues find their way onto the public policy agenda so that they become of widespread concern and deserve attention by government and corporations? These kinds of questions will be discussed in this chapter as part of an attempt to understand the social context in which public policy is developed.

VALUES Public policy reflects the values of society, or at least of significant segments of society, that are active in the public policy process. When particular values people hold strongly are threatened or when new values are adopted, pressures are generated. If the pressures are strong and widespread, they may result in the formulation of public policy, provided no other means can be used successfully. Thus it would seem that the concept of value is a good place to start in attempting to understand the origins of public policy. Values are fundamental and enduring beliefs about the most desirable conditions and purposes of human life and as such generate pressures for change when contradictions appear in society that are not immediately resolved.

Definition of Values   There is both a subjective and an objective definition of values. The subjective aspect of values has to do with values that are different among people and reflect individual desires and beliefs. Values are properties that human beings associate with or assign to certain forms of human behavior, institutions, or material goods and services. When something is valued, it is considered to be worthwhile, good, desirable, important, and esteemed or prized.[1] That something, whatever it is, is believed to contribute to one's well-being and be of benefit to him or her. Something that is valueless is considered to be worthless and is not desired for any reason. When one makes a value judgment about something, one is either attributing value to a certain action or entity and judging it to be worthwhile, good, or desirable to some degree, or deciding that the entity in question has little or no worth and is not desired. It is important to note that in the subjective sense, values reside in the human beings making value judgments and are not intrinsic to the objects or entities under consideration.

Value conflicts exist between people and within people. One person may value a new house quite highly, whereas another person may not deem it very important. One person may strongly desire a vacation in Hawaii. Someone else may want to buy a new car. A single individual may want both a vacation in Hawaii and a new car, but may not be able to afford both of these good things. The market system resolves these conflicts by forcing people to translate their conflicting desires into common economic values reflected in prices and make choices about which items are most worthwhile. The market system responds to this subjective definition of values by allowing people to express their desires in the marketplace for goods and services they value.

The objective view of values, on the other hand, deals with values in more absolute terms—that certain things are good for people whether they desire them or not, or conversely, that certain things are inherently bad and people shouldn't have them in spite of their desires. There is a large market for cocaine and other narcotics, for example, as many people desire these products. There are producers and drug dealers who try to meet these needs. Yet most societies believe it is a bad thing for people to use these products and try to prevent their production, sale, and usage through the use of sanctions and penalties. To use another example, government regulators have decided that auto safety is a good thing despite people's apparent disdain for safety measures, and at one point, required auto manufacturers to design cars so they could not be started until seat belts were fastened.

---

[1]*Webster's New Collegiate Dictionary* (Springfield, Mass.: G. & C. Merriam Company, 1977), p. 1292.

In this objective view, values are believed to be intrinsic to the objects or entities under consideration, and are not solely a function of human judgments. Value conflicts again exist as people differ over which objects have intrinsic value and which take priority when choices have to be made. Some people may value clean air quite highly and are willing to pay a high price for better air quality, whereas others may value energy independence (which means burning coal that dirties the air) and are willing to tolerate a lower air quality. The public policy process resolves such value conflicts through a process of negotiation and compromise where a common course of action is agreed upon with respect to a social objective, such as clean air or energy independence. Decisions have to be made collectively about the provision of public goods and services that will contribute to the enhancement of the society's welfare.

When many people in a society desire the same things or make the same kinds of value judgments, social values can be said to exist. These values show up in principles the society believes in strongly, the institutions that are most highly esteemed, the behavior a society believes is appropriate, and the objectives people pursue. Social values, then, are values held in common because it is believed that certain principles, institutions, behavior, and objectives will produce a desirable state of affairs for all members of that society. When these social values are relatively homogeneous over a period of time, that society is stable and experiences little social change. When a homogeneous value system begins to break up and large segments of society begin to express so-called nontraditional values, social change of some kind seems inevitable. Social change of this sort usually brings about changes in the major institutions of society to incorporate these new values.

Classification of Values   Values can be measured along several dimensions to evaluate their importance and strength in influencing a society's behavior. These dimensions are shown in Exhibit 4.1, which can be used as a model to determine the important values of a given society. If these dimensions can be measured accurately, one can get some idea of the dominant value system in a society and where values rank in a scale of priorities. This information should be helpful in attempting to forecast value changes and develop political strategies.

Extensiveness has to do with how widespread a value is throughout a society. Recent surveys show, for example, that support for cleaning up the environment is widespread throughout all segments of society. Economic growth is something Americans have valued throughout their entire history and are likely to do so for the foreseeable future. Freedom is something Americans value with great intensity and will go to great lengths to protect and preserve. Also, the heroic accolades given to winners of the Super Bowl and winners of other sports events show how strongly Americans value competition.

Values can also be classified into certain categories, such as those shown in Exhibit 4.2, which can aid in understanding how values relate to each other and

Exhibit 4.1
Value Dimensions

1. Extensiveness of the value in the total activity of the system. What proportion of a population and of its activities manifests the value?
2. Duration of the value. Has it been persistently important over a considerable period of time?
3. Intensity with which the value is sought or maintained, as shown by effort, crucial choices, verbal affirmation, and reactions to threats to the value—for example, promptness, certainty, and severity of sanctions.
4. Prestige of value carriers—that is, of persons, objects, or organizations considered to be bearers of the value. Culture heroes, for example, are significant indexes of values of high generality and esteem.

Source: Robin M. Williams, Jr. *American Society: A Sociological Interpretation,* 3rd. ed. (New York: Knopf, 1970), p. 448. Reprinted with permission.

simplify an analysis of value change. Values that fall in the same category relate to each other in a cluster and form a value system. Using such categories, one can make a comparative analysis in terms of which values are more dominant than others in our society. This procedure can also aid in understanding social change and predicting future developments in public policy that may affect corporate behavior.

Many would argue that American society is dominated by an economic value system. Elbing and Elbing, for example, believe that the business institution is the supreme institution in our society. What is good for business is believed to be good for the entire country. The ultimate social values for society are assumed to be the outgrowth of economic values created by business organi-

Exhibit 4.2
Value Systems

Theoretic:	The pursuit of knowledge for its own sake—the desirability of attaining knowledge because of the pleasure this brings to an individual.
Economic:	The pursuit of those material goods and services that can be bought and sold on the marketplace whose value is determined through the exchange process.
Aesthetic:	The importance of beauty in all aspects of existence, particularly in nature.
Social:	The desire to associate and interact with other people either individually or as members of a group and affirm one's existence in this manner.
Political:	The desire to make decisions that affect many people in society and exercise power over them.
Religious:	The pursuit of the ideas and precepts of a particular religious system.
Ethical:	The desire to do the right thing, take the right action, make the right decision in accordance with a particular ethical system.

Source: Adapted from Keith Davis and Robert L. Blomstrom, *Business and Society: Environment and Responsibility,* 3rd ed. (New York: McGraw-Hill, 1975), p. 175. Reproduced with permission.

[2]Alvar O. Elbing, Jr. and Carol J. Elbing, *The Value Issue of Business* (New York: McGraw-Hill, 1967), p. 57.

zations. Social and ethical problems not solved through the production of goods and services traded on the marketplace are viewed as peripheral problems.[2]

Others may not agree that economic values are so dominant, at least as far as their individual priorities are concerned, and perhaps even in the society at large. Some may believe that religious values are most important—that the ideals embodied in the Judeo-Christian tradition, for example, are most desirable and enduring as far as human fulfillment is concerned. Intellectuals may hold a certain disdain for economic values and believe the marketplace caters to the vulgar tastes of the masses. For them, the pursuit of knowledge may be the most important value in their scale of priorities.

Influences on Values Values change in response to many influences in society. *Technology* is one such influence. It may be possible for some things to be done that could never have been done before or to do something more easily or inexpensively than before, changing the benefit-cost ratio. The invention of the automobile, for example, eventually made it possible to travel long distances with relative ease and at increased speeds, making distant places accessible. The automobile has thus influenced many values with respect to freedom and adventure. But the automobile also pollutes the environment, and thus influences values with respect to the air we breath.

Information changes the importance of certain things in our society. When it became known that using the environment to dump our wastes into was having some disastrous side effects and might even change the climate of the world, the importance of the environment increased dramatically and more resources were allocated to cleaning it up. As we learn more about the effects of smoking on human health, people have changed their behavior toward tobacco use, and public policies have been adopted to protect the health of nonsmokers.

Shifts in population have an effect on the dominant value systems in society. If the aged come to constitute an increasing proportion of the population, the values they hold as a group will tend to exercise more influence over the society as a whole. The same will hold true if young people come to constitute an increasing proportion of the population, as was true of American society in the 1960s. Their values tended to dominate many segments of American society in those years, as both the market system and public policy process responded to their individual wishes and collective desires for the society as a whole.

Another factor influencing values is *education*. As people attain more formal education, they may question their desires and the things that they were raised to believe were important. They may come to reject these traditional values appropriated from their families and adopt a new set of desires and goals to pursue. Education supposedly broadens one's horizons and acquaints one with new sets of possibilities. Education gives people access to different dimensions of life and thus may change their beliefs about what is worthwhile.

Changes in basic institutions, such as the family and religion, also affect

91

values. These institutions, particularly the family, play a crucial role in the socialization of children and the transmission of values from generation to generation. Much evidence suggests that these institutions are changing. Increasing numbers of women are employed outside the home, leaving children in day care centers or nursery homes. The increasing divorce rate breaks up more and more families and leads to an increase of single-parent families. Attendance at religious institutions has declined and the authority of these institutions is severely questioned. As these basic institutions play a reduced role in value transmission, there is less continuity of values from one generation to the next. Children form their values on the basis of experience with peers rather than appropriating them from the previous generation.

Affluence also causes value changes. Society can be looked at from the standpoint of a Maslowian hierarchy of needs. As more and more people in society become affluent and thus fulfill their basic economic needs, they can move up the ladder to fulfill a higher order of needs. Things become important to them that were not within the range of possibility before. They may desire other goods and services besides economic ones and pursue other goals related to self-fulfillment or improving the quality of life for the whole society.

Value Changes in American Society Identifying specific value changes in American society is a risky proposition, but a good deal of evidence suggests that certain value changes have taken place in recent years. These changes have not necessarily occurred throughout the entire society, but are significant enough to have appeared in much of the literature related to American society. These changes, some of which are described below, are reflected in public policy and have impacted business organizations.

1. One traditional value is the importance that American society has attached to work and a corresponding disrespect for laziness. The traditional notion was that work had value in and of itself regardless of the nature of the work. Working contributed to the development of individual character and made a contribution to the wealth of society. Thus work had a transcendent meaning that made all jobs of equal value and made work a serious duty of humankind.

These beliefs have changed for many people. Work has lost this transcendent meaning and is valued more for what it contributes to the individual's personal enjoyment and fulfillment. Many people want a job that is fulfilling and challenging and shun jobs that involve drudgery and boredom. If they cannot find this kind of job, they try to gain more leisure time away from the job to pursue their interests. Leisure is seen as beneficial and fulfilling and is not necessarily believed to be contributing to the decadence of society.

2. Related to the importance of working hard was the traditional impor-

tance of deferring personal gratification until the future. There was value in providing for one's security in retirement, saving for a rainy day, building an estate for the children, and having such virtue rewarded in heaven rather than on earth. The growth of a credit-oriented society has destroyed this value, as it encourages instant gratification. Why wait? One can enjoy a particular product or service right now by purchasing it on credit and paying later through an installment plan. Homes can be purchased with long-term mortgages. The future is taken care of with social security or institutional retirement plans.

3. Americans have traditionally believed that opportunity for success should be—and is in fact—equal for all people in society. America was the land of opportunity to which people came from all over the world. The existence of such unbounded opportunity led to the conclusion that the successful are differentiated from the unsuccessful only by their moral virtue, their willingness to work hard and save, and their innate abilities. Recent years have seen the recognition that equal opportunity has not always existed for certain segments of society, most notably minorities and women. It has been discovered that systemic discrimination against these groups was built into the hiring, transfer, and other employment practices of our major institutions.

4. Since there was so much opportunity, Americans have always believed that it was important to make it on one's own in the world—that the world did not owe one a living but that one had to earn his or her own place in society by working hard to make a success of something. The Depression years saw the beginnings of a philosophy of entitlement that has grown stronger. People have a right to an income, a job, and good health, but, despite one's best efforts, the marketplace does not always provide opportunities to realize these goals. If the market system cannot respect these rights, the government should, by becoming the employer of last resort, providing in effect a guaranteed annual income (social security) or providing health care for all its citizens.

5. The tendency to pursue material wealth as a solution to many problems and a national belief in the desirability of economic growth and improved material living standards has been a social goal of the highest priority. This value was questioned in the 1950s and 1960s by many people who dropped out of the system to pursue something more meaningful for themselves than material wealth. Many public policy measures were also passed to promote social values such as clean air and safer workplaces that placed a check on the unregulated pursuit of economic growth and provided a means to attain some kind of balance between economic growth and social values.

6. The traditional American attitude toward the natural environment was that it is basically a hostile force to be subdued and exploited as a readily available source of economic growth. Our land and resources were believed to be infinite. Indeed, as the first pioneers saw the vast expanse of the western region of the country, this belief was a reasonable response. This is

so no longer. We know our resources are finite and we have nearly exhausted some of them. We also know that we have to live in harmony with nature and that our environment has deteriorated from many years of exploitation and neglect.

7. Technological progress is closely related to growth—a faith in the ability of science and technology, supported by money and economic resources, to ultimately solve all our problems. New technologies were introduced rapidly into society as a way to sustain growth and improve the quality of life. The side effects of many technologies, however, have now become all too apparent, and some technologies, such as nuclear power, are being questioned as to whether the risks involved make them worthwhile. Technology is seen as the source of many of our problems, and thus cannot be introduced into society without some thought given to its long-term effects on the environment.

8. Americans have come to have a health consciousness over the last several years that is a departure from traditional values. Although we have always been concerned about our health, this concern is now more intense and widespread. This health consciousness is evident in the physical fitness centers that have grown around the country, the efforts people put into physical exercise like jogging, and the increased expenditures for health care. This concern is partly a result of developments in medical technology, but it also reflects a change in values that shows a greater priority given to health matters. This value change affects business in terms of greater emphasis on product and workplace safety and health, increased concern about environmental pollution and health, and growing concern related to traditional American habits like cigarette smoking.

9. The increased litigiousness of Americans reflects a value change in that people value certain rights more highly than in the past and are willing to challenge institutions that violate those rights by pursuing them through the legal system. Changed thinking about product liability has made it easier for the average citizen to file suit against large companies and other institutions, and juries have been prone to award large settlements to plaintiffs for compensatory damages and in some cases punitive damages. Awards have also been made for new kinds of intangible damages like pain and suffering that are open-ended in nature. These increased liability awards have created a crisis in the liability system in this country as insurance costs have skyrocketed and in some cases is unavailable. Thus consumers and workers can assert their rights to safe products and safe workplaces through the legal system and do not have to rely solely on government and business to respond to these values.

10. Finally, and in a sense summarizing all the rest, there has been the predominance of economic values in our society. This predominance is reflected in the high priority and social approval granted to the economic institutions in our society and the men and women who manage them. Recently, the

term *quality of life* has come into vogue as a concept used to broaden people's conception of the kind of life they desire for themselves. Within this conception, social values play an increasingly important part and economic values begin to lose their dominant character. From this change comes pressure to make the corporation respond to social values—to view it as a socioeconomic institution that has both economic and social responsibilities.

These changes in values are not, of course, spread throughout the entire society. They tend to be concentrated among younger people, people with college educations, and people in the middle- and upper-income groups. This concentration may reflect differences in formal education or it may indicate that people are not willing to abandon traditional values until they have attained the material success inherent in the old value system. But it is important to note that values seem to be changing fastest among people one would expect to have the greatest influence over society's future.

It must also be noted that American society is not in the process of exchanging one set of values for another. It is changing from a nation with relatively homogeneous values to one in which a variety of values is tolerated and encouraged. This change is consistent with the movement toward a pluralistic society, as such a social structure allows a greater diversity of values to be expressed. More issues can be placed on the public policy agenda in a pluralistic society that may command the attention of public policy makers.

ETHICS

Advocates of the public policy approach have in many cases failed to acknowledge how thoroughly saturated the public policy process is with value-laden phenomena. There was a hope that by using the public policy approach, scholars could escape the subjectivity and vagueness of corporate social responsibility philosophizing and substitute a more objective and value-neutral basis for measuring and judging business social performance. If business adhered to the standards of performance expressed in the law and existing public policy, then it could be judged as being socially responsive to the changing expectations of society.[3]

However, when one digs beneath the surface of the public policy approach, one finds public policy plagued by the same kinds of ethical dilemmas that plagued earlier attempts to deal with the social responsibilities of business. The normative questions about corporate social responsibilities are still on the table and are still largely unanswered. Public policy is, in the final analysis, all about values and value conflicts, and public policy solutions to social problems are built on some conception of ethics that has to do with the promotion of human welfare. Thus there is an ethical dimension to public policy that needs to be discussed.

[3]William C. Frederick, "Toward CSR[3]: Why Ethical Analysis is Indispensable and Unavoidable in Corporate Affairs," *California Management Review*, vol. XXVII, no. 2, (Winter 1986), pp. 129–133.

Ethics is concerned with actions and practices that are directed to improving the welfare of people. Ethicists explore the concepts and language that are used to direct such actions and practices.

> Some are primarily concerned with the justification of this concern itself, others with the delineation or justification of principles that specify appropriate welfare-meeting conduct, and others with the relationship between these principles and the rules or character traits that guide people toward specific behavior to achieve human welfare. In essence ethics is concerned with clarifying what constitutes human welfare and the kind of conduct necessary to promote it.[4]

Ethics and values are terms that are often used interchangeably in many discussions. Ethics is usually considered to be the more general term, referring to conceptions of human welfare and the development of principles to attain human welfare. Values can be thought of as specific desires for concrete objects or beliefs that are held to be important. We can value specific goods and services that are available on the market or we can value more abstract concepts such as freedom or equality. Whatever we value, however, stems from some general conceptions of a good life or a life that is worth living. We value freedom because we believe freedom is a fundamental human characteristic or need that makes for a better society. Human welfare is promoted if people are free to pursue their own interests and objectives. Ethics and values are thus closely related and are used interchangeably in many discussions.

An ethical decision, as distinguished from a nonethical decision, is one that affects human welfare or human fulfillment in some significant manner. An ethical decision is one in which somebody's welfare is at stake—somebody will be positively or negatively affected by the decision. To speak of human welfare or human fulfillment is too vague and abstract to be of much help in clarifying the nature of an ethical decision and analyzing its components. Few decisions promote the welfare of everyone affected by the decision. Most public policy decisions benefit some people and groups and hurt others. Even when a decision seems to benefit everybody—a win-win situation—people and groups are benefited to a different extent. There are usually questions of tradeoffs involved in most public policy decisions, and the distribution of benefits and burdens is a relevant consideration.

An ethical decision can be further defined as a decision where questions of justice and rights are serious and relevant moral considerations. These concepts are central ethical considerations in human affairs, and an ethical decision is one where a consideration of these concepts is an important dimension of the decision. Can the decision be defended on grounds of justice? Is it fair and equitable in some sense to all the parties affected? Does the decision violate some basic

---

[4]Charles W. Powers and David Vogel, *Ethics in the Education of Business Managers* (Hastings-on-Hudson, N.Y.: The Hastings Center, 1980), p. 1.

human rights, such that it could be labeled an immoral decision? These are the kinds of questions that must be asked by all participants in the public policy process, including managers of business organizations.

Justice There are several kinds of justice. *Distributive* justice is concerned with a fair distribution of society's burdens and benefits—the goods and services society has available through its major institutions including business organizations and governmental institutions. Distributive justice poses a special problem for business which relies on inequalities as incentives to induce people to be more productive. How can these inequalities be morally justified?

Compensatory justice is concerned with finding a fair way of compensating people for what they lost when they were wronged by others. The amount of compensation should be somehow proportional to the loss suffered by the person being compensated. This type of justice is of particular relevance to business organizations facing huge lawsuits involving products that are alleged to have caused harm to human health. What is a just compensation for the loss of a loved one or the loss of one's health if, indeed, the product was the causal agent and the manufacturer was at fault? Theories of strict liability assign more of the responsibility to the manufacturer and make it easier for complaints about defective products to be brought against companies.

Retributive justice has to do with just imposition of punishments and penalties upon those who do wrong. The wrongdoer needs to be punished, especially if the wrong was done intentionally, so that justice is served and the transgressor's behavior is changed. Business is affected by this type of justice in the area of punitive damages, which some juries have been prone to award in damage cases. Punitive damages are awarded over and above compensatory damages and have no limit in most cases, although they should be consistent and proportional to the wrong committed.

Justice is often expressed in terms of fairness or what is deserved. One has been treated justly when one has been given what he or she deserves or can legitimately claim. The so-called formal principle of justice states that like cases should be treated alike—equals ought to be treated equally and unequals unequally. This is called the formal principle of justice because it states no particular respects in which equals ought to be treated the same or unequals unequally. The principle merely states that whatever particulars are under consideration, if persons are equal in those respects, they should be treated alike. Individuals who are similar in all respects relevant to the kind of treatment in question should be given similar benefits and burdens, even if they are dissimilar in other irrelevant respects. Individuals who are dissimilar in a relevant respect ought to be treated dissimilarly, in proportion to their dissimilarity.[5]

---

[5]Tom L. Beauchamp, *Philosophical Ethics: An Introduction to Moral Philosophy* (New York: McGraw-Hill, 1982), p. 223.

This formal principle of justice can be considered to be a minimal moral rule. It does not tell us how to determine equality or proportion, and therefore lacks substance as a specific guide to conduct. Material principles of justice, on the other hand, specify in detail what counts as a relevant property in terms of which people are to be compared, what it means to give people their due, and what are legitimate claims. These theories put material content into a theory of justice and identify relevant properties on the basis of which burdens and benefits should be distributed. Some of the most difficult questions about the nature of justice arise over the specification of the relevant respects in terms of which people are to be treated equally or unequally.[6]

> Each material principle of justice identifies a relevant property on the basis of which burdens and benefits should be distributed. The following is a sample list of major candidates for the position of valid principles of distributive justice: (1) to each person an equal share; (2) to each person according to individual need; (3) to each person according to the person's rights; (4) to each person according to individual effort; (5) to each person according to societal contribution; (6) to each person according to merit. There is no obvious barrier to acceptance of more than one of these principles, and some theories of justice accept all six as valid. Most societies use several in the belief that different rules are appropriate to different situations.[7]

Theories of justice have been developed to provide general guidelines in determining what justice requires in a given situation. These theories systematically elaborate one or more of these material principles of justice and show how they are relevant properties on which to distribute burdens and benefits. Egalitarian theories emphasize equal access to primary goods and services, libertarian theories emphasize rights to liberty, and marxist theories emphasize need as a relevant property. The acceptability of any of these theories depends on the quality of the moral argument they contain as to whether one or more of the material properties they advocate ought to be given priority.[8]

Rights   The notion of rights has received a great deal of attention in our society in the last several decades. Various movements have appeared to press for the rights of specific groups, such as the civil rights movement concerned about fundamental rights for blacks and other minorities, women's rights movements developed to press for equal treatment of women in our society, and, more recently, right to life movements that attempt to protect the rights of unborn children and oppose abortion. Where do these rights come from and what gives rise to these kinds of movements?

[6]Ibid., pp. 225–229.
[7]Ibid., p. 229.
[8]Ibid., p. 230.

People have used the concept of rights throughout history to overthrow systems of governance and establish new forms of social and economic power. In the middle ages, kings claimed a divine right to govern in order to throw off the shackles of the church, and they went on to claim even more extensive powers over the subjects they came to dominate. Fledgling democracies claimed a natural right to liberty in order to overthrow kings and establish a new system of government. Rights seem to emerge as a significant force in history when there are enough people who feel a basic injustice is being perpetuated and they are able to organize or be led to force a basic change of some kind in the society.

Today we speak more about human rights than natural rights, and attempt to promote some human rights throughout the world. Rights are no longer derived from the operations of natural reason, but rather from ideas of what it means to be human. It is assumed that human beings have some kind of an essential nature that determines the fundamental obligations and rights that are to be respected by other people and social institutions. The rights that are asserted as fundamental to the development of humanity are believed to stem from knowledge of these essential properties of human nature.

A person can exercise a right to something only if sufficient justification exists (i.e., a right has overriding status). Moral rights are important, normative, justifiable claims or entitlements. Basic human rights cannot be overridden by considerations of utility. Rights can be overriden only by another, more basic right of some kind. For example, property rights can be overriden by a program of affirmative action to promote equal opportunity, on the basis that equality of opportunity is a more basic human right, not because it promotes social welfare. The right to liberty on the part of employers can be overriden in the interests of the rights of workers to a safe workplace. In this respect, certain rights can be considered fundamental because other rights are derived from them yet they are not derived from any more basic rights, and they are preconditions or necessary conditions of all other rights.[9]

There is a difference between moral and legal rights. One may have a legal right to do something immoral, or a moral right without any corresponding legal guarantee. Legal rights are derived from political constitutions, legislative enactments, case law, and executive orders of the highest state official. Moral rights exist independently of and form a basis for criticizing or justifying legal rights. Legal rights can be eliminated by lawful amendments or by a coup d'etat, but moral rights cannot be eroded or banished by political votes, powers, or amendments.[10]

A right is an individual's entitlement to something. A person has a right when he or she is entitled to act in a certain way or is entitled to have others act in a certain way toward him or her. These entitlements may derive from a legal system that permits or empowers the person to act in a specified way or that

[9]Ibid., p. 194.
[10]Ibid., p. 189.

requires others to act in certain ways toward that person. Legal rights are limited to the particular jurisdiction within which the legal system is in force.[11]

Entitlements can also be derived from a system of moral standards independently of any particular legal system. They can be based on moral norms or principles which specify that all human beings are permitted or empowered to do something or are entitled to have something done for them. In this case, rights are not limited to a particular jurisdiction. The most important moral rights are those that impose prohibitions or requirements on others and that enable individuals to pursue their own interests.[12]

There are negative rights that can be considered as duties that others have not to interfere in certain activities of a person. A negative right is a right to be free to hold and practice a belief, to pursue an action, or to enjoy a state of affairs without outside interference. Negative rights protect an individual from interference from the government and from other people. Government is to protect this basic right to be left alone and is not to encroach on this right itself. Libertarian theories of justice emphasize negative rights because human beings are viewed as ends in themselves, free to act according to their own purposes, and this right is to be respected by other people as well as by the institutions of society.

Positive rights, on the other hand, mean some other agents have a positive duty of providing the individual with whatever he or she needs to freely pursue his or her interests. Positive rights are rights to obtain goods and services, opportunities, or certain kinds of equal treatment. Egalitarian theories of justice emphasize more positive rights in that society should correct for the arbitrariness of nature by providing goods and services to its least advantaged members and assuring them equal opportunities. These are fundamental rights that require an obligation on the part of people and institutions to respect.

Moral rights of either kind are tightly correlated with duties. Rights can be defined in terms of moral duties other people have toward a person. Even negative rights imply a duty of the part of other people to respect the right to be left alone. Negative rights imply a duty on the part of the government to protect these rights. Thesee correlative duties may not fall on any specific individual but on all members of a group or society.[13]

Moral rights provide individuals with autonomy and equality in the free pursuit of their interests. These rights identify activities or interests that people must be left free to pursue or not pursue as they themselves choose, and whose pursuit must not be subordinated to the interests of others except for special and weighty reasons. Moral rights provide a basis for justifying one's actions and for invoking the protection or aid of others. They express the requirements of morality from the point of view of the individual instead of society as a whole,

[11]Manuel G. Valesquez, *Business Ethics: Concepts and Cases* (Englewood Cliffs, N.J.: Prentice-Hall, 1982), p. 59.

[12]Ibid., pp. 59–60.

[13]Ibid., p. 60.

and promote individual welfare and protect individual choices against encroachment by society.[14]

Utilitarian standards promote society's aggregate utility and are indifferent to the welfare of individuals except insofar as it affects this social aggregate. Moral rights, however, limit the validity of appeals to social benefits and to numbers. If a person has a right to do something, then it is wrong for anyone or any institution to interfere, even though a large number of people might gain much more utility from such interference. If utilitarian benefits or losses imposed on society become great enough, they may be sufficient, in some cases, to breach the walls of rights set to protect a person's freedom to pursue his or her interests.[15]

Concepts of justice and rights are related. Rights most often stem from some basic feeling of injustice, and the assertion of rights is meant to correct these injustices. Rights are meant to serve justice and justice should take rights into account. The question for the decision maker to answer is whose rights should be respected and what concept of justice is appropriate. Libertarian theories of justice emphasize liberty and negative rights and seem to be more consistent with a free enterprise system. In the last several decades in our country, with the rise of a welfare system, government has emphasized more of an egalitarian concept of justice to correct for some of the inequalities produced by capitalism, and has emphasized positive rights to goods and services, opportunities, and health and safety.

Some kind of balance between these approaches would seem to be a reasonable solution to disagreements that arise over these theories. Our market economy and the government act as a counterweight to each other. The market gives priority to property rights and economic concerns, such as efficiency and growth, and is concerned about getting the economic job done in a manner that obtains the most useful output from labor, capital, and natural resources. The government is concerned with egalitarian and humanitarian values related to justice and respect for certain basic human rights related to equal opportunity and protection from fraud and abuse in the marketplace as well as from harm in the workplace.

Throughout our history, we have been able to reach compromises between these two sets of values and have reached different conclusions on particular policy issues that define the scope of the marketplace and governmental responsibility. We have traveled a road between a strictly lassiez-faire type of economy with severely limited government intervention and outright government ownership of the means of production and central planning. We have largely avoided polarizing ideological debates that threaten compromise and have been able to veer to the right or left of center but never to the extremes as economic and social conditions necessitate. The vital center in American politi-

[14]Ibid., p. 61.
[15]Ibid., p. 62.

cal and social attitudes generally prevails and keeps us somewhere near the middle of the road regarding rights to liberty and equality. It is within this ethical context that the manager of today's corporation must operate.

SOCIAL-POLITICAL STRUCTURE

Before a policy choice can be made with respect to a social or economic problem, that problem must be accepted as part of the agenda of the policy-making system. It must find its place in the range of problems deemed amenable to public action and worthy of the attention of policymakers.[16] The way in which a society goes about identifying problems and developing policies to solve these problems is also a function of the social-political structure. The structure of the social-political process has a great deal to do with the kinds of problems that get attention and the public policies that are eventually adopted. There are two different ways of viewing American society from the standpoint of its social-political structure that have implications for problem identification and public policy formulation.

The Power-Elite Model

One theory maintains that the major institutions in the United States are dominated by a ruling elite that determines the problems that get attention and the policies that are eventually adopted to deal with these problems. The composition of society in this theory is shown in Exhibit 4.3 According to this model there are three major classes in society: the ruling elite, often referred to as the establishment; the middle class, sometimes referred to as the silent majority; and the lower class, those at the bottom end of the income scale with little wealth in their possession.

The ruling elite or establishment is a class that is small in numbers relative to the total population. Members of this class share an upper-class background: they are most likely listed in the social register of the community in which they live, they most likely attended one of a fairly small number of preparatory schools, they are probably members of what used to be called men's clubs, and they have a good deal of wealth, much of which may have been inherited. Because of these characteristics, the establishment is a homogeneous class in that its members share similar values and ideologies.

The middle class is large, much larger than the establishment, and as a whole has control over a great deal of wealth. But it is composed of many different kinds of people with diverse backgrounds. It is a heterogeneous class in that its members do not share similar attitudes, values, and goals, and are often in conflict with one another over what issues are important and what policies should be adopted. It is difficult for the middle class to organize itself as

---

[16]B. Guy Peters, *American Public Policy: Promise and Performance*, 2nd ed. (Chatham, N.J.: Chatham House, 1986), p. 39.

Exhibit 4.3
The Power-Elite Model of Society

I. The Ruling Elite or Establishment
    A. Small in numbers
    B. Upper-class background
II. The Middle Class
    A. Large
    B. Conflictual
    C. Limited importance
III. The Lower Class
    A. Large
    B. Indifferent
    C. Alienated

Source: Rogene A. Buchholz, *Business Environment and Public Policy: Implications for Management and Strategy Formulation,* 2nd ed., © 1986, p. 127. Reprinted by permission of Prentice Hall, Englewood Cliffs, NJ.

a whole and exercise the power in society it theoretically possesses, and therefore its importance in making public policy for society is limited.

The lower class is again large in numbers, but its members have little or no wealth; in fact, many of its members may have negative wealth. Many members of the lower class are indifferent toward or alienated from the rest of society. Most of their energies are taken up in seeking out an existence in what is perceived to be a basically hostile environment. Many members of this class, particularly the poorest ones, probably believe their lives do not count for much in society, that they are a forgotten class with few or no avenues through which to express their needs and opinions. Thus this class is also not very influential as far as making public policy is concerned.

From the perspective of this particular model of society, the establishment largely "runs" society. The members of the ruling elite are the "gatekeepers" of the issues society considers. Unless a particular problem is identified by this class as important, it does not get on the public policy agenda. Once an issue is on the agenda, the public policy response to that problem is a reflection of the values and ideologies of this governing elite. They decide the shape of public policy and control its implementation. They exercise a broad scope of decision-making power in the major institutions of society and have the power to employ and reward people in these institutions.

Thus in elite theory, the people or the masses do not determine public policy through their demands and actions. The power elite dominate public decision making and their interests are served in the policy-making process. The elite use their power to decide which issues the political arena will or will not consider. "The stability of the system, and even its survival, depends upon elite consensus in behalf of the fundamental values of the system, and only policy alternatives that fall within the shared consensus will be given serious consideration." [17] The main tenants of elite theory can be summarized as follows.

1. Society is divided into the few who have power and the many who do not. Only a small number of persons allocate values for society; the masses do not decide public policy.
2. The few who govern are not typical of the masses who are governed. Elites are drawn disproportionately from the upper socioeconomic strata of society.
3. The movement of nonelites to elite positions must be slow and continuous to maintain stability and avoid revolution. Only nonelites who have accepted the basic elite consensus can be admitted to governing circles.
4. Elites share a consensus on the basic values of the social system and the preservation of the system. [In the United States the elite consensus includes private enterprise, private property, limited government, and individual liberty.]
5. Public policy does not reflect demands of the masses but rather the prevailing values of the elite. Changes in public policy will be incremental rather than revolutionary. [Incremental changes permit response to events, which threaten the social system, with a minimum of alteration or dislocation of the system.]
6. Active elites are subject to relatively little direct influence from apathetic masses. Elites influence masses more than masses influence elites. [18]

There was a good deal of literature from the 1960s to the 1970s suggesting that this structure was basically representative of our society. Studies were conducted that attempted to show that on all levels of government a behind-the-scenes concentration of elite power existed. Books with such titles as *The Protestant Establishment*, *Who Rules America?* and *America, Inc.* appeared, which tried to establish that a ruling elite did in fact exist that controlled society and ran it in their interests. [19] They were able to exercise control by dominating the following processes.

1. The special interest process, which comprises the various means utilized by wealthy individuals, specific corporations and specific sectors of the economy in influencing government to satisfy their narrow, short-run needs.

[17]Thomas R. Dye, *Understanding Public Policy*, 3rd ed. (Englewood Cliffs, N.J.: Prentice-Hall, 1978), p. 27.
[18]Thomas Dye and Harmon Zeigler, *The Irony of Democracy*, 3rd ed., p. 6. Copyright © 1975 by Wadsworth Publishing Company, Inc. Reprinted by permission of the publisher, Brooks/Cole Publishing Company, Monterey, California.
[19]Edward Digby Baltzell, *The Protestant Establishment* (New York: Random House, 1964); William G. Domhoff, *Who Rules America?* (Englewood Cliffs, N.J.: Prentice-Hall, 1967); Morton Mintz and Jerry S. Cohen, *America, Inc.: Who Owns and Operates the United States?* (New York: Dial Press, 1971).

2. The policy-formation process, which is the means by which general policies of interest to the ruling class as a whole are developed and implemented.

3. The candidate-selection process, which has to do with the ways members of the ruling class ensure that they have "access" to the politicians who are elected to office.

4. The ideology process, which involves the formation, dissemination and enforcement of the assumptions, beliefs and attitudes that permit the continued existence of policies and politicians favorable to the wealth, income, status and privileges of members of the ruling class.[20]

William G. Domhoff, for example, in *Who Rules America?*, tried to show with some empirical evidence that there is an upper class in the United States that is also a governing class primarily through the control it exercises over major institutions. Domhoff defined this governing class as a social upper class that owns a disproportionate amount of the country's wealth, receives a disproportionate amount of the country's yearly income, and contributes a disproportionate number of its members to the controlling institutions and key decision-making groups of the country.[21] He argued that the institutions in which the majority of decisions are made about American society (corporations, foundations, universities, the executive branch of the federal government, and the federal judiciary) are dominated by upper-class members, who can therefore be assumed to control the policies that flow from these institutions. Thus, according to Domhoff, the American upper class is also a governing class that by and large runs society, especially in light of the wealth owned and the income received by members of that exclusive social group.[22]

In *Who's Running America?*, Thomas R. Dye defined a national elite as those individuals who occupied the top positions in the institutional structure of American society. Dye divided society into three institutional sectors: corporate, governmental, and public interest. The corporate elite is composed of those individuals who occupy formal positions of authority in institutions that control over half the nation's total corporate assets. The governmental elite is composed of those individuals who occupy formal positions of authority in the major civilian and military bureaucracies of the national government. And finally, the public interest elite is composed of those individuals who occupy formal positions of authority in the mass media, prestigious law firms, major philanthropic foundations, leading universities, and recognized national civic and cultural organizations.[23]

[20]G. William Domhoff, *The Powers That Be: Processes of Ruling-Class Domination in America* (New York: Random House, 1978), p. 10.

[21]Domhoff, *Who Rules America?*, p. 5.

[22]Ibid., p. 11.

[23]Thomas R. Dye, *Who's Running America?: The Carter Years*, 2nd ed. (Englewood Cliffs, N.J.: Prentice-Hall, 1979), pp. 11–12.

Dye concluded that about 4,000 individuals in 5,000 positions exercised formal authority over institutions that controlled roughly half the nation's resources in industry, finance, utilities, insurance, mass media, foundations, education, law, and civic and cultural affairs. These individuals constituted an extremely small percentage of the nations's total population; in fact, their numbers represented less than two-thousandths of 1 percent of total population. Even within this number, there were important concentrations of combined corporate, governmental, and social power, centered about the great, wealthy, entrepreneurial families.[24]

The Pluralist Model

The pluralist model differs from the power-elite model of society in that there are no reasonably well-defined classes with one class exercising by far the most influence on public policy. A pluralist society is composed of a number of groups, all of which wield varying degrees of influence in the public policy process. These organizations can quite properly be called interest groups because they form around shared interests. People organize and support such groups because they share common attitudes and values on a particular problem or issue. They believe they can advance their interests better by organizing themselves into a group rather than pursuing their interests individually. These groups compete for access to formal institutions of decision making and for the attention of key policy makers in the hope of producing policy outcomes that favor their interests.

Such interest groups convey certain kinds of demands that are fed into the public policy process. They fill a gap in the formal political process by representing interests that are beyond the capacities of individuals acting alone or representatives chosen by the people. At times they perform a watchdog function by sounding an alarm whenever policies of more formal institutions threaten the interests of their members. They generate ideas that may become formal policies of these institutions and help to place issues on the public policy agenda.

Americans seem particularly inclined to form groups to pursue their common interests. There were 13,583 national associations in the United States in 1976, devoted to a variety of interests including religion, education, science, and business.[25] By 1980, there were nearly 15,000 nonprofit associations of one kind or another, and 28 percent of these were headquartered in Washington, D.C.—a sure indicator of political interest. In 1981, approximately 40,000 people were employed by these Washington-based associations.[26] One study reported that 75 percent of all American adults belonged to at least one organiza-

---

[24]Ibid., p. 240.

[25]Encyclopedia of Associations, vol. I, *National Associations of the U.S.*, 20th ed. (Detroit: Gale, 1976).

[26]Robert H. Salisbury, "Interest Groups: Toward a New Understanding," *Interest Group Politics*, Allan J. Cigler and Burdett A. Loomis, eds. (Washington, D.C.: Congressional Quarterly, 1983), p. 357.

tion and 57 percent were active in at least one group.[27] The importance of associations in American life was recognized by Alexis de Tocqueville many years ago in his famous book on American democracy.

> Americans of all ages, all conditions, and all dispositions, constantly form associations. They have not only commercial and manufacturing companies, in which all take part, but associations of a thousand other kinds—religious, moral, serious, futile, extensive or restricted, enormous or diminutive. The Americans make associations to give entertainments, to found establishments for education, to build inns, to construct churches, to diffuse books, to send missionaries to the antipodes, and in this manner they found hospitals, prisons, and schools.[28]

Functions of Interest Groups.   These interest groups perform a variety of functions for their members. Groups may perform a *symbolic* function simply by giving members the opportunity to express the interests or values they hold. Such activity serves to reinforce one's identity or provide legitimacy for certain ideas, a valuable function in and of itself. Closely related is an *ideological* function, whereby groups may provide an outlet for people who hold strong beliefs about a particular aspect of American life, such as free enterprise, and need a way to appeal to these strongly held principles. A common function of interest groups is to promote the *economic* self-interest of their members, a function most often associated with business and labor groups. Groups can also be *informational*, disseminating information relating to particular causes the group may be pursuing or more technical information in which members may be interested, such as information about stamps, coins, or antique cars. Most groups collect, analyze, and disseminate information to their members to some extent. Finally, groups can perform *instrumental* functions for their members— concrete goals that are noneconomic in nature. This goal can include the efforts of antismoking groups to ban smoking in public places or the right-to-life groups that seek to outlaw abortions.[29]

Classifications of Interest Groups.   Interest groups can be classified according to their primary functions. *Economic interest groups*, formed to promote the economic self-interest of their members, may not have been formed with political activity in mind, but eventually find such activity necessary to promote or protect their interests. Economic interest groups include business groups such as the National Association of Manufacturers or Business Roundtable, labor unions, and professional associations such as the National Education Association.

---

[27]Samuel H. Barnes, "Some Political Consequences of Involvement in Organizations," paper presented at the 1977 annual meeting of the American Political Science Association, quoted in Raymond E. Wolfinger, Martin Shapiro, and Fred I. Greenstein, *Dynamics of American Politics*, 2nd ed. (Englewood Cliffs, N.J.: Prentice-Hall, 1980), pp. 229–230.

[28]Alexis de Tocqueville, *Democracy in America*, vol. II (New York: Schocken, 1961), p. 128.

[29]Norman J. Ornstein and Shirley Elder, *Interest Groups, Lobbying and Policymaking* (Washington, D.C.: Congressional Quarterly Press, 1978), pp. 29–34.

Solidarity groups draw on feelings of common identity based on a shared characteristic such as race, age, or sex. The basis of the group is a sense of kinship. Examples of this classification include ethnic groups, composed of members from a particular part of the world, and women's rights organizations. These groups may have economic interests at stake, but their primary function seems to be in maintaining or promoting an identity or consciousness related to a common characteristic shared by all members of the group.

A third category is the *public interest group* that claims to speak for the public. Whether such groups should be called "public" interest groups or "special" interest groups is a subject of much debate. The fact is that such groups do not necessarily appeal to the economic self-interest of their members nor do they share common characteristics such as a solidarity group. They exist to promote noneconomic interests, such as the environment or equal opportunity. Thus they are somewhat ideological in nature but also have concrete goals in mind. Some of these groups tend to advance overall value positions covering a wide range of issues (liberalism or conservatism); others are strictly single-issue groups. Examples of public interest groups are the Natural Resources Defense Council and Common Cause.[30]

The Natural Resources Defense Council (NRDC) was launched in 1970 by the Ford Foundation, which brought together a group of recent Yale Law School graduates and establishment New York lawyers who shared a common ambition to set up a public interest law firm to pursue environmental interests. Since that time when the NRDC consisted of only a handful of attorneys writing briefs on a $100,000 grant, the organization has grown into a national group with 55,000 supporting members and a budget of $6 million. The NRDC acts as a kind of shadow EPA for forcing the agency to write and rewrite regulations and to take actions that have been postponed. The organization has had an impact on almost every piece of environmental legislation considered by Congress and has been rated higher than any other environmental group for lobbying effectiveness.[31]

Common Cause is one of the most prominent public interest groups operating in Washington. It was founded by John Gardner, a former secretary of Health, Education, and Welfare, in the mid-1970s. His public prestige and visibility helped make the organization an immediate success. Even though Gardner has since stepped down as chairman, membership remains at a high level. The organization focuses most of its efforts on governmental and institutional reform, including public financing of political campaigns, open meetings and hearings in Congress and executive agencies, and reform of laws related to lobbying disclosure.[32]

[30]Wolfinger, Shapiro, and Greenstein, *Dynamics of American Politics*, pp. 233–248.

[31]Robert E. Taylor, "Group's Influence on U.S. Environmental Laws, Policies Earns It a Reputation as a Shadow EPA," *The Wall Street Journal*, January 13, 1986, p. 46.

[32]Ornstein and Elder, *Interest Groups*, p. 47.

Table 4.1
The Organized Interests

Big Interests	Special Interests	Strategically Located Special Interests	General Cause Groups	Special Cause Groups
Chamber of Commerce, U.S.A.	American Bankers Association	Air Line Pilots Association	National Conference of Christians and Jews	Zero Population Growth, Inc.
Water Resources Congress	American Hot-Dip Galvanizers Association	Association of Oil Pipe Lines	Izaak Walton League	Zionist Organization
American Farm Bureau Federation	City of Philadelphia, Washington, D.C., office	Building and Construction Trades	Americans for Democratic Action	Federation of the Blind
National Federation of Business and Professional Women's Clubs	National Cotton Council	Department of AFL-CIO	John Birch Society	National Society, Daughters of the American Revolution
National Council on the Aging	Dairy Industry Committee	National Association of Real Estate Investment Trusts	Common Cause	Diabetes Association
AFL-CIO	Disabled American Veterans	American Association of State, County and Municipal Employees		National Abortion Rights Action League
	Hawaiian Sugar Planters Association	American Postal Workers		
	Poultry and Egg Institute of America	Brotherhood of Locomotive Engineers		
	National Association of Retail Druggists	Communications Workers of America		
	United Steelworkers			
	United Mineworkers			

Interest groups can also be classified by the scope of their activities and membership (See Table 4.1). Big interests are those that are representative of large instutitions or sectors of society. These big interests include masses of people that belong to a particular institution or constitute a class in society. They include business, labor, agriculture, religion, veterans, and race. When these big interests can be mobilized, as during the civil rights movement, they can have a major impact on public policy. Because they are so broad and include so many people, however, big interests are difficult to mobilize around a single interest.[33]

[33]Theodore J. Lowi, *Incomplete Conquest: Governing America*, 2nd ed. (New York: Holt, Rinehart and Winston, 1981), pp. 35–42.

Special interests are more narrow in scope and include smaller numbers of people. Some of the most influential special interests are organized around a narrowly defined sector, trade, or occupation, and are thus able to specialize and focus their energies on a few issues of concern to the membership. Strategically located special interests have a great deal of potential power because of their location in the production of goods and services or in the movement of people or communications. Due to the interdependence and specialization of society, a breakdown or stoppage in one of these key locations can affect the ability of many industries and groups to carry out their functions. General cause groups are activated by one very broad issue or several more specialized but related issues, whereas special cause groups have more narrowly defined goals and interests.[34]

Interest Group Tactics.   Interest groups have a number of tactics they can use to focus attention on the issue they are concerned with and win widespread support. *Boycotts* were particularly useful in the civil rights movement in the South because the black population was large and could be organized. When the blacks refused to ride the buses in Montgomery, Alabama, and boycotted white merchants in parts of the South, they had an effect because of the large numbers involved. Boycotts of lettuce in support of the California farmworkers were less successful.

The Supreme Court upheld the use of boycotts in a 1982 decision. This ruling revised a decision of a Mississippi Supreme Court that held the National Association for the Advancement of Colored People (NAACP) and ninety-one blacks liable for business losses of local merchants during the 1960s civil rights protests. The local businesses were asking for $3.5 million in damages. The Supreme Court ruled that nonviolent boycotts organized to achieve constitutional rights goals have the full protection of the First Amendment, which protects freedom of speech, and are not subject to damage suits.[35]

Interest groups can hold *public demonstrations* in support of an issue or a cause. The purpose of these demonstrations, particularly peaceful protests, is to show that a significant number of people feel very strongly about an issue and have not been able to make their voices heard through the normal political process. When such demonstrations attract thousands of people, as did some of the civil rights demonstrations and protests against the war in Vietnam, they attract widespread public attention and often induce official action through normal governmental channels. Such demonstrations can also turn violent and involve the destruction of life and property. Most public demonstrations, how-

[34]Ibid., pp. 42–46.
[35]"High Court Ruling on Boycotts May Lead More Groups to Use Them to Make a Point" *The Wall Street Journal*, July 6, 1982, p. 13.

ever, have limited political objectives and do not aim to upset the normal functioning of government and society.

The so-called "Big Business Day" was a mass demonstration organized by Ralph Nader and allies among union leaders, politicians, and economists. Demonstrations were held at 150 cities around the country charging big business with pollution, gouging of consumers, union busting, and governmental corruption, among other allegations. Nader called the demonstration the beginning of a long drive to pressure Congress to pass the Corporate Democracy Act, which would reform corporate boards of directors and require more public disclosure.[36]

The use of *terrorism* as a tactic to advance a particular interest or cause is fortunately not as widespread in the United States as it is in some parts of the world, but it is not entirely unknown. Terrorism can involve taking hostages, hijacking airplanes, killing government officials, slaying people with opposite interests, destroying property, and similar measures. Much terrorist activity is directed against "the system" and is intended to upset and interfere with the normal functioning of a society or its government.

Interest groups can also attempt to win public support through advertisements in newspapers, distributing leaflets to large segments of the population, buying time on television, and other *uses of the media*. Sometimes they become quite skillful in using the media to their advantage. The events that transpired in Selma, Alabama, at the height of the civil rights movement were no accident. This particular city was chosen by civil rights groups because all the ingredients were there to make the use of nonviolent demonstrations successful. The sight of dogs attacking humans and police beating people provoked moral outrage all across the country as people watched their television screens. This generated a great deal of support for the movement.

When the concern of an interest group gets picked up by the political process, it can then *lobby* to help shape the public policies that are being developed to deal with the problem. Some of the larger groups have a large membership that provides adequate financing to be able to support full-time lobbyists in Washington, D.C., and in some state capitals.

The word *lobbying* has a rather negative connotation in many people's minds, eliciting images of behind-the-scenes arm-twisting and money changing hands under the table. Looked at in its best light, lobbying can be defined as communication with public officials to influence their decisions in a manner that is consistent with the interests of the individual or group doing the communicating. The lobbyist's purpose is a selfish one in that a lobbyist seeks to persuade others that his or her position on an issue is meritorious. Lobbying behavior is thus designed to bring about favorable outcomes from government for the group represented by the lobbyist.

The lobbyist performs a number of functions. One activity is to provide

---

[36]"Nader's Antibusiness Bust," *Time*, April 28, 1980, p. 51.

members of Congress with information. Such information, of course, tends to portray the position of the group represented by the lobbyist favorably, but it must also be accurate enough to be acceptable to members of Congress. Lobbyists also keep their constituents informed about developments in Congress or in the executive branch that may affect their interests. This information may stimulate grass-roots efforts from the membership to contact their local representatives or senators. Finally, lobbyists can also use publicity to support or oppose a particular bill or to put pressure on the administration or Congress.[37]

Lobbying is presently regulated by the Regulation of Lobbying Act of 1946, which defines lobbyists as those individuals whose principal purpose is to influence legislation by direct contact with members of Congress. These legally defined lobbyists must register with Congress and give quarterly reports on their spending for lobbying activities. Lobbying in the executive branch is not currently regulated by statute.

The number of registered domestic lobbyists has more than doubled since 1976, growing from 3,420 to 8,800, but some experts put the actual number of influencers at about 20,000—or more than thirty lobbyists for every member of Congress. Registered lobbyists reported expenditures of $50 million in 1985, twice as much as a decade earlier, but the true figure may be closer to $1.5 billion.[38]

The 1946 law allows many people who do a great deal of lobbying to avoid registering because lobbying is not necessarily their principal purpose. People who run Washington offices of corporations, for example, are not required to register because lobbying is not their primary job, even though they may lobby on various occasions. There were attempts in 1978 to change the law and make the reporting and registering requirements more stringent. However, these reform efforts failed. Most large corporations probably employ lobbyists, who are located in the Washington office of the company. More than 500 corporations, including some small companies, have such offices. Many general business and industry and trade associations have their headquarters or offices in Washington for lobbying purposes.

Interest groups often form *coalitions* and work together with other groups to increase their influence in the public policy process. Such a coalition was formed byu the environmental groups in the early 1980s to counter the efforts of the Reagan administration to ease environmental constraints. These groups were able to put aside their differences and unite in a tightly knit movement or lobby, as it was called, to become a national power. As a united force, they were able to frustrate the efforts of business to make major changes in the Clean Air Act that would be more compatible with business interests.[39]

[37]Wolfinger, Shapiro, and Greenstein, *Dynamics of American Politics*, pp. 252–253.
[38]"Peddling Influence: Lobbyists Swarm Over Capitol Hill," *Time*, March 3, 1986, p. 27.
[39]William Symonds, "Washington in the Grip of the Green Giant," *Fortune*, October 4, 1982, pp. 137–141.

Finally, an interest group can use *litigation* to advance its interests. This has proven to be such a useful tactic for groups to use that recent years have seen a tremendous increase in litigation. Interest groups can sue the government or private parties they believe are violating the law. They can file "friend of the court" briefs, which are attempts to influence the courts through supplementary arguments. The Bakke case, regarding preferential admission of minorities to medical school, elicited more such briefs on both sides of the issue than any Supreme Court case in history.

Business groups file suit against government agencies blocking the issuance of new regulations. Environmental groups file suit against the Environmental Protection Agency pressuring it to speed up the issuance of regulations for hazardous waste disposal. Conservationists file suit against the government challenging a federal construction project, using the required environmental impact statement as the basis for their suit, claiming that the statement was improperly prepared or showing some serious impacts that justify stopping the project.

Because of the increase in litigation, the courts are deciding more and more public policy matters through interpreting laws, establishing precedent, and trying to discern the intent of Congress. As will be seen in later chapters, the courts play a crucial role in public policy making that is likely to continue. As our society becomes more litigous, the courts are increasingly going to pursue interests and seek redress for damages, and thus the courts are thrust into many areas of policy making.

The Operation of a Pluralistic System. Identification of problems in a pluralistic system occurs when people who are concerned about the problem organize themselves or join an existing organization to pursue their particular interests in the problem. If the problem is of widespread concern, and the group or groups dealing with it can attract enough financial and other kinds of support, the problem may eventually become public as people become aware of it and show varying degrees of support. Eventually government or other institutions may pick up on the problem and translate the issues being raised into formal legislation or other policy actions. These interest groups then continue to exercise influence in helping to design public policies to deal with these problems.

Thus in the pluralist model, problems are identified and policies designed in a sort of bottom-up fashion—concern about a problem can begin anywhere at the grass-roots level in society and eventually grow into a major public issue that demands attention. This is in contrast to the power-elite model, a sort of top-down process in which the upper class identifies the problems, designs public policy, and forces it on the rest of society. One could see the pluralistic process at work during the social revolutions of the 1960s. Various interest groups, such as the Southern Christian Leadership Conference, Nader's groups, and the Sierra Club, were active in identifying the problems of civil rights, consumerism, and pollution respectively, and in helping to shape public policies on these problems.

Public policy, then, reflects the interests of groups, and as groups gain and lose influence, public policy is altered to reflect the changing patterns of group influence. Public policy is the result of the relative influence of groups in the policy-making process, and results from a struggle of these groups to win public and institutional support. As one theorist claims, "What may be called public policy is the equilibrium reached in this [group] struggle at any given moment, and it represents a balance which the contending factions or groups constantly strive to weigh in their favor."[40]

In theory, a pluralistic system is an open system. Anyone with a strong enough interest in a problem can pursue this interest as far as it will take him or her. Membership in a particular social or income class or of a particular race does not prevent one from participating in the public policy process. Power is diffused in a pluralistic system and dominant power centers are hard to develop in such a competitive arrangement. The existence of many interest groups also provides more opportunities for leadership, making it possible for more people with leadership ability to exercise these talents. There are many opportunities for people to become political entrepreneurs who perform an organizing function by bringing together people with similar interests.[41]

But interest groups themselves, particularly as they become large, tend to be dominated by their own leadership. This leadership usually formulates policy for the group as a whole, and the public stance of an interest group often represents the views of a ruling elite within the interest group itself rather than all of the rank and file membership. Many interest groups may provide few, if any, opportunities for members to express their views on issues facing the group. Interest groups in many cases also draw most of their membership from better educated, middle- or upper-class segments of society. Many minorities and particularly the poorer elements of society are not adequately represented. Their problems are likely to be ignored unless championed by other people who are more likely to participate in public policy making.

Improved public policy decisions should also result from such a structure since more people, particularly those who are closest to the problem, have an input in decision making. Yet a pluralistic system is a system of conflict because interest groups compete for attention and influence in the public policy process, and such competing interests do not necessarily result in the best public policy decisions. Conflict can get out of control and result in social fragmentation, making a policy decision for society difficult to reach. This is particularly true when interest groups are unwilling to compromise, in which case reaching

[40]Earl Latham, *The Group Basis of Politics* (New York: Octagon Books, 1965), p. 36, as quoted in Anderson, Brady, and Bullock, *Public Policy and Politics* (North Sciuate, Mass.: Duxbury, 1978), p. 416.

[41]Andrew S. McFarland, "Public Interest Lobbies Versus Minority Faction," *Interest Group Politics*, Allan J. Cigler and Burdett A. Loomis, eds. (Washington, D.C.: Congressional Quarterly, 1983), p. 327.

a public policy decision for society as a whole may be impossible. Furthermore, some interests are not adequately represented.

A pluralistic system does seem to allow for more interests to be represented than does a society structured along the power-elite model. More people should have a chance to promote their particular values and interests and have a chance to govern society. This is a mixed blessing, however. As a society becomes more pluralistic, the interests represented will be more diverse, and the direction in which society is moving will be less clear. The lack of central direction for society, which an elite provides, can be a disadvantage as society is pulled to and fro by the competition of many different interests with varying degrees of power and influence. Thus a society may find it increasingly difficult to formulate possible solutions to complex policy questions.

The public choice school sees interest groups not so much as competitors against one another, but as competing against the public, which is largely unaware of what is happening. Interest groups are joint raiders on the U.S. Treasury and potential abusers of government's coercive power. As government expanded its activities, interests groups saw political competition rather than economic competition as the most effective way to insure their economic survival. They have found it profitable to manipulate the political process to redistribute wealth and insulate them from the uncertainties of the market.[42]

Any society is undoubtedly a mixture of both these models, with elements of an establishment and interest groups helping to identify problems and develop public policies to deal with them. It could be argued that societies tend to lean toward one model or the other at various points in their history. If this is true, a great deal of evidence suggests that our society is leaning toward the pluralistic model at present. Interest groups have proliferated in the last decade, have become sophisticated in the use of various tactics, and have wielded influence in the public policy process far beyond what their actual numbers would suggest. Many people active in these groups know how to pursue their own interests effectively. Few, if any, books are written about an "establishment" anymore, suggesting that it either has disappeared or is not influential enough to worry about. Congress itself is fragmented, without the power-brokers of past years, and is thus more subject to grass-roots lobbying. This kind of structure has implications for public policy making which has been the subject of much discussion.

Some observers have characterized our society as one of interest group pluralism, whereby the federal government is subject to the pressures of special interest groups. Because of the changes in the seniority system in Congress and the proliferation of subcommittees, Congress has become a collection of independent power centers. The interest groups can thus take their case directly to individual members of Congress and establish close working ties with the sub-

---

[42]"The Political Economy of Interest Groups," *Manhattan Report*, vol. IV, no. 2 (1984), p. 2.

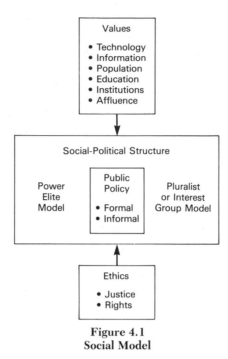

Figure 4.1
Social Model

committee(s) in their areas of interest. The result is the infamous "iron triangle" composed of the interest groups, the congressional subcommittee, and the relevant federal agency, which becomes the focus of public policy making. This kind of process encourages government to act on individual measures without attention to their collective consequences. Policy is not made for the nation as a whole, but for narrow autonomous sectors defined by the special interests. Although these groups may claim to be acting in the public interest, such claims are suspect.

> . . . the problem with the so-called public interest groups is not their venality but their belief that they alone represent the public interest. The confidence these groups have had in pursuing their numerous and sometimes far-reaching missions is not always warranted, especially when their activities—and their demands—are scrutinized in the context of the full effects of the government regulations which they so often instigate or endorse with tremendous zeal.[43]

---

[43]Reprinted, by permission of the publisher, from *The Future of Business Regulation*, by Murray L. Weidenbaum, p. 146 © 1979 AMACOM, a division of American Management Association, New York. All rights reserved.

Another problem with interest group pluralism is the removal of public policy making from public scrutiny. Decisions are being made behind closed doors, effectively removed from popular control. As stated by Everett Carl Ladd, "The public cannot hope to monitor the policy outcomes that result from the individual actions of 535 Senators and Representatives operating through a maze of iron triangles."[44] The solution to this fractionalism, according to some observers, is a revitalized party system where the claims of interest groups can be adjusted to mesh with a coherent program that represents more of a national interest. The proliferation of interest groups makes necessary strengthened parties that can cope with the multiple organized pressures of interest group pluralism.

These concepts of value, ethics, and social-political structure are tied together in Figure 4.1 to show how public policy originates in our society. Values, which are subject to various influences, and notions about justice and rights, work their way through the social-political structure whether organized along power-elite or pluralist lines or some combination thereof. All of these elements become mixed and intertwined in a very complex fashion, but the result may be that a particular issue finds its way onto the public policy agenda to become the subject of formal or informal public policy making where a common course of action is decided upon.

SELECTED REFERENCES

BAIER, KURT, and NICHOLAS RESCHER. *Values and the Future: The Impact of Technological Change on American Values.* New York: Macmillan, 1969.

BALTZELL, EDWARD DIGBY. *The Protestant Establishment.* New York: Random House, 1964.

BEAUCHAMP, TOM L., and NORMAN E. BOWIE. *Ethical Theory and Business,* 3rd ed. Englewood Cliffs, N.J.: Prentice-Hall, 1988.

BERRY, JEFFREY M. *Lobbying for the People: The Political Behavior of Public Interest Groups.* Princeton, N.J.: Princeton University Press, 1977.

BOWIE, NORMAN. *Business Ethics.* Englewood Cliffs, N.J.: Prentice-Hall, 1982.

CIGLER, ALLAN J., and BURDETT A. LOOMIS, EDS. *Interest Group Politics.* Washington D.C.: Congressional Quarterly, 1983.

DEGEORGE, RICHARD T. *Business Ethics,* 2nd ed. New York: Macmillan, 1986.

DES JARDINS, JOSEPH R., and JOHN J. MCCALL. *Contemporary Issues in Business Ethics.* Belmont, Calif.: Wadsworth, 1985.

[44]Everett Carl Ladd, "How to Tame the Special-Interest Groups," *Fortune,* vol. 102, no. 8 (October 20, 1980), p. 72.

DOLBEARE, KENNETH M. *Democracy at Risk: The Politics of Economic Renewal.* Chatham, N.J.: Chatham House, 1986.

DOMHOFF, WILLIAM G. *Who Rules America?* Englewood Cliffs, N.J.: Prentice-Hall, 1967.

DOMHOFF, WILLIAM G. *Who Rules America Now?: A View for the '80s.* New York: Simon & Schuster, 1983.

DONALDSON, THOMAS. *Corporations and Morality.* Englewood Cliffs, N.J.: Prentice-Hall, 1982.

ELLUL, JACQUES. *The Technological Society.* Trans. John Wilkinson. New York: Knopf, 1964.

FERGUSON, THOMAS, and JOEL ROGERS, EDS. *The Political Economy: Readings in the Politics and Economics of American Public Policy.* Armonk, N.Y.: M. E. Sharpe, 1984.

KELSO, WILLIAM A. *American Democratic Theory: Pluralism and Its Critics.* Westport, Conn.: Greenwood Press, 1978.

LOWI, THEODORE J. *Incomplete Conquest: Governing America.* New York: Holt, Rinehart and Winston, 1981.

MINTZ, MORTON, and JERRY S. COHEN. *America, Inc.: Who Owns and Operates the United States?* New York: Dial Press, 1971.

NICHOLLS, DAVID. *The Pluralist State.* New York: St. Martin's Press, 1975.

ORNSTEIN, NORMAN J., and SHIRLEY ELDER. *Interest Groups, Lobbying and Policymaking.* Washington, D.C.: Congressional Quarterly Press, 1978.

ROKEACH, M. *The Nature of Values.* New York: Free Press, 1973.

SCHUMPETER, J. A. *Capitalism, Socialism, and Democracy,* 3rd ed. New York: Harper & Row, 1950.

SUTTON, F. X., ET AL. *The American Business Creed.* Cambridge, Mass.: Harvard University Press, 1956.

TOFFLER, ALVIN. *Future Shock.* New York: Bantam Books, 1970.

VELASQUEZ, MANUEL G. *Business Ethics: Concepts and Cases,* 2nd ed. Englewood Cliffs, N.J.: Prentice-Hall, 1988.

WALTON, CLARENCE C. *Ethos and the Executive: Values in Managerial Decision Making.* Englewood Cliffs, N.J.: Prentice-Hall, 1969.

WALTON, CLARENCE C. *The Ethics of Corporate Conduct.* Englewood Cliffs, N.J.: Prentice-Hall, 1977.

WERHANE, PATRICIA W. *Persons, Rights, and Corporations.* Englewood Cliffs, N.J.: Prentice-Hall, 1985.

WOLFINGER, RAYMOND E., MARTIN SHAPIRO, and FRED I. GREENSTEIN. *Dynamics of American Politics,* 2nd ed. Englewood Cliffs, N.J.: Prentice-Hall, 1980.

THE PUBLIC POLICY PROCESS

The public policy process refers to all the various methods by which public policy is made in our society. Formulation of public policy is not limited to formal acts of government, but can be achieved by interest groups that bring issues to public attention and attempt to influence public opinion as well as government. If interest groups are successful in raising issues and public opinion becomes strong enough to generate significant pressures on corporations, there may be no need for formal government action. Pressures were developed outside of government, for example, by stockholders and other groups to "encourage" American companies who had facilities in South Africa to sell off those holdings and withdraw from the country entirely. The public policy process consists of society as a whole, so to speak, and may or may not involve formal government action. This process is a complex mixture of interest groups, public opinion, the media, government, and other elements. Thus some kind of an overview of this larger process may be helpful.

Most public policy that affects business, however, is the result of formal government action, particularly at the federal level. Interest group pressure and public opinion eventually translate into some kind of legislation or regulation that prescribes a specific form of business behavior. Thus it is worthwhile to spend some time describing the processes by which the federal government formulates public policy for the society as a whole. If one wants to influence government, one must understand how it works and where to intervene for maximum effect. This chapter will present both an overview of the larger public policy process and a detailed examination of the way in which government translates public preferences into specific public policies.

MODELS OF THE PUBLIC POLICY PROCESS

There are various ways to describe the larger public policy process in order to understand its operation. Anderson, Brady, and Bullock describe six stages of the public policy process (see Table 5.1). The first stage, *problem formation,* involves a situation where human needs, deprivation, or dissatisfaction appear that must be addressed. If enough people believe the nature of the problem is such that government should respond, it then becomes a public rather than a private problem. Public problems involve large numbers of people and have broad-ranging effects, including consequences for people not directly involved, such as a strike by railroad workers that affects the entire society.[1]

Not all problems get the attention of government, however, and reach the *policy agenda* stage. Those that do reach this stage get there by a variety of routes. Whether the problem gets on the public policy agenda or not depends on the power, stature, and number of people in the interest group. Political leadership is another factor in agenda setting, with the President of the United States being most important in this regard because of the nature of this position. Crisis events, such as wars and depressions, as well as protests and demonstrations, also put problems on the policy agenda.[2]

The stages of *policy formulation* and *adoption* involve the development of proposed courses of action for dealing with public problems. Policy formulation does not automatically mean adoption, of course, as many policy proposals are never formally adopted by the government. Public policies to address particular problems are formulated by the President and his immediate advisors, other members of the executive branch, career and appointed administrative officials, specially appointed committees and commissions, and legislators who introduce bills for consideration by the Congress. Whether these policies are adopted, of course, depends on winning enough support from everyone whose approval is necessary. Although the most formal adoption strategy is one of proposal, congressional approval, and presidential signature, there are other adoption strategies that exist in government.[3]

[1]James E. Anderson, David W. Brady, and Charles Bullock, III, *Public Policy and Politics in America* (North Scituate, Mass.: Duxbury Press, 1978), p. 7.

[2]Ibid., p. 9.

[3]Ibid., pp. 9–10.

Table 5.1
The Policy Process

Policy Terminology	1st stage Problem Formation	2nd Stage Policy Agenda	3rd Stage Policy Formulation	4th Stage Policy Adoption	5th Stage Policy Implementation	6th Stage Policy Evaluation
Definition	Relief is sought from a situation that produces a human need, deprivation, or dissatisfaction	Those problems, among many, which receive the government's serious attention	Development of pertinent and acceptable proposed courses of action for dealing with public problems	Development of support for a specific proposal such that the policy is legitimized or authorized	Application of the policy by the government's bureaucratic machinery to the problem	Attempt by the government to determine whether or not the policy has been effective
Common Sense	Getting the government to see the problem	Getting the government to begin to act on the problem	The government's proposed solution to the problem	Getting the government to accept a particular solution to the problem	Applying the government's policy to the problem	Did the policy work?

Source: James E. Anderson, David W. Brady, and Charles Bullock, III, *Public Policy and Politics in America*, p. 8. Copyright © 1978 by Wadsworth Publishing Company, Inc. Reprinted by permission of the publisher, Brooks/Cole Publishing Company, Monterey, California.

Policy implementation, the fifth stage of the policy process, involves the actual application of an adopted policy. The administrative agencies are the primary implementors of public policy, but the courts and Congress are also involved. Congress may override the decisions of an agency such as the Federal Trade Commission, and the courts interpret statutes and administrative rules and regulations when there is a question about a specific application. The agencies, often delegated substantial authority by Congress, have a wide range of discretion in implementing policy because their mandates are often broad and ill-defined in their enabling legislation. The Federal Trade Commission Act, for example, specifies that unfair methods of competition are illegal. It is left up to the FTC and courts to decide what specific methods are unfair on a case-by-case basis. Thus the agencies make "administrative law" through implementing the statutes passed by Congress. The application of a public policy passed by Congress can actually change the nature of the policy itself, as implementation often affects policy content.[4]

Policy evaluation, the last stage, involves an attempt to determine whether the policy has actually worked. Such an evaluation can lead to additional policy formulation to correct deficiencies. According to Anderson, Brady, and Bullock, there are two types of policy evaluation. The first is a "seat of the pants" or political evaluation that is usually based on fragmentary evidence and may be ideologically biased. The other is a systematic evaluation that seeks to objectively measure the impact of policies and how well objectives are actually accomplished. Such an evaluation focuses on the effects a policy has on the problem to which it is directed.[5]

Preston and Post present other models of the public policy process that focus more on the dynamics of decision making rather than on stages of policy making. They describe three models: optimization, incrementalism, and power-bargaining. The *optimization* model is epitomized by most economists and many bureaucrats who regard the public policy process as the rational search for optimal solutions to well-defined problems. The elementary principles of such an approach are maximization (attaining the highest level of output for a given level of input) and minimization (incurring the least possible cost or inconvenience in order to achieve a given result). The optimization model is a useful analytical construct, but it is limited by its stringent analytic requirements and limited scope. It is an intellectual abstraction, according to Preston and Post, setting forth formal relationships among given conditions. But it takes no account of the

---

[4]Ibid., pp. 10–11.

[5]Ibid., pp. 11–12. Evaluation is a problem in U.S. government because there is almost no incentive to evaluate federal programs. After going through the difficulty of getting a program started and funded, a federal bureaucrat is highly unlikely to agree to an independent evaluation that could allow political opponents a chance to have the program discontinued. Thus there have been few instances where an important policy initiative has been tried and tested in any rigorous manner. See "Intellectuals' Niche in Public Policy," *Insight,* September 19, 1988, pp. 62–63.

way in which policy goals are articulated, alternatives proposed, and preferences discovered. Thus it is, at best, only a partial model of the public policy process.[6]

> The problem, of course, is that government is not supposed to be just a unified, efficient, economic machine but a responsive, disjointed, political apparatus that is accessible at many points and reflects the great variety of perspectives found in an open society.[7]

The *incrementalist* approach holds that policy formulation proceeds by small steps and changes rather than a comprehensive analysis in search of some optimal state of affairs. Incrementalism involves fragmenting a complex problem that no one fully understands, into smaller manageable problems. Thus a piece of a larger problem is first coped with by a specific policy, then the consequences of this first policy are dealt with, and so on, until the larger problem is alleviated or is no longer of concern. Rather than adopting a comprehensive revision of the welfare system, for example, and searching for an optimal solution such as a guaranteed income or other sweeping change, welfare reform from an incrementalist perspective focuses on small changes in one or more programs such as food stamps or medicaid, coping with the consequences of these changes, making other small changes, and so on ad infinitum.

Some argue that incrementalism is the only possible approach to such large problems as poverty because of political constraints. Any suggestion of comprehensive reform exposes every aspect of the existing system to endless debate because of vested interests, guaranteeing political stalemate. Thus every administration is politically constrained to pursue an incremental strategy of reform.[8] Such a strategy, however, leaves much to be desired. Incrementalism has been called the science of "muddling through," without a clear sense of direction or idea of what policy would be most preferred from the standpoint of some overriding principle or objective.

The *power bargaining* model is more of a political model, focusing on the strength and goals of various power centers within society, and on the processes of conflict bargaining and cooperation. Public policy is to be explained primarily in terms of the interaction of groups possessing some degree of social and political power. Conflict between these groups is resolved and an equilibrium reached through bargaining and compromise. The essence of power is the ability to impose penalties or distribute rewards. The outcome of the policy process depends on the penalizing and rewarding abilities of conflicting groups.

---

[6]Lee E. Preston and James E. Post, *Private Management and Public Policy* (Englewood Cliffs, N.J.: Prentice-Hall, 1975), pp. 62–64.

[7]Charles T. Goodsell, *The Case for Bureaucracy: A Public Administration Polemic*, 2nd ed. (Chatham, N.J.: Chatham House, 1985), p. 175.

[8]See Frederick Doolittle, Frank Levy, and Michael Wiseman, "The Mirage of Welfare Reform," *The Public Interest*, no. 47 (Spring 1977), p. 77.

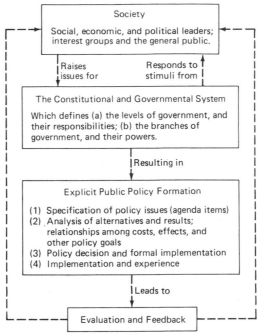

Figure 5.1
Institutional Systems Model of the Public
Policy Process

Source: Lee E. Preston and James E. Post, *Private Management and Public Policy,* © 1975, p. 72. Reprinted by permission of Prentice Hall, Englewood Cliffs, NJ.

Preston and Post then go on to describe what they call an *institutional-systems* model of the public policy process that integrates these three models into a comprehensive framework (see Figure 5.1). The primary initiative in identifying issues for public policy consideration in this model is based in society at large and its various constituent elements. Formal policy making takes place within the constitutional and governmental system that defines the levels and branches of government, their responsibilities and power, and relationship to each other. These aspects of the system are of long duration and subject to only incremental change. The process of explicit policy formation involves the stages of problem identification, analysis, policy decision, implementation, and experience. This last stage, experience, leads to evaluation and feedback to the society at large which may require policy changes. This model accommodates the optimization model with its inclusion of analysis, acknowledges incrementalism in the relative permanence of the constitutional and governmental system, and includes power and bargaining at all stages.[9]

[9]Preston and Post, *Public Policy*, pp. 67–73.

THE INSTITUTIONAL CONTEXT OF PUBLIC POLICY

These general models of the public policy process highlight the crucial importance of governmental institutions in formulating public policy for the society as a whole. Thus to gain a more detailed knowledge of the public policy process, these institutions must be described and examined. The constitution established three branches of government: the legislative, executive, and judicial. We will describe in more detail the institutional structure of Congress, the policy-making powers of the executive branch, and the role and structure of the courts in policy making. There is a fourth aspect of the institutional structure, however, that is often called a fourth branch of government. This consists of the administrative agencies that actually implement most public policies, and may actually determine policy content through the implementation process.

Congress

The Constitution grants the Senate and House of Representatives all legislative power, which, on the surface, seems to give Congress the sole power to approve formal public policy measures. As will be seen later, this is not true, as other branches of government also have legislative power. The Constitution may have intended a separation of power between the legislative, executive, and judicial branches of government, but what the Constitution really did was to establish three institutions with shared power acting as a check and balance on each other. Whereas the most important function of Congress is indeed legislative—enacting laws—it has many other powers and responsibilities: it plays an essential role in amending the Constitution; it appropriates money to operate the federal government and, through the numerous grant-in-aid programs, much of state and local government; it has the power to impeach and try the President, Vice-President, and all civil officers of the United States for grave criminal offenses; it creates administrative agencies and performs certain oversight functions with respect to these agencies; it confirms Presidential appointees to the courts and high executive posts in government; and it has broad investigative powers regarding matters of public policy and administration. These are just some of the responsibilities Congress has of a nonlegislative nature.

Article I of the Constitution contains the so-called "great compromise" under which members of the House are chosen for two-year terms on the basis of population, and two senators from each state are chosen for six-year terms. This arrangement was a compromise between representatives to the Constitutional Convention from heavily populated states, who wished representation to be based on population, and from less populated states who demanded equal representation for all states. This compromise resulted in some inevitable differences in the power and organization of the two houses of Congress.[10]

Bills concerning the raising of revenue must originate in the House, for

---

[10]H. H. Liebhafsky, *American Government and Business* (New York: Wiley, 1971).

example. It is believed that tax legislation will then be made more responsive to the electorate because representation in the House is based on population and its members are elected every two years. The Senate, on the other hand, has the power to approve or disapprove most Presidential appointments to regulatory commissions and federal judgeships as well as concur in treaties with foreign countries.[11]

Since Congress has so much work to accomplish, organization is of crucial importance. The committee system has been developed over the years to handle this workload and provide a degree of specialization regarding public policy problems. Each house is divided into standing committees with respect to subject matter, and these committees, in turn, may have a number of subcommittees. Each committee has a fairly stable membership and a fixed jurisdiction, such as taxes, agriculture, defense, regulation, and environment. Most of the work of Congress is done through this committee structure. When a bill is introduced into Congress, it is referred to the relevant committee, which discusses it (probably by first assigning it to a subcommittee), may amend it in some fashion, and either report on it to the entire membership or fail to do so, thus killing the bill at the committee level.[12]

There are twenty-two standing legislative committees in the House and sixteen in the Senate (see Exhibit 5.1). Each representative serves on one or two of these committees, each senator on two or three of them. Once assigned to a committee, a member remains there until he or she leaves office or voluntarily moves to another committee. The ratio of party representation on each committee is roughly proportional to the ratio of Democrats and Republicans in the House or Senate as a whole. Some of the committees in the House are exclusive committees, meaning that a member may not belong to any other House committee except the Budget Committee. These exclusive committees are the Appropriations, Rules, and Ways and Means Committees. These are the three most powerful committees in the House. The Rules Committee, for example, specifies the conditions under which a bill will be considered. If the Rules Committee refuses to grant a rule to a bill, the bill can go no further.[13]

Committee chairpersons used to have dominant power over almost every aspect of a committee's activity. The chair had complete control of the subcommittees, for example, in that he or she could create or abolish them, pick their members, and determine their jurisdiction. The Subcommittee Bill of Rights adopted in 1973 by the House Democrats changed this procedure. Each committee has to have a minimum number of standing subcommittees with fixed jurisdictions. Decisions about the organization of the subcommittee are made by the full committee's Democratic caucus. Thus committee chairpersons suf-

[11]Ibid., p. 83.

[12]Raymond E. Wolfinger, Martin Shapiro, and Fred I. Greenstein, *Dynamics of American Politics* (Englewood Cliffs, N.J.: Prentice-Hall, 1980), p. 329.

[13]Ibid., p. 330.

Exhibit 5.1
Standing Committees of Congress

Standing Committees of the House

Agriculture	Interior and Insular Affairs
Appropriations	Judiciary
Armed Services	Merchant Marine and Fisheries
Banking, Finance, and Urban Affairs	Post Office and Civil Service
Budget	Public Works and Transportation
District of Columbia	Rules
Education and Labor	Science, Space, and Technology
Energy and Commerce	Small Business
Foreign Affairs	Standards of Official Conduct
Government Operations	Veterans' Affairs
House Administration	Ways and Means

Standing Committees of the Senate

Agriculture, Nutrition, and Forestry	Finance
Appropriations	Foreign Relations
Armed Services	Government Affairs
Banking, Housing, and Urban Affairs	Judiciary
Budget	Labor and Human Resources
Commerce, Science, and Transportation	Rules and Administration
Energy and Natural Resources	Small Business
Environment and Public Works	Veterans' Affairs

Source: 1987–88 Official Congressional Directory—100th Congress (Washington, D.C.: U.S. Government Printing Office, 1987),

fered some loss of power from these developments, but they still have considerable influence over committee activities.[14]

The seniority system was the sole basis for selecting committee chairpersons. The member of the majority party with the longest continuous service on a committee was automatically appointed to chair that committee. This meant, of course, that chairs went disproportionately to older members of Congress. It also meant that chairships went to members from safe seats who returned to Congress year after year to build up seniority. The seniority system eventually became controversial because members with safe seats mostly came from rural areas and were more conservative than the party's congressional membership as a whole. This was a particular problem for the Democratic party because most of these safe seats were in southern states, where conservatism, particularly with regard to civil rights, was strong. Thus liberal legislation was being frustrated because of the power of committee chairpersons.[15]

[14]Ibid., pp. 334–335.
[15]Ibid., p. 336.

Some changes were made in this seniority system by both parties in the 1970s. In 1971, the Republican Conference decided to take an automatic secret vote on the ranking minority member of each committee. In 1973, the House Democrats did the same for the more important job of picking committee chairpersons. Nominations for committee chairs came from a new body—the Democratic Steering and Policy Committee. This revolution did not completely overturn the seniority system, as the most senior member of each committee is still likely to be its chairperson. But the threat of being deposed, makes that individual subject to majority sentiment in the party. Chairs can no longer use their power to flout the wishes of a strong majority of the party.[16]

The legislative process itself is complex and often cumbersome. Once a bill is introduced, it is first assigned to the committee having jurisdiction over its subject matter. This committee, in turn, usually refers the bill to a subcommittee for further discussion. Hearings are usually held by the committee or subcommittee where witnesses present facts and arguments in support of or in opposition to the bill. Expert witnesses are called on to testify as are representatives of private groups that the bill will affect. These hearings are critical for any group that may be affected, and such groups should be represented at the hearings. The hearings serve three functions: (1) they help in polishing the draft of the proposed legislation, (2) they help committee members assess the strength of support and opposition to a particular measure, and (3) they provide time to mobilize additional support or opposition by bringing the bill to public attention.[17]

After the hearings, the subcommittee then drafts a final version of the bill to be presented to the full committee. This is the final point of decision as to the exact wording of the bill for all but the most controversial items. The whole discussion process of the subcommittee is then repeated at the full committee level. If the bill is noncontroversial, the full committee may pass the bill without much discussion. The bill then goes to the House or Senate for further consideration. Scheduling in the Senate is usually accomplished by the majority leader in cooperation with the bill's floor manager, who is usually chairperson of the committee where the bill was initially considered. In the House, the bill must first get through the House Rules Committee and have the rules approved by the House before the substance of the bill itself is considered.[18]

Since there are many House members, controlling floor debate is more crucial than in the Senate. Floor action is thus more tightly scheduled than in the Senate where unlimited debate is permitted. The House thus disposes of much legislation more quickly than the Senate, where a more leisurely approach is usually taken. Minority rights are more respected in the Senate, where a small group can prevent a bill's passage by filibustering (i.e., refusing

[16]Ibid., pp. 337–339.
[17]Ibid., p. 354.
[18]Ibid., pp. 355–356.

to stop talking about the bill so a vote can be taken). A filibuster can be stopped by a successful vote for cloture, which requires the approval of sixty members.[19]

Most bills are introduced into both houses of Congress, because both houses must approve the bill before it can be sent to the President. But to clear Congress, both houses must pass it with exactly the same wording. The final versions of the same bill are usually different as passed by each house, sometimes substantially different. These differences are usually worked out by a Conference Committee composed of senior members of each party, who served on the relevant committee in each House. A Conference Committee is appointed for every bill as necessary and must work out a compromise between the two versions. The compromise bill is then voted on by each House, and if passed, finally goes to the President, unless held back by the Congress for political reasons.

Literally thousands of bills are introduced separately into both houses of Congress during each two-year congressional session. These bills reflect the concerns of constituents, pressures of special interest groups, requests of the administration, and the personal views of the elected representatives themselves. Only about 4 percent of these bills eventually become the law of the country. Successful bills are those that have strong lobbyist and constituent support or bills that are necessary to maintain the funding and operation of government services.

The Executive Branch

The President of the United States is the chief figure in the executive branch, if not of the entire government. The functions and powers of the President are unmatched within the government, and thus the impact the President can have on public policy is quite significant. One academic authority on the Office of the Presidency identified the following ten functions as being most important. (Although all of these functions are important, from the standpoint of public policy that affects business, some functions are much more important than others.)

Chief of State (by acting as ceremonial head of government)
Chief Executive (in supervising day-to-day activities of the Executive Branch)
Commander-in-Chief (of the military forces)
Chief Diplomat (in formulating and executing foreign policy and conducting foreign affairs)
Chief Legislator (by guiding Congress in its law-making activity)
Chief of the Party (by serving as number one political boss in his party)
Voice of the People (in calling the attention of the nation to its unfinished business)

[19]Ibid., pp. 357–358.

Protector of the Peace (in taking actions in times of national disaster to restore domestic order)

Manager of Prosperity (by seeking to maintain full employment, high level production, a high rate of growth, price stability, etc.)

World Leader (in serving as leader of the "Free World")[20]

As chief legislator, the President can submit proposals for legislation to Congress, but has no formal authority to force Congress to adopt the proposals. Thus the President must rely on techniques of persuasion, the granting or withholding of favors, and television appearances to influence public opinion to exert pressure on members of Congress. The framers of the Constitution did not anticipate that the President would become a major source of legislation. Congress was supposed to propose the laws, and the President dispose of them by signing or vetoing the bills sent by Congress. But during the administration of Franklin D. Roosevelt, the presidency itself became a major source of legislation, initiating hundreds of bills to deal with the Depression. In the first "Hundred Days" of FDR's term, Congress passed an impressive list of major laws initiated by the President and his advisors.[21]

The presidential practice of submitting legislation to Congress became institutionalized with the Truman administration. It is now customary for the State of the Union message to be accompanied by an official Presidential legislative program. As manager of prosperity, a role given to the President by the Employment Act of 1946, the President submits a legislative package he believes will promote a healthy economy. The economy has become too complex and governmental policy too significant to permit the government to rely on whatever bills happened to be introduced by congressional members. Thus the President can take the lead in developing a comprehensive package of legislation to deal with economic and social problems. Congress, of course, often does not go along with the President's proposals and has its own ideas of what public policies are appropriate.[22]

The President has thus come to play a far greater role in the legislative process than the mere exercise of veto power granted him by the Constitution. The veto remains, however, an important part of public policy formulation. More than 2,000 bills have been vetoed in the history of Congress and fewer than 100 of these have been overriden. The difference betwen a simple majority needed to pass a bill and a two-thirds vote needed to override a veto is significant. The veto is more likely to be used by a president facing a Congress controlled by the opposite party. With the veto, a president can virtually stymie an opposite party's legislative program.[23]

[20]Clinton P. Rossiter, *The American Presidency*, 2nd ed. (New York: Harcourt, Brace, and World, Inc., 1960), as quoted in Liebhafsky, *American Government and Business*, p. 93.

[21]Wolfinger, Shapiro, and Greenstein, *Dynamics*, p. 409.

[22]Ibid., p. 410.

[23]Ibid., p. 415.

As the chief executive, the President has power of appointment regarding high-level cabinet positions as well as heads and commissioners of government agencies. This power carries a great deal of influence over public policy, as agency heads and commissioners determine the actions taken by the agencies. During the first term of the Reagan administration, for example, people were appointed to head the Federal Trade Commission and Environmental Protection Agency who were opposed to increases in government regulation. They tried to reverse the activist role these agencies had played in previous administrations by changing policies and cutting budgets. The individual appointed to head the Interior Department changed the role of that agency from one of conservation to one of opening up more federal land to exploration and mining.

The President can also issue executive orders which are really legislative acts affecting the various departments and agencies within the executive branch. For example, President Johnson issued an executive order requiring affirmative action plans of most government contractors—an act that went beyond the intent of Congress in passing civil rights legislation. Upon taking office, President Reagan issued an executive order requiring a benefit-cost analysis to be performed by executive branch agencies issuing new regulations, something Congress had not done in the legislation creating the Occupational Safety and Health Administration (OSHA), for example, an executive agency affected by the order.

The executive branch of government also contains the Cabinet and its departments, which carry out a great deal of the work of government. The President may or may not rely on the Cabinet to play a significant policy-making role in the administration. The cabinet departments themselves, however, are quite large and some, such as Health and Human Services and Defense, administer budgets larger than most countries of the world. The impact they have in affecting public policy is significant as they implement legislation and carry out executive functions. Very often, the cabinet departments move in directions not entirely to the satisfaction of the President.

Modern presidents are more likely to rely on advisors in the Executive Office of the President, such as the Chairman of the Council of Economic Advisors or the Director of the Office of Management and Budget, and on the White House staff for major inputs to the policy-making process. The impact these individuals can have on the President and the policy-making process depends on the power they are able to accumulate. Particularly important in this regard is the White House staff, which has been able to accumulate more power over the years. People on the White House staff generally have access to the President on a day-to-day basis, something most cabinet members do not have. The White House staff performs the functions of legislative liaison, handling press relations, writing the President's speeches, and controlling the President's schedules and relations with major interest groups and party figures. Because of these functions, the White House staff has become a key factor in formulating legislative proposals of the President and in running the executive branch in general. The existence of these positions, which are largely independent of the bureaucratic departments, has contributed to what some call the "institutionalization of the presidency." The expansion of agencies within the Executive Office of the President and the growing power of the White House staff "reflects not just a need for coordination and advice, but the president's desire for officials loyal to his goals, not to the interests of career bureaucrats."[24]

Given all these powers, however, it is important to note that the President does not run the government. According to some authorities, the President more accurately *leads* the government, which is a far different matter. As important and powerful as the President is, he does not have authority over Congress, the courts, or even many of the agencies in the federal government. The President has to lead by example, by using powers of persuasion and by mustering what political power is available to the presidency. But the President does not run the government the way a manager runs a company, nor should presidential supporters attempt to run the government in his or her name.[25]

The Courts

The courts play an important role in the public policy process through applying the law to specific situations when a dispute arises between affected parties. Such disputes will involve disagreements about the legal rights and duties of the parties. For example, OSHA has the responsibility to set standards to protect the health of workers. But business might complain that a particular standard is too stringent, that OSHA has not presented conclusive evidence that the new standard will actually improve health, that proper procedures were not used in setting the standard, or that OSHA did not take economic factors into account in developing the standard. Similarly, institutions may develop affirmative action programs to comply with the civil rights laws passed by Congress, but these programs may bar certain individuals, particularly white males, from obtaining jobs and promotions they would otherwise be awarded. Some of these individuals may claim they are a victim of reverse discrimination. These disputed claims will be resolved through the court system which will define and enforce the rights and duties of the affected parties.

The courts, however, do not just play a passive role in discerning the intent of Congress and applying the complexity of the law to particular situations. They can and have played an active role in ways Congress may not have intended and thus have been accused of actually legislating rather than just adjudicating disputes. The intent of Congress in passing the Sherman Anti-Trust Act of 1890, for example, was clearly to curb the growth of trusts and other business combinations. Yet the Justice Department lost seven of the first eight cases it brought under the act because the courts were pro-business. The first

[24]Ibid., p. 427.
[25]Goodsell, *Bureaucracy*, p. 175.

132

applications of the Sherman Act were to Unions. In 1894, the Supreme Court issued an injunction against the union in the Pullman strike on the basis that it was a conspiracy in restraint of interstate commerce. It was not until 1911 that two trusts (Standard Oil and American Tobacco) were found guilty of violating the Sherman Act and ordered dissolved into separate entities.

Laws cannot be written that provide a solution to every possible quarrel that can arise in a society. Most laws passed by Congress are thus written in rather broad language and contain words like *unfair* and *reasonable* that are subject to interpretation. What, for example, is an "unreasonable" restraint of trade or an "unfair" method of competition? Thus the courts have to give meaning to these general phrases in specific situations. In this sense the courts make public policy, with the Supreme Court being final policy maker. The courts have to discern the intent of Congress by reading the record and applying the law to a specific situation. It is claimed that the Supreme Court spends more of its energies making legal interpretations for the guidance of lower courts that will best serve the interests of society in the future, than on satisfying the interests of the parties to a specific quarrel.[26]

Article III of the U.S. Constitution states that "the judicial power of the United States shall be vested in one Supreme Court and in such inferior courts [courts subordinate to the Supreme Court] as the Congress may from time to time ordain and establish." Over time, the federal court system has evolved into a three-level system, consisting of United States District Courts, the United States Courts of Appeals, and the U.S. Supreme Court (see Figure 5.2).

The ninety-four district courts are the basic trial courts of the system, applying the rules of law or of equity. Since they are trial courts, juries are used. The area of district court jurisdiction does not extend across state lines, as each state has at least one federal district court and some have as many as four. The work of the district courts has expanded dramatically over the past several years, as Congress has passed more laws creating federal statutory rights enforceable in federal courts. The various civil rights statutes, for example, have made it possible for many Americans, who believe they have been discriminated against, to sue somebody in a federal court. Environmental and consumer legislation has given many people access to the federal courts to pursue their policy preferences. Environmental groups have used the courts to stop or slow down projects that they claim are violating the environmental laws passed by Congress.

If either party to the litigation is not satisfied with the district court's ruling, it has the right to appeal to a court of appeals for a review of the case. There are eleven such courts of appeals, one for each of the circuits into which the United States is divided, and a twelfth for the District of Columbia (see Figure 5.3). Each of these courts hears appeals from the district courts within its circuit. Decisions by a court of appeals are normally rendered by three-judge panels named by the chief judge of the circuit. In some situations, however,

---

[26]Wolfinger, Shapiro, and Greenstein, *Dynamics*, pp. 480–481.

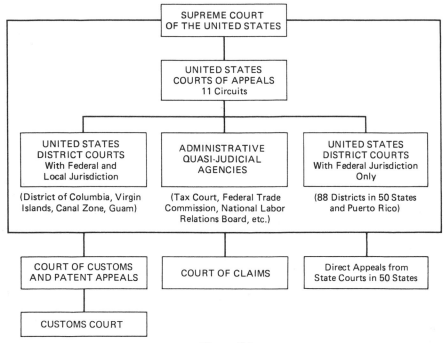

Figure 5.2
Federal Judicial System

Source: Robert N. Corley, Robert L. Black, and O. Lee Reed, *The Legal Environment of Business*, 5th ed. (New York: McGraw-Hill, 1981), p. 42. Reprinted with permission.

cases may be decided by all the judges in a given council sitting together. District court cases normally reach the Supreme Court only after having been reviewed by an appeals court. Since it is so difficult to be granted an appeal to the Supreme Court, the decision of the appeals court represents the final review for most litigants. In addition to appeals from district court decisions, the appeals court also hears appeals from the legal decisions of federal administrative agencies and regulatory commissions.[27]

There are several specialized courts in the federal system that have authority to hear cases involving specific subject matters. The Court of Customs has jurisdiction over disputes involving customs duties. Appeals from this court go to the Court of Customs and Patent Appeals, which also review decisions made by the U.S. Patent Office. The Claims Court deals with money claims against the United States. The Tax Court, however, is an executive agency that reviews decisions of the Internal Revenue Service. Despite its name, it is not really a court in the true sense of the word.[28]

[27]Ibid., p. 491.

[28]Roger E. Meiners and Al H. Ringleb, *The Legal Environment of Business* (St. Paul, Minn.: West Publishing Co., 1982), p. 44.

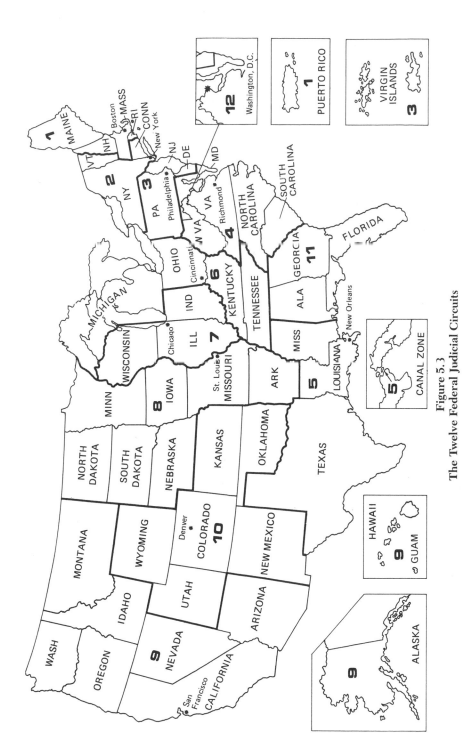

Figure 5.3
The Twelve Federal Judicial Circuits

The Supreme Court is the highest court in the land, and is primarily an appellate review court. Cases reviewed by this Court are generally heard by nine judges, one of whom is appointed Chief Justice of the Supreme Court. Appeals are brought to the Supreme Court from a U.S. Court of Appeals, the Court of Customs and Patent Appeals, the Court of Claims, and the highest courts in the states. Review is usually obtained by filing a petition for certiorari by a lower court, which, if granted, directs the lower court to send the record of the case to the Supreme Court for review. Granting of the writ, however, is at the discretion of the Supreme Court, and is not a right on the part of the parties affected. The Supreme Court cannot hear all the cases that are appealed, and thus picks those that are of substantial national importance or in which an abvious conflict exists between decisions of appeals courts. One of the important functions of the Supreme Court is to assure that there is national uniformity in interpreting federal legislation. The Supreme Court also reviews decisions of state supreme courts when a violation of the U.S. Constitution is alleged.[29]

If the Supreme Court does not grant certiorari and refuses to hear a case, the decision of the last court to deal with the case stands. Decisions made by the Supreme Court are final, in the sense that there is no further judicial review. This does not always end the matter, however, as Congress may change a statute to better reflect its intent if dissatisfied with the Supreme Court's interpretation.[30] The Supreme Court's decisions usually take the form of an order to a lower court or a government agency to carry out the mandate of the Supreme Court as reflected in the decision. Such follow-up work can take many years if complex plans are necessary to implement the Court's decision.[31]

Administrative Agencies   The fourth branch of government consists of all the administrative agencies created by Congress to implement legislation in a specific area. The agencies that have the most direct impact on business are the regulatory agencies. When Congress began to pass laws to regulate business, it created administrative agencies to carry out its wishes. The first such agency was the Interstate Commerce Commission (ICC), created in 1887 to deal with the railroad problem. Other regulatory agencies followed, dealing with specific industries such as communications, transportation, and financial institutions. In the 1960s and 1970s, Congress enacted hundreds of laws dealing with the environment, civil rights, consumer issues, and other social matters, and created many new agencies to implement this legislation. This new type of regulation has come to be called *social regulation* to distinguish it from the earlier type of regulation that dealt with a specific industry. Figure 5.4 presents an historical perspective to

[29]Wolfinger, Shapiro, and Greenstein, *Dynamics*, pp. 497–498.

[30]Meiners and Ringleb, *Legal Environment*, p. 44.

[31]Wolfinger, Shapiro, and Greenstein, *Dynamics*, p. 499.

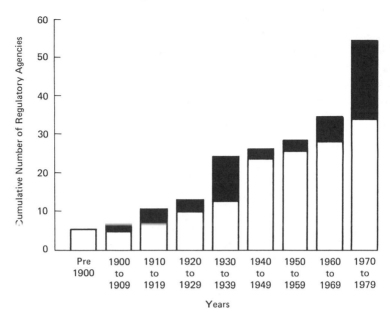

Figure 5.4
A Historical Perspective to Agency Growth

Source: Kenneth Chilton, *A Decade of Rapid Growth in Federal Regulation* (St. Louis, Mo.: Washington University, Center for the Study of American Business, 1979), p. 5. Reprinted with permission.

agency growth, showing the growth of traditional industry regulation in the New Deal era, and the surge of social regulation that is of more recent vintage.

An administrative agency has been defined as "a governmental body other than a court or legislature which takes action that affects the rights of private parties."[32] These agencies may be called boards, agencies, administrative departments, and so on, but in the regulatory area they are most often called commissions. The State Governmental Affairs Committee defined a regulatory commission as "one which (1) had decision making authority, (2) establishes standards or guidelines conferring benefits and imposing restrictions on business conduct, (3) operates principally in the sphere of domestic business activity, (4) has its head and/or members appointed by the president . . . [generally subject to Senate confirmation], and (5) has its legal procedures governed by the Administrative Procedures Act."[33]

These regulatory commissions have specialized functions to implement governmental policy in specifically defined fields. Congress cannot immerse itself in all the details of each activity regulated or pass legislation that mandates

[32]John D. Blackburn, Elliot I. Klayman, and Martin H. Malin, *The Legal Environment of Business: Public Law and Regulation* (Homewood, Ill.: Irwin, 1982), p. 65.

[33]Robert E. Healy, ed., *Federal Regulatory Directory 1979–80* (Washington, D.C.: Congressional Quarterly, Inc., 1979), p. 3.

specific forms of business behavior. Thus it passes laws that are broad in scope and sets general goals to be accomplished. The task of implementing these laws is given to the regulatory agencies which are largely composed of so-called experts in areas like safety and health or the environment. Congress, for example, gives OSHA the power to set standards to improve safety and health in the workplace, but Congress does not specify what kind of standards should be established and for what substances. It is up to OSHA to determine these standards based on its expertise. In this manner, OSHA and other regulatory agencies make public policy.

Congress creates an administrative agency by passing a statute that specifies the name, composition, and powers of the agency. This statute is called the *enabling legislation* for the agency. The agencies are theoretically a creature of the Congress and accountable to Congress for agency activities. Congress can amend the enabling legislation to change agency behavior. Each House has oversight committees that review the work of the agencies, hold hearings, and propose amendments to the enabling legislation. Congress can also control agency activities through the appropriations process by attaching riders forbidding the agency to spend any money on particular cases. Congress did also use the legislative veto to rescind specific regulations issued by the agencies. However, critics argued that the legislative veto was an encroachment on executive powers, and thus its usage was eventually found to be an unconstitutional practice.

Agencies are also subject to specific statutes that govern their activities. The Administrative Procedures Act (APA), passed in 1946, specifies formal procedures with which agencies must comply and establishes standards and prerequisites for judicial review of agency action. Agency actions that are going to affect the environment are subject to the National Environmental Policy Act (NEPA) that requires the development of an environmental impact statement before undertaking the action. Finally, the Freedom of Information Act (FOIA) and Government in the Sunshine Act require, with certain exceptions, that agency documents be publicly available and that agency proceedings be open to the public.[34]

Judicial review of agency action is important because many of the regulations issued by agencies that are opposed by business wind up in the courts. Despite Congressional oversight, the primary task of assuring that agencies comply with congressional dictates has fallen on the courts. The courts may overturn an agency's action for any of the following reasons: (1) the agency failed to comply with the procedures specified in its enabling legislation, the APA, NEPA, or FOIA; (2) the agency's action conflicts with its enabling legislation and therefore exceeds the scope of its authority; (3) the agency's decision is premised on an erroneous interpretation of the law; (4) the agency's action conflicts with the Constitution; and (5) the agency erred in the substance of its

---

[34]Blackburn, Klayman, and Malin, *Legal Environment*, p. 67–68.

action. The last reason has to do with standards of evidence to support an agency's findings and the consideration of all relevant factors in a decision.[35]

There are two general types of regulatory agencies. Some agencies are independent in the sense that they are not located within a department of the executive branch of government. Since they are not part of the legislative or judicial branch either, a fourth branch of government seems to have emerged that combines the functions of the other three in the making, interpreting, and implementing of legislation. These independent agencies include the Consumer Products Safety Commission (CPSC), Equal Employment Opportunity Commission (EEOC), Federal Trade Commission (FTC), Securities and Exchange Commission (SEC), and the ICC. In creating these agencies and making them independent, Congress sought to fashion them into an arm of the legislative branch and insulate them from presidential control. But many presidents have considered these commissions to be adjuncts of the executive branch and have argued that they should be able to coordinate and direct the independent agencies.[36]

Critics of this structure argue that the independent character of these commissions can hinder political monitoring by the executive branch and Congress that would make the agencies more responsive to social and economic change. Since Congress in particular does not always exercise its oversight function very well, the agencies can become complacent in their functions. On the other hand, these agencies can also become too zealous in their efforts, requiring new congressional action to reign them in, such as efforts directed toward the FTC and its rule-making authority.[37]

Another criticism is that the independent character of these agencies has weakened them by removing the benefits of more direct congressional and presidential support. In the case of industry regulation, this makes the agencies more vulnerable to pressure from the regulated industries. They become timid in defending the public interest and developing effective regulatory programs. In the case of social regulation, the independence of the agencies makes them subject to pressures from various interest groups, which may make them ignore the economic impact of their actions.[38]

Other agencies are located within the executive branch in one of the cabinet departments. These agencies include the Food and Drug Administration (FDA) as part of the Department of Health and Human Resources, the Antitrust Division of the Department of Justice, the Labor-Management Services Administration and OSHA in the Department of Labor, and the National Highway Traffic Safety Administration (NHTSA) in the Department of Transportation. Even here, however, there is some question whether these agencies are

[35]Ibid., pp. 70–71.
[36]Healy, *Regulatory Directory*, p. 25.
[37]Ibid.
[38]Ibid., p. 26.

subject to presidential influence and guidance or whether they are free to use the regulatory authority granted them by Congress. Some believe that the President's power to appoint and dismiss cabinet officers carries with it an implicit authority to direct actions by regulatory agencies within the executive departments. Others argue that these agencies may accept White House advice, but that ultimately they are as independent as the separate regulatory commissions.[39]

Regulatory activities may be pursued in a number of ways: rate making, licensing, granting of permits, establishing routes, establishing standards, requiring disclosure of information, and pursuing formal litigation against violators of federal standards. In general, however, the traditional industry-oriented agencies have used adjudication procedures more than rule-making procedures to carry out their functions. Rates and routes for air carriers, for example, were set in trial-like circumstances, where interested parties presented their oral arguments and were cross-examined. After a lengthy process of review, the agency eventually reaches a decision, which may be appealed in the courts. The agency thus proceeds on a case-by-case basis, making law and policy much the same as a court. This procedure gives the agency considerable flexibility in developing an area of regulation over time.

The rule-making procedure is generally preferred by the newer social regulatory agencies. Rule making is the process of promulgating rules, resulting in regulations of greater certainty and consistency and allowing for broader input from the public. The APA definition of a rule is "an agency statement of general or particular applicability and future effect designed to complement, interpret, or prescribe law or policy."[40] Thus rule making is the enactment of regulations that will generally be applicable at some future time period.

Under the rule-making process, an agency must first publish a proposed regulation in the Federal Register. The Federal Register is a legal newspaper in which the executive branch of the United States government publishes regulations, orders, and other documents of government agencies. It was created by Congress for the government to communicate with the public about the administration's actions on a daily basis.

This procedure provides an opportunity for public comment. Any interested individual or organization concerned with a pending regulation may comment on it directly in writing or orally at a hearing within a certain comment period. The Federal Register gives detailed instructions on how, when, and where a viewpoint can be expressed. After the agency receives and considers the comments, it may publish a final version of the regulation in the Federal Register or discontinue the rule-making procedure. If a final regulation is published, the agency must also include a summary and discussion of the major comments it received during the comment period. The final regulation may

---

[39]Ibid., p. 31.
[40]Blackburn, Klayman, and Malin, *Legal Environment*, p. 77.

take effect no sooner than thirty days following its publication. After a final rule has been adopted by the agency, it is also published in the Code of Federal Regulations. The Code contains all the rules and regulations that any given agency has passed over the course of its existence.

On February 17, 1981, President Reagan issued an executive order that required agencies in the executive branch to prepare a regulatory impact analysis for each major rule being considered. The purpose of this analysis was to permit an assessment of the potential benefits and costs of each major regulatory procedure. The executive order also required that agencies choose regulatory goals and set priorities to maximize the benefits to society and choose the most cost-efficient means among legally available options for achieving the goals. This regulatory impact analysis must be submitted to the Office of Information and Regulatory Affairs (OIRA) located in the Office of Management and Budget (OMB). This analysis must pass OIRA's scrutiny before a regulation can be published. OIRA has the power to delay issuance of the regulation either in its proposed or final form.

Government agencies are very important actors in the public policy process. They combine the functions of the legislative branch in making administrative law, the executive branch through enforcing agency actions, and the judicial branch in adjudicating disputes. The administrative process has grown because of the need for specialized application of the laws Congress passes. The Congress did not wish to increase executive power by giving these functions to the President, and thus created administrative agencies as an alternative. These agencies are subject to control by the other three branches through Congressional oversight, the Presidential power of appointment and issuance of executive orders, and judicial review. They also have shown a great deal of autonomy at times in formulating public policy. Business can therefore be surprised when a law passed by Congress often turns out to be quite different than anticipated after being implemented by the agencies.

> Administrative agencies wield power because they constitute mobilizations of resources that can be used to allocate political values. They develop distinctive institutional points of view on what policies are deemed in the public interest. They push unabashedly within political arenas to advance these viewpoints. Moreover, agencies are supported by external political groups as well as opposed by them, and thus they engage fully in the political conflict that inevitably envelopes those possessing power.[41]

This political conflict limits the power agencies can exercise in the government. There are several features in the bureaucratic environment, some of which have been already mentioned, that limit the power of agencies. Because of the separation of powers concept, Congress and the executive branch have some ability to control agency behavior. The press makes the exposure of agency

[41]Goodsell, *Bureaucracy*, p. 126.

scandal a principal objective. The Freedom of Information Act requires agencies to open themselves to public scrutiny. The power of public interest lobbies and built-in mechanisms of client advocacy also provide limits on agency behavior. Statutory encouragement and protection of whistle blowing is also a factor in the environment. Finally, the institutionalization of citizen participation in decision making provides another check on agency power. This system of checks and balances leads one author to comment that bureaucratic power in the United States is "probably more inhibited than in any other country on earth."[42]

OPERATION OF THE PUBLIC POLICY PROCESS   The preceding section described the structure of government in terms of the three branches established by the Constitution and a fourth branch consisting of administrative agencies designed to carry out specialized functions related to implementation of legislation. This overall organization of government is shown in Figure 5.5, which shows a number of independent agencies and government corporations in a separate section. It must be remembered that many other agencies are part of the cabinet departments and are also considered to be part of the fourth branch of government because of their quasi-independent status.

The role these branches play in formulating public policy was outlined insofar as formal responsibilities are concerned. This kind of description and diagram, however, says nothing about the relative power of these branches in relation to public policy making and the relative impact particular actors have in the public policy process. Such information would be extremely useful for a business executive who desires to participate in public policy formulation and use his or her time effectively.

The problem is one of finding where the power lies in government. Is Congress more powerful than the executive branch? What parts of Congress make the most impact on public policy formulation? Are the regulatory agencies the place where one should expend time and effort to affect the actual application of legislation? What role do the courts actually play in the public policy process?

The so-called traditional models of the public policy process, those which show how a bill becomes a law, for example, are of little use in this regard. They are too formal and mechanistic in their approach. Like the formal organization chart of a business, they may tell us little about how the organization really works and who has actual power to affect policy. Dan Fenn, writing in the *Harvard Business Review*, has the following to say about these traditional models.

> Like the textbook chart with the pipes and valves showing how a bill goes through Congress, they leave people and power out. They mislead us about the true nature of executive-legislative relations and make a consciously

[42]Ibid., p. 133.

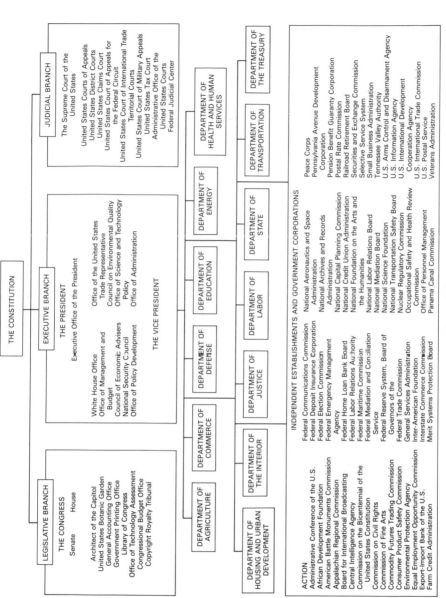

Figure 5.5
The Government of the United States

Source: Office of the Federal Register, *U.S. Government Manual 1987/88* (Washington, D.C.: U.S. Government Printing Office, 1987), p. 21.

143

contrived system of controlled power and maximum access look centralized and monolithic.[43]

Thus we must look to nontraditional models of government to tell us how public policy is actually formulated. One such model was developed by Wallace S. Sayre and reconstructed by Walter G. Held in a Brookings publication. According to Held, "Sayre developed a model that identifies nine sets of actors or power structures in the decision-making system, sets forth their principal interests, motivations, and values, and describes the interplay among them that results in the formulation, adoption, and implementation of policies and programs by the federal government."[44]

The focal point of Sayre's analysis is the bureau leader (see Figure 5.6), the level immediately below the political level in the executive branch. By bureau leader, Sayre means the head of an administrative agency. These administrative agencies include: (1) subdivisions of cabinet departments, (2) administrative agencies outside the departments such as the Veteran's Administration, (3) independent regulatory boards and commissions, (4) independent administrative boards and commissions like the Federal Home Loan Bank Board, and (5) federal corporations such as the Tennessee Valley Authority.[45]

The bureau unit has major powers for carrying out programs and proposals, which makes the bureau leader pivotal in policy making. The bureau leader can function both as an expert staff person to political superiors and a general manager to subordinates within the agency. He or she is in a key position to influence the specific application of public policy measures. Bureau leaders direct large federal projects and programs or participate in determining policies and actions. Their activities draw the attention of many interest groups who wish to influence public policy.

This is not to suggest that the bureau leader is autonomous in the policy-making process. In reality, the head of an administrative agency is subject to many lines of influence, as shown in Figure 5.6, that compete for his or her time and attention. According to Held, these other sets of power structures in the federal decision-making process that affect the bureau chief's decisions, include the following:

The presidential line of influence, which includes executive departments and agencies and special presidential staff organizations.

The congressional line of influence, which includes the various committees, subcommittees, staffs, and special organizations established as aids to Congress.

[43]Dan H. Fenn, Jr., "Finding Where the Power Lies in Government," *Harvard Business Review*, vol. 57, no. 5 (September–October 1979), p. 153.

[44]Walter G. Held, *Decisionmaking in the Federal Government: The Wallace S. Sayre Model* (Washington, D.C.: The Brookings Institution, 1979).

[45]Ibid., p. 3.

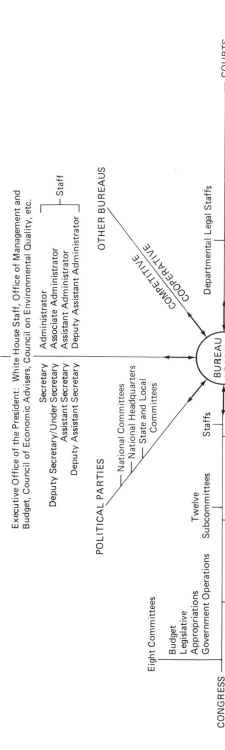

Figure 5.3

The Wallace S. Sayre Model of the Federal Decisionmaking System[a]

Source: Walter Held, *Decisionmaking in the Federal Government: The Wallace S. Sayre Model* (Washington D.C.: The Brookings Institution, 1979), p. 2.

[a] The presidential and congressional lines of influence have been modified to reflect organizational changes since the Sayre model was developed.

PRESIDENT

Executive Office of the President: White House Staff, Office of Management and Budget, Council of Economic Advisers, Council on Environmental Quality, etc.

Administrator
Associate Administrator ⎤
Assistant Administrator ⎥ Staff
Deputy Assistant Administrator ⎦

Secretary
Deputy Secretary/Under Secretary
Assistant Secretary
Deputy Assistant Secretary

OTHER BUREAUS

COMPETITIVE

COOPERATIVE

Departmental Legal Staffs

COURTS

ALLEGED LIMITATIONS:
Rationality Lacking
Innovation Depressed
Public Interest Not Represented

Justice Department
Office of Legal Counsel
Solicitor General

BUREAU LEADER

GENERAL

SPECIAL

MEDIA

POLITICAL PARTIES

National Committees
National Headquarters
State and Local Committees

Staffs

Office of Technology Assessment

Advisory Committees

CAREER STAFF

FRIENDLY

HOSTILE

INTEREST GROUPS

Twelve Subcommittees

Congressional Budget Office

Eight Committees

Budget
Legislative
Appropriations
Government Operations

General Accounting Office

CONGRESS (House and Senate)

THE PROCESS:
Alliance Building
Bargaining/Negotiation
Compromise

The courts' line of influence, which is mainly exerted through legal officers in the executive branch who try to interpret what the courts are likely to do or say about actions taken or contemplated.

Other bureaus, whose activities may compete for jurisdiction, money, and other resources, or whose cooperation is required for successful performance.

The political parties, which seek to influence governmental actions to achieve their goals.

The media, both general and specialized, communicating in print or electronically.

The interest groups, whose constituents expect their agents to see that their values and desires are reflected in federal decisions.

The career staff, who are associated with the bureau leaders, and the employees under their direction.[46]

To survive, a bureau leader must understand the nature of this system of influences and work within it to influence the outcome of the decision-making process. The leader must educate the many power centers in government about his or her activities and goals and induce them to help the bureau leader perform effectively. He or she must build alliances with other power centers in and out of government, must bargain with these power centers, and be able to reach compromises with other interests on a given issue who have power.[47]

Thus the Sayre model places primary emphasis on the heads of administrative agencies in the public policy process. It identifies the implementation stage as being the most crucial in policy making. The agencies actually determine the specifics of a program or proposal and carry out the wishes of Congress, the executive branch, and the courts. While Congress may pass legislation, the agencies apply it to specific situations. The President may issue an executive order affecting some agencies, but the agencies implement the order. The courts may rule on a particular public policy issue, but the agencies may be able to circumvent much of the impact of this ruling. The bureau leader thus sits at the seat of power, according to Sayre, and others try to influence his or her actions.

Dan Fenn uses this wheel model developed by Sayre to determine where the power lies in government. But he makes the point that one cannot answer a general question, such as who really runs the government, with this model. One can only answer the question of why a particular piece of public policy came out the way it did.[48] Thus the wheel model is not limited to bureau chiefs,

[46]Ibid., p. 5.
[47]Ibid., p. 18.
[48]Fenn, "Power," p. 147.

but can be used to analyze decision-making processes where the bureau chief may not be the central figure.

To use the wheel model, one has to identify the key decision maker on a given issue. It may indeed be a bureau chief, but it could also be a legislator or the President. Once the key decision maker is identified and the power centers around him or her have been listed, one must assess the degree of interest these power centers have, evaluate their clout, and explore the possibility of forming common causes with them.[49] This wheel model, according to Fenn, can be a guide to a rational, systematic strategy for business, helping an executive select the tactics that are likely to work best in a given policy situation.[50]

Another view of where the power lies in government is presented by Clifford M. Hardin, Kenneth A. Shepsle, and Barry R. Weingast. They argue that the root of the nation's economic difficulties during the early 1980s lay in Congress itself. During the decade of the 1970s, a collection of powerful subcommittees, about 150 in each house of Congress, provided the motivation for much of the unrestrained and uncoordinated growth of the federal government. Subcommittees have grown more numerous and powerful over the past several years, and have been used more and more by Congress to conduct the main business of the nation's legislature.[51]

Indeed, according to the authors, both Congress as a collective entity and the presidency have been eclipsed by the now autonomous committees and subcommittees of Congress. These committees and subcommittees have developed a relatively free hand in policy making within their own narrow jurisdictions. They have positioned themselves with respect to a handful of issue areas to protect relevant constituencies from changes that would adversely affect their interests.[52]

This trend toward the decentralization of Congress, transferring power from strong institutional and party leaders initially to committees and later to subcommittees, has been accelerated by seversl recent developments, according to the authors. "The Legislative Reorganization Act (1970), the Subcommittee Bill of Rights (1973), and the Committee Reform Amendments in the House (1974), served to strengthen the hand and assure the independence of the now numerous subcommittees."[53] The destruction of institutional and party power centers has resulted in the creation of new power centers, namely the committees and subcommittees of Congress.

These committees and subcommittees operate with relative independence in well-defined policy jurisdictions. They tend to be populated by those

[49]Ibid., p. 151..

[50]Ibid., p. 153.

[51]Clifford M. Hardin, Kenneth A. Shepsle, and Barry R. Weingast, *Public Policy Excesses: Government By Congressional Subcommittee* (St. Louis, Mo.: Washington University Center for the Study of American Business, 1982), p. 1.

[52]Ibid.

[53]Ibid., p. 6.

who have the highest stake in a given policy area. Thus, for example, farm-state Congressmembers dominate the agricultural committees and urban legislators dominate the banking, housing, and social welfare committees.[54] Legislators tend to gravitate to the committees and subcommittees whose jurisdictions are most pertinent to their geographic constituencies.[55]

There are three reasons, according to the authors, why committees and subcommittees occupy such a key position in policy making. First, they originate legislation in specific areas of public policy. Second, they act as oversight agencies directing the activities of adminstrative agencies. The wise bureau chief, say the authors, "had best attend to the concerns of the relevant committee and subcommittee members who can embarass or otherwise complicate his life through the adverse publicity of oversight, and who can directly affect his bureau's authority and budget through the annual authorization and appropriations process."[56] Third, the committees and subcommittees can protect a program or agency from policy changes they deem undesirable. Reform proposals to alter bad programs can fall on deaf ears or have little effect if actually put into operation, if they are not consistent with the interests of committee and subcommittee members.[57] They are in a position to sabotage, water down, or simply ignore ameliorative changes. Policies to reform programs are often held hostage by these legislators whose constituents benefit from the current arrangements.

Thus there are several alternative ways of viewing the operation of government in addition to the separation of powers doctrine of the constitution or the organizational chart approach. It is important to know where the power lies in government, whether it resides in the bureau chiefs, the committees and subcommittees of Congress, the presidency, or the courts, or whether it is constantly shifting with given issues.[58] In order to be effective in the public policy process, business must be aware of where the power lies and how the system actually operates.

SELECTED REFERENCES

ALLISON, GRAHAM T. *The Essence of Decision: Explaining the Cuban Missile Crises.* Waltham, Mass.: Little, Brown and Co., 1971.

[54]Ibid., p. 10.
[55]Ibid., p. 9.
[56]Ibid., p. 11.
[57]Ibid., p. 12.
[58]"In the final period of the twentieth century, we Americans have a more fluid system of power than ever before in our history. Quite literally, power floats. It does not reside in the White House, nor does it merely alternate from pole to pole, from president to opposition, from Republicans to Democrats. It floats. It shifts. It wriggles elusively, like mercury in the palm of one's hand, passing from one competing power center to another . . . gravitating to whoever is daring enough to grab it and smart enough to figure out the quickest way to make a political score." Hedrick Smith, *The Power Game: How Washington Works* (New York: Random House, 1988), pp. 14–15.

BAUER, RAY, ITHIEL DE SOLA POOL, and LEWIS A. DEXTER. *American Business and Public Policy*, 2nd ed. Chicago: Aldine-Atherton, 1972.

COBB, ROGER W., and CHARLES D. ELDER. *Participation in American Politics*. Baltimore: John Hopkins University Press, 1975.

DYE, THOMAS R. *Understanding Public Policy*, 3rd ed. Englewood Cliffs, N.J.: Prentice-Hall, 1978.

FRITSCHLER, A. LEE, and BERNARD H. ROSS. *How Washington Works: The Executive's Guide to Government*. Cambridge, Mass.: Ballinger, 1987.

GOODSELL, CHARLES T. *The Case for Bureaucracy: A Public Administration Polemic*, 2nd ed. Chatham, N.J.: Chatham House, 1985.

HELD, WALTER G. *Decisionmaking in the Federal Government: The Wallace S. Sayre Model*. Washington, D.C.: The Brookings Institution, 1979.

JONES, CHARLES O. *An Introduction to the Study of Public Policy*, 2nd ed. Belmont, Mass.: Duxbury Press, 1977.

LANE, FREDERICK S. *Current Issues in Public Administration*. New York: St. Martin's Press, Inc., 1978.

LINDBLOM, CHARLES E. *Politics and Markets: The World's Political-Economic Systems*. New York: Basic Books, Inc., 1977.

NAVARRO, PETER. *The Policy Game: How Special Interests and Ideologues Are Stealing America*. Lexington, Mass.: Lexington Books, 1984.

PRESTON, LEE, and JAMES POST. *Private Management and Public Policy*. Englewood Cliffs, N.J.: Prentice-Hall, 1975.

REDMAN, ERIC. *The Dance of Legislation*. New York: Simon & Schuster, 1974.

SMITH, HEDRICK. *The Power Game: How Washington Works*. New York: Random House, 1988.

STARLING, GROVER. *The Politics and Economics of Public Policy*. Homewood, Ill.: Dorsey Press, 1979.

TRUMAN, DAVID. *The Governmental Process: Political Interests and Public Opinion*, 2nd ed. Westminster, Md.: Alfred A. Knopf, 1951.

INTERNATIONAL DIMENSIONS
OF PUBLIC POLICY

<== IDEAS TO BE FOUND ==>
IN THIS CHAPTER

- The international regulatory environment
- The foreign payments controversy
- Economic sanctions and trade policies
- International public affairs

The previous chapter focused on the public policy process in the United States, but this by no means is the only dimension to public policy with which a manager needs to be familiar. As business becomes increasingly international-ized, public policies that affect business in the international arena have also become of increasing importance. The term *internationalization* refers to an increased foreign influence on national trends and policies.[1] When countries trade with each other and when they are open for foreign investment and technology, they are also more open to outside influences. The increased magni-tude of international trade and investment that has taken place over the past several decades has led to greater independence among individual national economies as they have become internationalized.[2]

This internationalization of domestic economies around the world is most directly the result of decisions made by private firms to engage in international trade and investment. Thus some attention needs to be given to the role of the

---

[1] H. Hal Mason and Robert S. Spich, *Management: An International Perspective* (Homewood, Ill.: Irwin, 1987), p. 2.

[2] Ibid., p. 9.

multinational corporation (MNC) in the international economy. Because of its role in promoting trade and investment between countries, the MNC has become a major force in internationalizing national economies. The MNC is the major institutional means through which international trade and investment is accomplished.

> The multinational corporation is probably the most visible vehicle for the internationalization of the world economic system. As the economies of different nations have become increasingly linked and functionally integrated, the multinational corporation seems to have been the institution most able to adapt to a transnational style of operation. Indeed, multinational corporations are a major result of and a prime stimulus for furthering the number and complexity of transnational interactions.[3]

A multinational corporation has been defined as any enterprise that undertakes foreign direct investment, owns or controls income-gathering assets in more than one country, produces goods or services outside its country of origin, or engages in international production.[4] Multinational corporations are generally headquartered in industrialized countries and pursue business activities in one or more foreign countries. They exercise influence over the various entities (branches, subsidiaries, joint ventures) in those countries. This allows them to adopt a common globally oriented corporate policy with respect to sharing information, using resources, and dividing responsibilities. Thus the term *multinational* can refer to many different kinds of business enterprises and is not limited to a single type of business.[5]

Multinationals have gained importance over the past several years as an international economy has developed. In 1966, the total value of direct foreign investment by MNCs originating in industrialized countries amounted to $90 billion. One-third of this investment was in developing countries. In 1970, the value of this investment was estimated at $250 billion, and by 1983, the global stock of foreign direct investment was about $625 billion. Roughly $150 billion of this investment, or about one-quarter of the global stock, was in developing countries.[6] There are about 10,000 multinationals throughout the world; 4,534 of these based in Europe and about 2,570 in the United States. The United States is the largest investor, however, with about 50 percent of the total to its credit. Most of this total is invested in developed countries.[7]

---

[3]David H. Blake and Robert S. Walters, *The Politics of Global Economic Relations* (Englewood Cliffs, N.J.: Prentice-Hall, 1983), p. 83.

[4]Thomas J. Biersteker, *Distortion or Development? Contending Perspectives on the Multinational Corporations* (Cambridge, Mass.: MIT Press, 1981), p. xii.

[5]The term *transnational corporation* (TNC) is often used to refer to this same entity. See Kwamena Acquaah, *International Regulation of Transnational Corporations: The New Reality* (New York: Praeger, 1986), p. 48.

[6]Ibid., pp. 43–44.

[7]Donald A. Ball and Wendell H. McCulloch, Jr., *International Business: Introduction and Essentials*, 2nd ed. (Plano, Tex.: Business Publications, 1985), pp. 5, 32. See also Simcha Ronen, *Comparative and Multinational Management* (New York: Wiley, 1986), pp. 13–16.

This kind of growth means that MNCs have significant economic and social impacts on national economies and political systems. Their activities have become highly visible, making them subject to criticism from many quarters. They have somewhat of a love-hate relationship with many developing countries who welcome MNCs because the multinationals have the potential to assist these countries in pursuing their own economic growth and development. Yet these same countries view MNCs as a threat to their national sovereignty and autonomy. They do not want to become economically and technologically dependent on institutions outside of their control. They often find MNCs hard to live with—and yet impossible to live without.[8]

> Nations of the world as a matter of national policy are seeking to improve their social and economic development. Multinational business has a significant and perhaps leading role in achieving these social goals. The people have needs, and business has the technology and resources to meet these needs. The result is that modern business relationships have become worldwide. Multinational business is a significant social institution.[9]

Generally speaking, there are at least four reasons why a business enterprise might decide to become international in scope. The first reason is to find new markets for products. These new markets may be needed to provide a sufficient demand to allow for economies of scale to be realized from large production runs. Large production runs may permit output to be produced at a level where the marginal cost of producing an extra unit is substantially less than the average cost. Thus the more goods that are produced, the lower the average cost per unit and the greater the profitability of the firm. Because of these economies, some business executives look for international markets to provide this extra demand for their products.

The second reason is the desire of business managers to find opportunities to earn greater returns on capital. These opportunities may be better in foreign countries, especially in the third world, where competition may be much less keen than it is in the United States (or other advanced industrialized countries) and where consumption is rising more rapidly. Growth of foreign consumption in the developing countries has become especially important in recent years. Firms can sometimes introduce new products overseas faster than they can in their home country, and thus start earning a return on investment sooner.

A firm may also become international in order to obtain resources that are needed for its operations. These resources may not be available in the firm's home country and thus it is necessary for the firm to go abroad and search for

---

[8]Acquaah, *International Regulation*, p. 44. As an indication of the power of MNCs, it is useful to note that in 1984, only twenty-five nations had GNPs greater than the total sales of Exxon, the world's largest MNC, and the total sales of Exxon surpassed the sum of the gross national products of forty-four African countries. Ball and McCulloch, *International Business*, p. 5.

[9]Keith Davis and William C. Frederick, *Business and Society: Management, Public Policy, Ethics*, 5th ed. (New York: McGraw-Hill, 1984), p. 409.

Table 6.1
Importance of Reasons for Foreign Investment

	Mentioned by Number of Companies
1. Maintain or increase market share locally	33
2. Unable to reach market from U.S. because of tariffs, transportation costs, or nationalistic purchasing policies	25
3. To meet competition	20
4. To meet local content requirements and host government pressure	18
5. Faster sales growth than in the United States	15
6. To obtain or use local raw materials or components	13
7. Low wage costs	13
8. Greater profit prospects abroad	11
9. To follow major customers	10
10. Inducements connected with host government investment promotion programs	8

Source: U.S. Department of Commerce, Domestic and International Business Administration, *The Multinational Corporation: Studies on U.S. Foreign Investment,* Vol. 2. (Washington, D.C.: U.S. Government Printing Office, 1973), p. 6.

these resources on the best terms available. In other cases, foreign countries may have specialized skills that are significant factors in the decision to establish overseas operations. A firm that is located in an advanced industrial country where wages are relatively high may invest in developing nations in order to take advantage of low-cost labor. These lower costs may give it a competitive advantage.[10]

Finally, foreign markets are a must for corporations making products for which domestic demand has been satiated. Such corporations must either find new markets for their products or develop new lines of business. The best course of action in many of these cases is to find new markets for existing products by attempting to penetrate foreign countries. For example, infant formula companies turned to overseas markets for exactly this reason. As the baby boom generation grew up and the birthrate declined in developed countries, the developing countries offered new potential markets for such products.

The United States Department of Commerce has had a long-standing interest in the area of foreign investment of U.S. multinational corporations. Concerning the principal reasons for making investments in foreign countries, the Department conducted a series of interviews with 76 chief executives in charge of international operations, covering most U.S. manufacturing industries.[11] Table 6.1 shows the results of this survey, listing the reasons in order of importance as measured by the frequency of mention by the executives interviewed.

[10]Mason and Spich, *Management*, p. 18.

[11]U.S. Department of Commerce, Domestic and International Business Administration, *The Multinational Corporation: Studies on U.S. Foreign Investment*, Vol. 2 (Washington, D.C.: U.S. Government Printing Office, 1973), pp. 1–2.

The growth of multinational corporations is paralleled by a growth in government regulation of economic activity, including regulation of multinational activity both within and without national borders. This growth increases the chances that the regulations of different countries will clash, with multinationals caught in the middle.[12] In effect, expansion beyond national boundaries is much more than a step across the geographical line of a country. It is also a step toward new and different social, educational, political, and economic environments. Different values and cultures mean that there are different ways of conducting business in various countries. These differences cause problems for managers of multinational corporations, as conflicts arise between MNCs and host and home countries, and find their way into public policy measures regulating the conduct of multinational enterprises. Public policies are often adopted to resolve these differences, making public policy important to companies operating in the international economy as well as in the domestic economy.

THE INTERNATIONAL REGULATORY ENVIRONMENT

Many countries find it difficult to control the activities of multinational corporations within their territories. The flexibility of MNCs enables them to move capital, goods, personnel, and technology across national boundaries. This flexibility enables MNCs to play one country off another to get the best deal for themselves. Since the activities of MNCs affect the level of social and economic development in many countries, particularly developing countries, there has been an increasing interest in developing some form of international regulation over the activities of MNCs and giving host governments some control over their activities. Third-world nations in particular believe that in the absence of international regulation, MNCs would only show interest in profit maximization without any regard to the development needs of host nations.[13]

Most conflicts arise from the fact that MNCs have some degree of economic power because of the decisions they make concerning product lines, location of plants, technology employed, trade flows, and other business considerations. These decisions are made with regard to corporate objectives related to profits and market share, and are not necessarily made in the interests of the host country or even the home country. MNCs do not and cannot take into account the interest of each and every country in the decisions it makes because the interests of the various countries rarely coincide. MNCs must maintain that they are looking after their own interests within a worldwide strategy they have developed for themselves. Yet governments are not likely to let important

[12]Douglas E. Rosenthal and William M. Knighton, *National Laws and International Commerce: The Problem of Extraterritoriality* (Boston: Routledge & Kegan Paul Ltd., 1982), p. 1.

[13]Acquaah, *International Regulation*, p. xii.

decisions be made by a foreign private institution without exercising some kind of influence.[14]

Host governments influence multinationals in a variety of ways. The underlying motive is to set the rules of the game. Government regulation is theoretically nondiscriminatory, since all the parties are nominally subject to the same rules of the game. In reality, however, governments are political creations and are often motivated by purely political considerations. Another major problem facing multinationals is that the regulatory environment varies considerably from country to country. Many regulations governing multinationals are difficult to interpret and are not consistently enforced. Moreover, in large parts of the third world there is a distinct absence of regulations or mechanisms for enforcing those regulations that do exist. Such countries often lack the necessary legal and administrative institutions and the technical proficiency to implement and enforce national policies.

MNCs are accused of creating numerous negative externalities for host countries, including the following: (1) the benefits of foreign investments are poorly or unfairly distributed between the MNC and the host country; (2) MNCs preempt the development of an indigenous economic base by squeezing out local entrepreneurs; (3) they employ inappropriate capital-intensive technology, adding to host country unemployment; (4) MNCs worsen the distribution of income in the host country; (5) they alter consumer tastes in the host country, thus undermining the culture; and (6) foreign investors subvert host country political processes by coopting the local elites, using their influence to keep host governments in line, and structuring the international system to respond to their needs to the detriment of host authorities.[15]

These negative externalities are the result of investment decisions and operational practices that are geared to the need of MNCs to survive and grow. They exist by maintaining or increasing world market shares, gaining a competitive edge over rivals, shifting operations to take advantage of access to natural resources or cheap labor markets, and other such factors where policies and strategies are developed that are global in nature, scope, and character. Regulation is developed to deal with some of these negative externalities, as it is difficult for any one country to deal with these unilaterally, particularly countries in the third world. This regulation takes place at various levels of institutional development.

International Level

Conceived and born amid the idealism and hopes that came with peace at the end of World War II, the United Nations is probably the best known of the international organizations. Of particular interest is the United Nations Centre

---

[14]Jack N. Behrman, *Essays on Ethics in Business and the Professions* (Englewood Cliffs, N.J.: Prentice-Hall, 1988), p. 240.

[15]Ibid., pp. 59–60.

on Transnational Corporations (UNCTC). It provides numerous services for member nations with respect to the operation of what it calls Transnational Corporations (TNCs) within their borders. The UNCTC has been in the process of developing an international code of conduct to regulate the activities of TNCs with regard to the internal affairs of host countries and to encourage TNCs to facilitate the achievement of the development activities of third-world countries. This code represents the first time a comprehensive international instrument is being developed for regulating a wide range of issues arising from relations between TNCs and host governments.[16]

The code is meant to provide a stable, predictable, and transparent framework that can facilitate the flow of resources across national boundaries, thereby enhancing the role of foreign investment in economic and industrial growth. The code is also meant to minimize the negative effects of TNCs by establishing the rights and responsibilities of TNCs and host governments. As a result of this twin focus, it is hoped the code will help reduce friction between TNCs and host countries and enable the flow of direct foreign investment to realize its full potential.

The first part of the code consists of a preamble and statement of objectives. The second part deals with definitions and the code's scope of application. The next portion concerns the activities of TNCs including (1) the general political implications flowing from the operations of TNCs; (2) specific economic, financial, and social issues; and (3) disclosure of information. The fourth part of the code covers the kind of treatment TNCs should expect from host governments, including issues of nationalization and compensation and choice of jurisdiction for settlement of disputes. The fifth section deals with inter-governmental cooperation for application of the code, and the sixth and final part is concerned with development at national and international levels.[17]

The problem with all such international codes is to make them general enough to secure ratification by a number of nations with diverse interests and yet specific enough to have some real meaning in concrete situations. Another problem is implementation. Third-world countries generally want such codes to be binding and are in favor of setting up some institutional machinery for enforcement purposes, whereas industrialized countries generally want such codes to be voluntary without any binding authority. This problem of international enforcement authority has undermined other efforts of this nature and is likely to produce the same result regarding the UNCTC code. Perhaps the major benefit of the code will be to provide a model for other such efforts at regulating TNCs at regional or national levels.

The complexity of problems on the global level has led the major trading nations to seek better solutions in the form of trade agreements. Two international trade organizations that have an important impact on the international

[16]Ibid., p. 111.
[17]Ibid., p. 114.

economic environment are the General Agreement on Tariffs and Trade (GATT) and the United Nations Conference on Trade and Development (UNCTAD). A third organization, the Organization of Economic Cooperation and Development (OECD), is also discussed.

The General Agreement on Tariffs and Trade.   The unhappy experience of the Great Depression led the major trading nations to seek better commercial policies after World War II. As one outcome of their efforts, the General Agreement on Tariffs and Trade was formed on October 10, 1947, as the world's trading club. Its initial membership was only twenty-three countries; today, GATT counts over ninety members and associates who account for well over 80 percent of total world trade. The communist countries are also represented by five members.

GATT provides a framework for multilateral trade negotiations and allows nations to work out differences in trade policies that might otherwise create a no-win situation for all the major trading nations. It was designed to provide a multilateral framework for tariff negotiations on a product-by-product basis. One of GATT's guiding principles to promote trade is that of nondiscrimination. Each contracting party must grant all others the same rate of import duties, that is, a tariff concession granted to one trading partner must be extended to all members of the organization. Another principle is the concept of consultation. When trade disagreements arise, GATT provides a forum for consultation. Disagreeing members are more likely to compromise than resort to arbitrary trade-restricting actions.

World-trade cooperation since World War II has led to a better open-door trading policy than might have been expected. GATT has been a major contributor to this policy. Since 1947, GATT has sponsored seven major tariff negotiations. As a result, the tariff rates for tens of thousands of items have been reduced, and a high proportion of the world trade has seen an easing of restrictions. The organization has undoubtedly contributed to the expansion of world trade since its inception. However, GATT has not prevented industrialized nations from adopting protectionist measures when it is in their interest to adopt such measures.

The United Nations Conference on Trade and Development.   UNCTAD was formed in 1964 as a permanent organ of the United Nations General Assembly. It counts 147 member countries, which is more than the UN itself and more than any other international organization in the world. UNCTAD was established because of the dissatisfaction of less-developed countries with GATT's performance. These countries felt that the results and benefits of GATT were not equally distributed. They have been dissatisfied because their share of the world trade was declining, and because the prices of their raw material exports were not consistent with the prices of imported manufactured goods.

At least three major goals can be cited for the UNCTAD: (1) to further the development of emerging nations by trade as well as other means, (2) to improve the prices of primary goods exports through commodity agreements, and (3) to establish a tariff preference system favoring the export of manufactured goods from less-developed countries.[18] However, major achievements of UNCTAD have been modest. One major achievement is organizational. A new club for world trade matters has been established with a large membership and financing from the UN budget. A second achievement is all the publicity and attention given by many countries to the trade aspects of a major world problem—the gap in economic development between the "have" and "have not" nations. UNCTAD has made few concrete achievements to date, however.[19]

The Organization of Economic Cooperation and Development. The OECD was formed in 1960, and has since grown into an international organization uniting the views and interests of the developed market countries. One of its first efforts to regulate MNCs was in 1967 when it proposed a code for the protection of foreign private investments. In 1975, voluntary standards of conduct to be used as guidelines in regulating MNCs were proposed. These efforts were directed toward integrating the activities of MNCs into national economic and social systems. But the OECD guidelines represent an attempt by the industrialized countries to regulate MNCs to suit their objectives. Thus the organization is often in conflict with communist and developing countries regarding international economic negotiations.[20]

Regional Level On the regional level, the tendency toward economic cooperation between nations of the same region to attain goals that they cannot achieve in isolation of each other has also led to the creation of a number of regional economic associations. The tendency to form regional groupings has been growing in the world economy since World War II. Regional groupings are agreements between nations in the same region to cooperate in various economic matters, even though political matters enter the picture. As described below, the European Free Trade Association, the Latin American Free Trade Association, and the European Economic Community are good examples of regional groupings.

The European Free Trade Association (EFTA) was formed in 1959 and originally included Austria, Denmark, Norway, Portugal, Sweden, Switzerland, and the United Kingdom. Finland and Iceland were added later. Tariffs between the member countries were reduced by successive cuts and in 1966 were abolished altogether. This action greatly stimulated trade between the member countries. EFTA does not maintain a common external tariff since each member country retains its own tariff structure applicable to non-EFTA countries.

Argentina, Brazil, Chile, Colombia, Ecuador, Mexico, Paraguay, Peru, Uruguay, and Venezuela agreed to form the Latin American Free Trade Associa-

---

[18]Vern Terpstra, *International Marketing*, 2nd ed. (Hinsdale, Ill.: Dryden, 1978), p. 36.
[19]Ibid., p. 37.
[20]Acquaah, *International Regulation*, pp. 139–142.

tion (LAFTA) in 1961 in the Treaty of Montevideo. The treaty provided for the elimination of all customs duties, surcharges, deposits, and other obstacles to trade between the member countries by 1973. This timetable had to be set back because of difficulties between the member countries. There has not been a great number of tariff concessions granted within this regional organization, thus its success has been limited.

The European Economic Community (EEC) was established by the Treaty of Rome in 1958 and includes Germany, France, Italy, Belgium, Luxembourg, the Netherlands, the United Kingdom, Ireland, and Denmark. Greece became the tenth member in 1981, and negotiations began in 1980 regarding the membership of Spain and Portugal. A gradual reduction of internal customs duties on industrial goods resulted in their complete removal by July 1, 1968, by EEC countries. At the same time, a common external tariff applying to goods imported from other countries also was created. Since that time, a common agricultural policy has been adopted and the removal of internal agricultural duties has been completed. The EEC has also made progress in abolishing restrictions on the movement of capital between member countries, in the alignment of taxes, in developing a community policy on competition, and on restrictive practices such as price fixing and company mergers.

Most of the international trading by communist countries comes within the framework of the Council for Mutual Economic Assistance (CMEA), which is the Russian counterpart of the EEC. The CMEA includes most of the communist countries as members (USSR, Czechoslovakia, East Germany, Hungary, Poland, Romania, Cuba, and Vietnam). It has objectives similar to those of western organizations, but is concerned only with the communist countries. The Soviet Union seems to be directing its efforts to turn the organization into a planning agency, with Moscow deciding where new factories should be built and what should be traded where.[21]

National Level

One of the major costs of joining regional groupings is having to give up some degree of sovereignty in terms of economic matters. Nations do join, however, because they expect benefits to outweigh costs. A variety of benefits are expected by economic integration, such as countervailing power, the benefits of free trade in a limited region, or economies of scale for their industries. These benefits, however, are often not enough to prevent nations from engaging in unilateral action with regard to regulations of MNCs in order to accomplish national goals and objectives.

The political and regulatory climate in which MNCs have to function flow from these goals and objectives. Governments develop policy areas that represent statements of their intentions to achieve national goals and objectives. These policy areas define national interests in terms of specific development

[21]Ball and McCulloch, *International Business*, p. 511.

Table 6.2
Country Goals, Policies, and Policy Tools

Country Goals	Policy Areas	Policy Tools
Autarky/Self sufficiency	Price stability	Tariff controls
Economic welfare	Economic competition	Nontariff controls
Border integrity and control (National security)	Free trade	Export promotion
	Industrial and basic resource development	Import substitution
Employment stability		Foreign direct investment: disincentives/incentives
Financial performance of economy growth rates and in balance of payments	Infrastructure development	
	Technology transfer	Official grants and loans
	Defense	Fiscal and monetary policy
Economic development through technological (Development)	Foreign aid	Exchange rate adjustment or control
	Ecological Balance	
Economic/political relations	Agriculture/food supply	Design of Governmental organization
External assistance	Labor/employment	
	Consumer protection	Government procurement programs
	Education/science	Cross national agreements

Source: R. Hal Mason and Robert S. Spich, *Management: An International Perspective* (Homewood, IL: Irwin, 1987), p. 61.

problems that need attention. Policy tools are then available to deal with these problem areas in order to attain national goals and objectives. These tools may include monetary and fiscal policies, trade policies, policies related by technology transfer, and other national policies that directly affect a firm's operations.[22] A representative list of these goals, policy areas, and tools is shown in Table 6.2

The United States has numerous laws and regulations that apply to the operations of MNCs, most of which deal with MNCs in foreign countries. Two of these areas of regulation will be discussed in detail in order to show how social and cultural differences complicate the international environment and how public policies to deal with international issues affect the operations of business organizations that are multinational in nature.

THE FOREIGN PAYMENTS CONTROVERSY

The foreign payments controversy erupted in the early 1970s as a result of (1) the Watergate investigations into illegal political contributions by corporations to the 1972 reelection campaign of President Richard Nixon and (2) the Security and Exchange Commission's investigations into questionable practices of corporations with regard to payments in foreign countries for political or business purposes. These investiga-

[22]Mason and Spich, *Management*, pp. 59–60.

tions eventually uncovered the fact that not only had many large corporations made contributions to political campaigns in this country, but the same had been done abroad on a rather large scale. These payments were most often contributions to politicians for political campaigns or favors and payments made to agents of government officials to win contracts. The term most often used in the media to refer to these contributions was *questionable payments* because there was some question about the ethics of these payments.

Revelation of the extent to which these questionable payments were made abroad to further the interests of U.S. businesses aroused great concern among government officials and other public and private figures in the 1970s and resulted in broad condemnation of these practices. In its report on questionable foreign payments by corporations, the Ad Hoc Committee on Foreign Payments stated, "No single issue of corporate behavior has engendered in recent times as much discussion in the United States—both in the private and public arenas—or as much administrative and legislative activity, as payments made abroad by corporations."[23]

The revelations shook foreign government officials, rocked U.S. corporate management, and tarnished the image of U.S. private enterprise at home and abroad. For example, the discovery shook the governments of Belgium, Holland, Honduras, Italy, and Japan, and contributed to the decline of confidence in U.S. business leadership. One commentator stated that " . . . the leadership of American big business has never been held in such low regard since perhaps the days of the Great Depression . . . big business is now close to the bottom rung in measures of public trust and confidence."[24]

Foreign payments have been defined as "any transfer of money or anything of value made with the aim of influencing the behavior of politicians, political candidates, political parties, or government officials and employees in their legislative, administrative and judicial actions."[25] These payments can be classified by legal type, by type of foreign recipient, by mode of payment, and by purpose of payer. Thus foreign payments were made in a variety of situations and in different manners for different purposes.

> The term "corporate payments abroad" encompasses a variety of practices, some legal under local law and some not, designed to influence the political process of a foreign country—to aid a political party, to expedite governmental services, or to shape a policy decision. Some payments have been agents 'or consultants' fees, which may be tax-deductible business expenses. Some

[23]Ad Hoc Committee on Foreign Payments of the Association of the Bar of the City of New York, "Report on Questionable Foreign Payments by Corporations: The Problem and Approaches to a Solution," March 14, 1977, p. 1.

[24]Nicholas Wolfson, U.S. Senate, Committee on Banking, Housing and Urban Affairs, *Foreign Corrupt Practices and Domestic and Foreign Investment Disclosure: Hearing on S. 305*, 95th Congress, 1st Session, March 16, 1977, p. 215.

[25]Neil H. Jacoby, Peter Nehemkis, and Richard Eells, *Bribery and Extortion in World Business* (New York: Macmillan, 1977), p. 86.

evidently have been bribes to government officials, which are widely prohibited. Others have been political contributions, the legality of which differs from country to country. Many payments, whether legal or illegal, have been made indirectly through special funds, sales agents, or foreign subsidiaries. The flow of money has been obscured by a variety of devices.[26]

Lawful payments included contributions to political parties or candidates in countries where this behavior is not illegal (as it is in the United States). Many countries allow corporations to make such contributions. Even where such payments were unlawful, it may not be appropriate to call them bribes, as they were not meant to abuse government authority. It is also true that in some cases the initiative for many payments came from foreign officials who demanded payments and may even have threatened sanctions. These payments could not be called bribes either, since a bribe is a payment made to induce the payee to do something for the payer that is improper and is an inducement to any person acting in an official or public capacity to violate or forebear from his or her public duty. Extortion, on the other hand, is a situation in which the recipient of the payment is the initiator, and the motivating force behind the payment is a threat of harm to the payer. Sometimes it is difficult to tell the difference between a bribe and extortion, and some actions, such as facilitating payments to customs officials to speed customers' clearances, are a little of both.

In many other instances, payments were made on the initiative of U.S. corporate officials. When a few companies were discovered to have made payments of these types, the Securities and Exchange Commission (SEC) developed a voluntary disclosure program to discover how widespread this practice was among U.S. corporations. On March 8, 1974, the Securities Act Release Number 33-5466 announced a voluntary disclosure program whereby firms could report questionable domestic and foreign payments and accounting practices to the SEC in the 8–K of 10–K filings.[27] This program was based on the SEC's mandate to protect shareholders' interests and enforce their right to full disclosure of "material" information, defined as encompassing all those matters of which an average prudent investor ought reasonably to be informed before purchasing securities. With respect to foreign payments, materiality was defined as (1) cases where the payment itself was large, (2) situations where the payment itself was not necessarily large but where it related to large transactions or where the deals were an important part of the firm's total business, or (3) cases where the payoff reflected on the lack of integrity of management, especially top management, in setting up overseas slush funds and secret bank

[26]Charles R. McManis, "Questionable Corporate Payments Abroad: An Antitrust Approach," *Yale Law Journal*, vol. 86 (December 1976), pp. 217–218. Reprinted by permission of the Yale Law Journal Company and Fred B. Rothman & Company.

[27]George C. Greanias and Duane Windsor, *The Foreign Corrupt Practices Act* (Lexington, Mass.: Lexington Books, 1982), p. 19.

accounts from which the payments were made but about which investors knew nothing.[28]

Under this program, news stories appeared day after day describing yet another corporation that had discovered such payments and was making this fact public knowledge. By March 1977, 360 firms had voluntarily disclosed their questionable payments. Eventually 527 companies, including some of the largest corporations in the country, were alleged to have made foreign payments over a six-year period to foreign governments and agents. Some of the largest payments were attributed to Exxon ($59.4 million), Lockheed ($55.0 million), Boeing ($50.4 million), and General Tire and Rubber ($41.3 million).[29]

Business tried to defend these practices by explaining that these payments were a necessary cost of doing business—that payments of this kind were an accepted practice in other countries. Business was transacted in many of these countries through agents who collected high fees for their services and passed some of this money on to government officials. In other cases, government officials were paid directly to award favors to companies. Customs officials were paid low salaries or wages with the expectation that their income would be supplemented by payments from foreign corporations. The reasoning was if companies in this country did adhere to "higher" standards, the business would simply go to a non-U.S. corporation that was not so virtuous and we would be shut out of many foreign markets. One company, for example, defended its payments with these words:

> The discontinuance of such payments at this time would needlessly hamper the conduct of the business of the company in numerous foreign locations, would contravene local practices, in some cases would imperil the safety of company employees on the protection of its property, and would be detrimental to the best interests of the stockholders.[30]

The public's concern about these payments was based on the belief that such payments corrupted the free enterprise system, under which the most efficient producers with the best products are supposed to prevail. As one treasury official stated, "When the major criterion in a buyer's choice of a product is the size of a bribe rather than its price and quality and reputation of its producers, the fundamental principles on which a market economy is based are put in jeopardy."[31] Such payments were believed to subvert the laws of supply and demand and result in free markets being replaced by contrived markets.

---

[28]Richard L. Baravick, "The SEC Unleashes a Foreign Payoffs Storm," *Business and Society Review*, no. 19 (Fall 1976), pp. 48–50.

[29]"Business Without Bribes," *Newsweek*, February 19, 1979, pp. 63–64.

[30]Gordon Adams and Sherri Zann Rosenthal, *The Invisible Hand: Questionable Corporate Payments Overseas* (New York: The Council on Economic Priorities, 1976), p. 5.

[31]Ibid., p. 3.

On the other hand, the public's concern for these payments stemmed from our beliefs about the proper relationships between the economic and political systems, and the behavior of public officials and private managers. The idea that official power vested by the state in government officials can be bought and sold on the marketplace is repugnant to the American mind. We make a clear separation between business and government, between the commercial and the political, and draw a boundary line between marketable goods and services and nonmarketable political rights, duties, and authority.[32]

Despite the pleas of business for an acceptance of special ethics in this situation, the government continued its relentless pursuit of questionable payments. The SEC continued to apply pressure for disclosure of these payments and supported legislation to deal with the problem. The Internal Revenue Service developed a special audit program of companies suspected of having slush funds. It was believed that some companies committed tax fraud by deducting payoffs as an expense on income-tax returns. The Federal Trade Commission investigated possible antitrust violations in countries where only U.S. competitors were involved. And finally, the Treasury Department accused one company of violating the Bank Secrecy Act, which requires anyone transporting more than $5,000 between the United States and a foreign country to file a report with the government.

The Foreign Corrupt Practices Act   Theoretically, the best way to deal with foreign bribery would be for some international body to pass measures regulating this practice. And in fact, resolutions on foreign payments were prepared by the secretariats of both the United Nations and the Organization of American States. But these resolutions were never formulated into an international code that could be implemented in countries all over the world. Despite pressure from the United States for such a code, the issue faded away on the international level. Many countries believed their national laws were already adequate to deal with the situation. Some countries did not consider such payments to be unethical and were not motivated to eradicate them from the system. If the United States wanted to do something to stop foreign payments, at least for those corporations headquartered in this country, it appeared that unilateral action was the only course available.[33]

Eventually, a new public policy measure was passed by Congress and signed into law by the President. The Foreign Corrupt Practices Act (FCPA) of 1977 has been characterized as the most extensive application of federal law to corruption since the passage of the 1933 and 1934 securities acts.[34] The law

[32]Jacoby, Nehemkis, and Eells, *Bribery and Extortion*, p. 127.

[33]Behrman, *Essays on Ethics*, p. 289.

[34]American Bar Association, Committee on Corporate Law and Accounting, "A Guide to the New Section 13(b)(2) Accounting Requirements of the Securities Exchange Act of 1934 (Section 102 of the Foreign Corrupt Practices Act of 1977)," *The Business Lawyer*, vol. 34, no. 1 (November 1978), p. 308.

contains both antibribery provisions and accounting provisions. The act makes it a criminal offense for any U.S. business enterprise—whether or not incorporated or publicly held—to pay money or give anything of value to a foreign official, foreign political party, or any candidate for a foreign political office for purposes of (1) influencing any act or decision of a foreign official, foreign political party, or party official or candidate acting in an official capacity (including a decision to fail to perform official functions); or (2) inducing a foreign official, political party, or party official or candidate to use influence with a foreign government (or instrumentality thereof) to influence any act or decision of such government or instrumentality.[35]

The law also prohibits offering money or anything of value to any person (foreign or domestic) while knowing or having reason to know that all or a portion of such money or thing of value will be used for the purposes just described. The law does not, however, cover facilitating or so-called "grease" payments that are intended merely to move a matter toward an eventual act or decision not involving discretionary action. (For example, payments or gifts to a customs duties officer of a foreign government to facilitate the passage of material to a plant facility may not be considered practices in violation of the act.)[36]

Companies that have corporate codes of conduct were encouraged to review their existing policy statements with legal counsel to determine whether they were adequate in light of the provisions of the FCPA. Companies that are involved in international trade or are contemplating doing business in a foreign country and that did not have formal codes of conduct should give serious consideration to the need for such a document. In addition, companies should carefully consider their policies for monitoring compliance with their corporate codes of conduct and, in particular, the provisions of this law.[37]

In terms of the accounting provisions, the Foreign Corrupt Practices Act consists of two basic requirements: (1) the maintenance of books, records, and accounts that accurately and fairly reflect, in reasonable detail, the transactions and dispositions of the assets (the word transactions encompasses all asset, liability, equity, income and expense accounts); and (2) the development of a system of internal accounting controls that provides reasonable assurance that transactions are executed in accordance with management's general or specific authorization, that transactions are recorded as necessary (a) to permit preparation of financial statements in conformity with generally accepted accounting principles or any other criteria applicable to such statements and (b) to maintain accountability for assets, that access to assets is permitted only in accordance

---

[35] *An Analysis of the Foreign Corrupt Practices Act of 1977* (Chicago: Arthur Andersen and Co., 1978), p. 4.

[36] Ibid.

[37] On the act in general, see Judah Best, "The Foreign Corrupt Practices Act," *Review of Securities Regulation*, no. 11 (February 13, 1978), pp. 975–982; reprinted in *The Foreign Corrupt Practices Act of 1977: Do You Know This Act Covers Domestic Business Activities?* (New York: New York Law Journal Seminars Press, 1978), pp. 127–134.

with management's general or specific authorization, and that the recorded accountability for assets is compared with the existing assets at reasonable intervals and appropriate action is taken with respect to any differences.[38]

Subject Parties   The provisions of the Foreign Corrupt Practices Act are applicable to every U.S. business enterprise, public or private, incorporated or unincorporated, that either is organized under the laws of a state territory, possession, or commonwealth of the United States or has its principal place of business in the United States. As stated, the prohibitions of the FCPA apply to both issuers and domestic concerns. An issuer is any company, domestic or foreign, that has a class of securities registered pursuant to Section 12 of the 1934 act, or any company that is required to file reports under Section 15(d) of the Securities Exchange Act of 1934. Other "publicly held companies," such as investment companies registered under the Investment Company Act of 1940 and limited partnerships with less than 300 partners, also are subject to the law on the same basis as any other "domestic concern." Domestic concerns (other than SEC registration) include: (1) any individual who is a citizen, national, or resident of the United States; and (2) any corporation, partnership, association, joint-stock company, business trust, unincorporated organization, or sole proprietorship that: (a) has its principal place of business in the United States or (b) is organized under the laws of a state, territory, possession, or commonwealth of the United States.[39]

Penalties   Failure to maintain accurate books and records and a sufficient system of internal accounting controls does not give rise to criminal liability. Registrants and controlling persons (any person[s] who has the power to control the direction, management, and policies of a corporation) found to have willfully violated the accounting provisions mentioned before would be subject to the general penalties contained under the Security Exchange Act of 1934. These penalties include a fine of not more than $10,000, or imprisonment of not more than five years, or both. A company also might be subject to civil litigation brought by a third party because of failure to comply with the accounting provisions or failure to disclose what might be contended to be a material fact.[40]

The law contains the following criminal penalties with regard to the antibribery provisions: (1) SEC registrants and domestic concerns (other than an individual) can be fined up to $1 million in fines; (2) any individual who is a domestic concern, and any officer, director, or stockholder acting on behalf of a registrant or domestic concern, who willfully violates the law can be fined up to

[38]Arthur Andersen and Co., *An Analysis*, pp. 8–9.
[39]Ibid., p. 3.
[40]Ibid., p. 8.

$10,000 and imprisoned for five years; and (3) any employee or agent who is a United States citizen, national, or resident or is otherwise subject to the jurisdiction of the United States and who willfully carried out the act or practice constituting the violation can be required to pay up to $10,000 in fines and given five years' imprisonment.

Employees and agents other than officers, directors, or stockholders of the registrant or domestic concern may be held liable under the FCPA only if the registrant or domestic concern on whose behalf the employee or agent acted itself was found to be in violation of the antibribery provisions. This provision was incorporated in the Act to avoid making a low-level employee or agent of a corporation the scapegoat for corporate wrongs.[41] The law also prohibits fines imposed on individuals from being paid directly or indirectly by the registrant or domestic concern on whose behalf such individual acted. Thus, although not specifically covered in the FCPA, this provision would appear to prohibit the reimbursement of a fine in any form or manner whatsoever.

Implications

U.S. business corporations were deeply concerned about three major aspects of the Foreign Corrupt Practices Act.[42] First, they would come under civil and criminal liabilities for accounting-and-reporting procedures as well as for questionable payments and falsification of records without clear materiality standards. In effect, the FCPA contains no standards for determining how to reflect "accurately and fairly" all transactions on the books and records. By implication, every transaction is subject to "potential criminal liability."[43] Second, in terms of our competitive position abroad, some companies expressed a fear that prohibition of payments would affect their competitiveness. Third, the adequacy of internal-accounting controls to provide reasonable assurances of management supervision over all transactions and assets without regard to materiality remained something of an enigma.

The passage of the FCPA raises many questions related to public policy that have ethical and moral dimensions. The negative effects of bribery were generally considered to be (1) the warping of economic and social objectives in the country as a result of altered decisions, (2) the upsetting of political processes resulting in undesirable decisions, (3) a potential reduction in national security, and (4) the destabilization of international relations.[44] But who is responsible for dealing with these negative effects? In which country should

[41]Ibid., pp. 4–5.

[42]See Robert K. Mautz, "Corporate Management and the FCPA: Reaction and Response," in Robert K. Mautz et al., *Internal Control in U.S. Corporations: The State of the Art* (New York: Financial Executives Research Foundation, 1980), pp. 291–300.

[43]Thomas L. Holton, Chairman of the AICPA's Committee on SEC Regulations, in U.S. House of Representatives, Committee on Interstate and Foreign Commerce, Subcommittee on Consumer Protection and Finance, *Foreign Payments Disclosure: Hearings on H.R. 15481 and S. 3664, and H.R. 13870 and H.R. 13953*, 94th Congress, 2nd Session, September 21 and 22, 1976, pp. 160–161.

[44]Behrman, *Essays on Ethics*, p. 290.

ethical criteria originate to deal with this issue? And if international action proves impossible to attain, should one country act unilaterally to deal with what is an international issue?

ECONOMIC SANCTIONS AND TRADE POLICIES

The benefits of international trade are numerous and have occupied the attention of government policy makers and academic theorists for hundreds of years. The advantages to be gained from international division of labor and specialization are widely recognized to have an expansionary effect on aggregate world products as well as on the national product of participating nations. The benefits from trade basically derive from differences in comparative costs, which result from a variety of causes such as unequal factor endowments, differing technologies, and diverse utility and preference functions.[45]

Even though the benefits from trade are real and substantial, however, nations impose economic sanctions from time to time that restrict trade between nations. Economic sanctions can be defined as penalties inflicted upon one or more nations by one or more other nations to coerce the target nation(s) to comply with certain norms of behavior that the initiators deem proper or necessary. Sanctions generally involve the movement of goods and services—the refusal to export to the target nation(s), restrictions on imports from the target nation(s), or both. But economic sanctions can also take the form of restrictions on capital flows, wealth held in the boycotting nations, and movement of tourists and other citizens.

Boycotts, which are one form of an economic sanction, are "instruments of foreign policy by which one state tries to bring about a change in the domestic or foreign policies of another."[46] They are a form of nonmilitary coercion in which economic weapons are used to inflict hardship on a country for political purposes. Having had no success through diplomatic channels and wishing to avoid military conflict, nations initiate boycotts or other economic sanctions hoping to cause sufficient economic damage to force change in the target nation's economic and social policies. The great advantage of economic sanctions is that they can be used to bring about change without resorting to the use of force and violence that is repugnant to a peaceful resolution of conflict.

Boycotts can be classified into two major categories: by the number of nations imposing the boycott and by the range of commodities covered by the boycott. In terms of the number of nations involved, the boycott could be unilateral, multilateral, or universal. If the boycott is imposed by only one nation, as was the case initially in the Cuban and Rhodesian situations, it is

---

[45]Donald J. Losman, *International Economic Sanctions* (Albuquerque: University of New Mexico Press, 1979), p. 7.

[46]Ibid.

unilateral. If it is imposed by more than one nation, as was true in the Arab boycott of Israel and the boycott of Cuba after Latin American nations joined with the United States, the boycott is *multilateral.* If most of the world community participates, the boycott can be regarded as *universal.* The sanctions against Rhodesia could be regarded as universal, since most of the world community participated in accordance with UN resolutions.

In terms of the range of commodities covered, the boycott could be classified as general or limited (selective). A *general* boycott covers any and all trade relations with the targeted nation(s), with the possible exception of trade related to humanitarian needs. *Limited* or *selective* boycotts cover only a limited number of commodities. The initial boycotts of Cuba and Rhodesia, for example, were limited to only one item (sugar and tobacco respectively).

The success of boycotts can be ascertained by using economic and political criteria to measure effectiveness. Economic effectiveness refers to the volume of monetary damage or disruption inflicted on the target nation(s), whereas political effectiveness refers to the degree that the changes desired by the boycotting nation(s) are actually undertaken by the target state(s).[47] One would generally expect that if a boycott is economically effective and causes serious damage, the target nation(s) would change its (their) behavior to comply with the wishes of the boycotting nations to avoid further economic damage. But there may be cases where nations do not respond to economic sanctions of this kind. Thus is it possible for a boycott to be both economically successful and yet a failure as far as attaining political objectives are concerned.

Other types of economic sanctions have been used in the South African situation. Because of our opposition to the racial policies of that country, two forms of economic sanctions have been used by U.S. organizations to pressure South Africa to change its policies toward blacks. One type of sanction is called *divestiture,* which consists of universities, churches, and some cities and states divesting themselves of stocks they hold in banks that make loans to South Africa and of companies that do business in South Africa. In this way they hope to pressure these other American institutions to stop doing business with the country. The other form of sanction is actual *disinvestment* by U.S. companies that have plants or other forms of investment in the country, by pulling out of the country and refusing to do business with South Africa until some kind of constructive social and political change has taken place.

The success of either of these sanctions is questioned by many critics. Some argue that it is better for U.S. companies to stay in South Africa, particularly since many of them adhere to the Sullivan principles that have benefited the blacks who work for them. These companies, it is argued, are able to promote social change much more effectively if they stay there than if they leave and thus are able to have no impact on the country. Others argue that any economic sanctions have much more of an economic impact on the blacks than

[47]Ibid., p. 1.

on the white minority, and thus such sanctions may actually make the situation worse for the people they are designed to help. South Africa can get loans elsewhere and can find companies from other countries to move in and take the place of U.S. companies that leave.

The costs of economic sanctions have been classified by Donald Losman as direct, indirect, and foregone potential. *Direct costs* are those additional financial or real outlays that are immediately and directly related to the imposition of sanctions. Examples of direct costs include increased transportation expenses that could result and the loss of traditional export revenues. Unemployment in the foreign trade sector would be another example of a direct cost to the target nation(s).

Indirect costs are those that result from the many domestic dislocations and slowdowns that are caused by a disruption of normal trade patterns. These indirect costs particularly relate to imports of intermediate products and raw materials. Adverse production effects can result when it is difficult to substitute domestic inputs for imported materials. Disruptions of intermediate product imports may significantly increase costs when technical adaptability to use domestic substitutes is poor or lacking entirely. This has been termed an "import bottleneck."[48]

Foregone potential refers to the failure of some economic sectors to grow or improve as rapidly as would have been the case if trade had not been disrupted. The growth of the tourist industry is often cited as an example of foregone potential. As a result of boycotts, the potential exchange earnings from this industry have never been realized. Economies on the cost side may also remain unrealized. In many cases, growth in the scale of the market can lead to production economies that go unrealized if the market is restricted.

Because trade is a two-way street, economic sanctions cannot be imposed upon other nations without costs to the nation(s) initiating the sanctions. Initiating countries may have to shift to more costly and distant suppliers and may suffer a significant reduction in the demand for their products. As a general rule, however, the loss to the boycotting nation(s) is far less than to the target nation(s) because they are economically larger and can turn to a variety of alternative suppliers and markets. In sum, the greater the number of nations imposing sanctions, the higher the costs are likely to be to the target nation(s). The larger the ratio of imports and exports to national income in the target nation(s), the greater are the disruptive effects that sanctions are likely to cause.[49]

Technology Transfer

On September 29, 1979, an act was passed by Congress that provided authority to regulate exports, to improve the efficiency of export regulation, and to

[48]Ibid.
[49]Ibid.

minimize interference with the ability to engage in commerce. This act, originally passed in 1969 and amended several times since, was called the Export Administration Act of 1979, the broadest of all public policy measures dealing with the extraction of U.S. technology by a potential adversary. This act gave the President of the United States the power to limit the export of certain products to certain nations through a system of "validated licensing." These controls could be imposed for reasons of national security, foreign policy, or limited domestic supply.[50] The act states:

> It is the policy of the United States to use export controls only after full consideration of the impact on the economy of the United States and only to the extent necessary:
>
> 1. to restrict the export of goods and technology which would make a significant contribution to the military potential of any other country or combination of countries which would prove detrimental to the national security of the the United States;
>
> 2. to restrict the export of goods and technology where necessary to further significantly the foreign policy of the United States or to fulfill its declared international obligations; and
>
> 3. to restrict the export of goods where necessary to protect the domestic economy from the excessive drain of scarce materials and to reduce the serious inflationary impact of foreign demand.[51]

Congress stated that exports of goods or technology without regard as to whether they may make a significant contribution to the military potential of individual countries or combinations of countries may adversely affect the national security of the United States. It also stated that the availability of certain materials at home and abroad is so variable that the quantity and composition of U.S. exports and their distribution among importing countries may have an important bearing on fulfillment of the foreign policy goals of the nation.

The act states that the President and the Secretary, defined as the Secretary of Commerce, may issue such regulations as are necessary to carry out the provisions of the act. These regulations may apply to the financing, transporting, or other servicing of exports and the participation therein by any person. Penalties for violating these regulations are divided into three major categories.

> 1. General Violations: whoever knowingly violates any provision of the Act or any regulation, order, or license issued under the Act shall be fined not more than five times the value of the exports involved, or $50,000, whichever is greater, or imprisoned not more than 5 years, or both.

---

[50]Christopher Madison, "Congress, Administration Split on How to Plug Technology Leaks to Soviets," *National Journal*, February 19, 1983, pp. 380–81.

[51]Export Administration Act of 1979, Public Law 96–72 (S. 737), September 29, 1979, p. 504.

2. Willful Violations: whoever willfully exports anything contrary to any provision of this Act or any regulation, order, or license issued under the Act, with knowledge that such exports will be used for the benefit of any country to which exports are restricted for national security or foreign policy purposes shall be fined not more than five times the value of the exports involved or $100,000, whichever is greater, or imprisoned not more than 10 years, or both.

3. Civil Penalties and Administrative Sanctions: civil penalties may be imposed either in addition to or in lieu of any other liability or penalty which may be imposed under provisions of the Act. These civil penalties may not exceed $10,000 for each violation of the Act or any regulation, order, or license issued under the Act.[52]

The Export Administration Act is used most extensively for national security reasons. The Commerce Department draws up a list of items that could have military value to adversaries. No item on this list can be exported without a license. The list runs more than seventy pages and includes thousands of items. Included on the list are items of direct military value as well as items of less obvious military use, such as semiconductors and microprocessors.[53]

Foreign policy controls are used less frequently, but they usually get more public notice and can have severe impacts on business organizations. For example, in 1982, President Reagan imposed export trade sanctions on U.S. oil and gas equipment that was to be used by the Soviet Union for its natural gas pipeline that was to extend into Western European countries. The trade ban was extended to include U.S. subsidiaries and foreign companies holding U.S. licenses on technology equipment.[54] This was the first time that trade sanctions had been applied to corporations outside the United States.

The Reagan administration placed the ban on U.S. and foreign sales of pipeline equipment for the following reasons: (1) the military rule imposed on Poland by the Soviet Union, (2) the possibility that our NATO allies could be blackmailed with the threat of a cut-off of gas supplies, and (3) curtailment of the flow of technology to the Soviet Union. President Reagan had earlier warned that stringent action would be taken if the Soviet repression was not eased in Poland and if U.S. manufacturers of oil and gas equipment and technology continued to supply the Soviet Union. The Western European countries, Great Britain, France, Italy, and West Germany opposed the U.S. embargo. Italy called the application of U.S. law outside the United States unacceptable, charging that it amounted to an infringement of national sovereignty.[55]

The question of the sanctity of a contract, of international free trade being important for business, and the mixing of political pressures with business as

[52]Ibid., p. 529.
[53]Madison, "Technology Leaks," p. 381.
[54]"An Anti-U.S.-Backlash Over Russia's Pipeline," *Business Week*, July 5, 1982, p. 21.
[55]"A Deal in the Pipeline," *Time*, November 22, 1982, p. 77.

well as the nation are all questions that management must address. Many businesspeople see the action taken by the Reagan administration in this situation as having only damaging results to American industry and resulting in little change in behavior on the part of the Soviet Union. In effect, we shot ourselves in the foot by restricting trade on nonmilitary items.

The issue in these situations is the relationship between U.S. business and foreign policy. Most foreign operations are subject to the risk of changes of government policy that are contrary to sound business practice. When legitimate national objectives are at stake, some regulation of trade with hostile nations can be expected. In this situation, the U.S.-imposed sanctions against the Soviet Union could not be termed successful. The tensions created over our handling of the pipeline sanctions split the Atlantic Alliance more effectively than the Soviets could ever have done by themselves. And some segments of the U.S. economy were severely hurt by the loss of foreign markets.

Dresser Industries' 1982 Annual Report provides an excellent synopsis of the situation. "While the effect in terms of dollar cost is difficult to measure, we do not feel that Dresser's global financial picture was materially impacted. The more serious long-term result we share with other U.S. companies. The reliability of U.S. suppliers has been seriously eroded in the world marketplace as a result of vacillating governmental policies."[56] And finally, as stated in the *Chicago Tribune*, "If sacrifices are going to be asked from American industry in the interest of foreign policy, then it is fair to expect, first, that foreign policy be identifiable and reasonably consistent, and second, that the sacrifice come close to achieving what is expected of them."[57]

One expert argues that what is needed is a balanced approach to technology transfer that tightens controls without choking creativity. Such a balanced approach must treat four core issues that exist in the relationship between national security and technology transfer: (1) determining the extent and implications of the use of the same technology in both military and civilian applications, (2) determining how critical a technology is to improving the military capability of potential adversaries, (3) determining whether a particular technology is freely available from a foreign source, and (4) determining which technology transfer mechanisms must be controlled.[58]

In 1985, the Export Administration Act was amended again to provide a better balance between enhancing the commercial interests of the United States and protecting its national security interests. The amendments shortened the licensing process, decontrolled low-technology items, liberalized licensing where comparable goods were widely available in the international marketplace, and provided for expanded congressional and private sector roles

[56]Dresser Industries, Inc., Dresser's 1982 Annual Report.

[57]"U.S. Industry and Foreign Policy," *Chicago Tribune*, August 29, 1982, p. 42.

[58]Roland W. Schmitt, "Export Controls: Balancing Technological Innovation and National Security," *Issues in Science and Technology* (Fall 1984), p. 122.

in the export control program. The President, however, continues to retain ultimate authority to break existing contracts between U.S. and foreign firms and to impose whatever export restrictions are deemed necessary in the interests of national security and foreign policy. The continuation of this provision effectively maintains previous uncertainties regarding U.S. business dealings with foreign nations.[59]

The Results of Economic Sanctions   The theory behind economic sanctions is that sufficient economic pressure applied to the target nation(s) can induce or compel a change in behavior that is more acceptable to the boycotting nations. For boycotts to be politically successful, economic hardship must be inflicted upon the target nation(s). However, after examining three boycotts in detail, Donald Losman concludes that economic effectiveness is only a necessary condition for success, but not a sufficient condition. In other words, political objectives are not likely to be attained without economic sanctions, but effective economic sanctions do not guarantee political success.[60] With regard to the three boycotts studied, Losman makes the following comments.

> Less than three million Israeli's hold out against the economic warfare of more than 100 million Arabs. Nine million Cubans have been able to withstand their economic isolation by the vast majority of Western Hemisphere nations, while less than 300,000 Rhodesian whites have prevailed for more than a decade against economic measures launched on a global scale by the United Nations.[61]

The direct and indirect costs to Cuba were the greatest of the three boycotts and loomed large relative to the Cuban economy. There were also significant opportunity costs, such as rising tourist revenues, that were foregone. Rhodesia experienced significant opportunity costs related to growth in foreign investment and foregone tobacco revenues. The major impacts of the boycott in the Israeli situation were in terms of foregone potential. Yet in all three of these cases, political aims of the boycotting nations were not attained.

There are many reasons for the failure of boycotts to attain their political objectives. Among the more important reasons, Losman mentions the following:

1. Partial sanctions, covering only some goods while allowing other goods to be exchanged, have no hope for success. As soon as sanctions are allowed to be selective rather than comprehensive, a debate ensues concerning which items are to be allowed and which embargoed. Even if agreement is reached, effective policing of such an effort is almost impossible.

[59]Ronald Reagan and Walter J. Olson, "Export Administration Amendments Act of 1985," *Business America*, September 2, 1985.

[60]Losman, *International Economic Sanctions*, p. 125.

[61]Ibid., p. 139.

2. Embargoes against countries with large, relatively affluent economies are not likely to succeed. Large economies have less recourse to international trade and are therefore less vulnerable. Furthermore, if they are important participants in world trade, the imposition of sanctions against them would probably hurt some of the boycotting nations and lead to circumvention of the boycott.

3. The use of trade sanctions changes the economic situation in a boycotted country. The targeted nation(s) can be expected to take steps to minimize the boycott's impact. They can reduce the impact by domestic diversification and import substitution. If infant industry potential exists, the boycott may bring about an improvement in real output in certain areas of the economy. Trade patterns may be restructured so that foreign substitutes relative to both markets and supply sources can be secured.

4. Another response to the imposition of sanctions is a conditioned adaptation to self-sacrifice. If the goods that are being boycotted cannot be produced or obtained at a reasonable cost, the nation may simply adjust to the new situation and alter its life style to live within its means rather than capitulate. If boycotts can be depicted by the government(s) of the targeted nation(s) as attacks from the outside upon the nation as a whole or upon its way of life, resistance will be strong. If no acceptable substitutes can be found, life under sanctions will remain preferable to capitulation.

5. Loopholes in sanctions enforcement are important considerations. Loopholes take the form of open noncompliance or various forms of clandestine trade including smuggling. Related to the problems of enforcement is that the boycotting states may become weary of their efforts over time and relax their enforcement efforts or pull out of the boycott altogether. This will most likely happen as the effects of the boycott in terms of accomplishing political objectives are not immediately apparent.[62]

Losman concludes that boycotts are most likely to be successful in the short run when their economic effectiveness tends to be greatest. But again, economic effectiveness in no way guarantees the desired political outcomes. Economic damage is not a sufficient condition for success.[63] Economic sanctions should be used sparingly, if at all, and even then, the costs and benefits to the boycotting nations need to be carefully considered.

INTERNATIONAL PUBLIC AFFAIRS

As foreign trade and direct foreign investment by U.S. companies in overseas countries grows, the role of international public affairs also becomes more significant. Because of the complexity of the environments faced by multinationals in overseas markets, U.S. companies

[62]Ibid., pp. 126–139.
[63]Ibid., p. 139.

need to take a long-term view of the business opportunities abroad and develop public affairs programs to influence the social, political, and economic environments of the local, national, and regional levels. Multinational companies need to cultivate markets and adjust products and services to the needs and tastes of foreign consumers, and to adapt to the priorities and values of host governments. Domestic public affairs serve as a bridge between the corporation and the external environment. This is basically the same function that should be performed by international public affairs (see Exhibit 6.1).

The basic components of an international public affairs program, accord-

Exhibit 6.1
Elements of an International Public Affairs Program

Environmental assessment/issue identification and management
- Identify, track, and assess issues and trends
- Achieve systematic internal issues awareness and coordination
- Assess political, social, and cultural elements of risk in projects, products, investments, and operations
- Issue research and analysis
- Emerging issue forecasting

Government relations activities
- Washington, D.C.
- Foreign-country level
- Regional level: EEC, OECD, ASEAN, etc.
- International level: UN, ILO, WHO, WIPO, etc.

Community action/involvement
- Community outreach
- Assess company impact on communities where located
- Philanthropy
- Corporate social responsibility activities
- Development activities
- Political involvement

Corporate public affairs training and constituency development
- Public affairs staff development
- Relations with line managers and other staff groups
- Employee relations
- Shareholder relations
- Media relations
- Academic relations
- Interest group relations
- External constituency group relations, e.g., suppliers

Corporate policy and strategy development
- External factor assessment in strategy planning and management decision-making
- Effect change in corporate strategy and policy to minimize risk and/or maximize opportunity
- Cost/benefit analyses of policy options based on external factors
- Assess impact/compliance with codes of conduct and company ethical standards

Source: Douglas Bergner, "International Public Affairs: A Preliminary Report by a PAC Task Force," *Perspectives,* Public Affairs Council, Washington, DC, April 1983, p. 3.

ing to one commentator, include the collection of social, political, and economic information and the analysis and forecasting of issues that are perceived to be important by a country's leadership. The forecasting task includes political and economic risk evaluation, identification of public policy issues that would be material to a company's activities in a host country, and ways in which issues are likely to affect a company's performance and operations. The assessment and management of risk in foreign environments requires skills that are often lacking in executives whose traditional business acumen was honed in the United States, and thus the public affairs function can perform a valuable service to the company by doing this assessment.[64]

Another important component of an international public affairs program is corporate strategy and policy development. This component includes benefit-cost analysis of the various policy options that are available to manage potential social, political, and economic risks, and making appropriate changes in corporate strategy as a result of this analysis. The company should also plan to reduce such risks in the future. Action programs that can be developed by the public affairs function include community action and government relations programs with participation in international, national, regional, and local organizations and programs, both public and private.[65]

There are differences between domestic and international public affairs that need to be addressed. The international environment is manifestly more complex and multifaceted than that of any single country, making the potential for system overload a real problem. Issues identification is more complex as MNCs face different sets of stakeholders in different countries. There are also differences with respect to corporate organizational problems. There is a tendency in many companies to leave all international responsibilities to the subsidiaries or regional offices located overseas with little or no role for public affairs. And finally, there are differences in how the international public affairs programs are focused. Each county's government is different and political power is located in different places. Thus each country needs to be analyzed independently to determine the critical junctures and influences in the development of issues and public policies that will affect the company. This complicates the process enormously.[66]

There are three different levels at which issues can arise in the international environment: (1) global issues that are often played out at the international organization level, (2) regional issues that are distinct to a particular area of the world, and (3) country-specific issues. These issues will have differing impacts on the company. Some issues will involve only one division or strategic business unit; others will cut across divisions; a third type will affect the com-

[64]Robert A. Kilmarx, "International Public Affairs," *The Public Affairs Handbook*, Joseph S. Nagelschmidt, ed. (New York: AMACOM, 1982), p. 178.

[65]Ibid.

[66]Douglas Bergner, "International Public Affairs: A Preliminary Report by a PAC Task Force," *Perspectives* (April 1983), p. 2.

pany's competitive environment and/or the entire industry; and some will relate to the company's economic environment.[67]

A survey conducted by the Public Affairs Council in 1984 of selected multinational firms with Washington offices found that 78 percent of the respondents
conducted varying amounts of international public affairs from their Washington
offices. More public affairs activities were being conducted by Washington-based
staff and more functional responsibility for international public affairs was being
located in the Washington office. Although it was still a relatively low-profile
activity, there had been continued development of the Washington-based international public affairs function for four years. Internal functions of international
public affairs included issues analysis, forecasting, planning, relations with overseas executives, political risk analysis, international philanthropy, community
relations, and the development of international codes of conduct.[68]

SELECTED REFERENCES

ACQUAAN, KWAMENA. *International Regulation of Transnational Corporations.* New
York: Praeger, 1986.

ADAMS, GORDON, and SHERRI ZANN ROSENTHAL. *The Invisible Hand: Questionable
Corporate Payments Overseas.* New York: The Council on Economic Priorities,
1976.

BALL, DONALD A., and WENDELL H. MCCULLOCH, JR. *International Business: Introduction and Essentials,* 2nd ed. Plano, Tex.: Business Publications, 1985.

BASCHE, JAMES R. JR. *Unusual Foreign Payments: A Survey of the Policies and Practices
of U.S. Companies.* New York: The Conference Board, 1976.

BIERSTEKER, THOMAS J. *Distortion or Development? Contending Perspectives on the
Multinational Corporations.* Cambridge, Mass.: MIT Press, 1981.

BLAKE, DAVID H., and ROBERT S. WALTERS. *The Politics of Global Economic Relations,* 2nd ed. Englewood Cliffs, N.J.: Prentice-Hall, 1983.

CONTRACTOR, F. J. *International Technology Liscensing: Compensation Costs and Negotiation.* Lexington, Mass.: D.C. Heath, 1981.

DANIELS, JOHN D., and LEE H. RADEBAUGH. *International Business: Environments
and Operations,* 4th ed. Reading, Mass.: Addison-Wesley, 1986.

DOZ, YVES L., and C. K. PRAHALAD. *The Multinational Mission.* New York: Free Press,
1987.

FAYERWEATHER, JOHN. *International Business Strategy and Administration,* 2nd ed.
Cambridge, Mass.: Ballinger, 1982.

[67]Douglas Bergner, "Managing International Issues," *Perspectives* (July 1982), p. 2.

[68]Douglas Bergner, "Washington-Based International Public Affairs: A Growing Corporate Function," *Perspectives* (July 1984), pp. 1–4.

FRANK, ISIAH. *Foreign Enterprise in Developing Countries.* Baltimore: Johns-Hopkins University Press, 1980.

GARLAND, JOHN, and RICHARD N. FARMER. *International Dimensions of Business Policy and Strategy.* Boston: Kent, 1986.

GLADWIN, THOMAS M., and INGO WALTER. *Multinationals Under Fire: Lessons in Management of Conflict.* New York: Wiley, 1980.

GREANIAS, GEORGE C., and DUANE WINDSOR. *The Foreign Corrupt Practices Act.* Lexington, Mass.: Lexington Books, 1982.

HEENAN, DAVID, and HOWARD PERLMUTTER. *Multinational Organization Development.* Reading, Mass.: Addison-Wesley, 1979.

JACOBY, NEIL H., PETER NEHEMKIS, and RICHARD EELLS. *Bribery and Extortion in World Business.* New York: Macmillan, 1977.

KOBRIN, STEPHEN J. *Managing Political Risk Assessment: Strategic Response to Environmental Change.* Berkeley: University of California Press, 1982.

LOSMAN, DONALD J. *International Economic Sanctions.* Albuquerque: University of New Mexico Press, 1979.

MASON, HAL R., and ROBERT S. SPICH. *Management: An International Perspective.* Homewood, Ill.: Irwin, 1987.

MORAN, THEODORE H., ED. *Multinational Corporations: The Political Economy of Foreign Direct Investments.* Lexington, Mass.: D.C. Heath, 1985.

PERLMUTTER, H. V., T. SAGAfi-NEJAD, and R. W. MOXON. *Controlling International Technology Transfer.* New York: Pergamon, 1981.

ROBINSON, RICHARD D. *Internationalization of Business: An Introduction.* Hinsdale, Ill.: Dryden, 1984.

TERPSTRA, VERN, and KENNETH DAVID. *The Cultural Environment of International Business*, 2nd ed. Cincinnati: South-Western, 1985.

UNITED NATIONS CENTRE ON TRANSNATIONAL CORPORATIONS. *Transnational Corporations in World Development: Third Survey.* New York: United Nations, 1983.

7

PUBLIC ISSUES MANAGEMENT

⟸ **IDEAS TO BE FOUND** ⟹
IN THIS CHAPTER

- Public issues management system
- Environmental analysis
- Public issues and strategy formulation
- Evaluating public issues management

The public policy process described in Chapter 5 has produced a great deal of legislation and regulation in the last two decades that affected business organizations and the management of those organizations. Changes have taken place in every area of public policy—antitrust legislation, economic management, labor-management relations, entitlement programs, and particularly in the area of social regulation—that have changed the way business can be operated and altered the management task to include a public policy dimension.

No other area of public policy has made as significant an impact on business and management in recent years as the area of social regulation. Before the election of Ronald Reagan, this area of regulation constituted a real growth industry in terms of regulations issued, budgetary increases, staff increases, and creation of new regulatory agencies. The growth of this new kind of regulation has been referred to as a second managerial revolution.[1]

The first managerial revolution is based on the idea that ownership and control have been separated in the modern corporation—that decision-making

[1]Murray L. Weidenbaum, *Business, Government and the Public* (Englewood Cliffs, N.J.: Prentice-Hall, 1977), p. 285.

power has shifted from the formal owners or stockholders, to a class of professional managers.[2] This second managerial revolution involves a further shift of decision-making power from these professional managers to a vast cadre of government regulators who are influencing, and in many ways controlling, managerial decisions of the typical business corporation. These decisions, which are increasingly subject to government influence and control, are basic to the operation of a business organization.

> No business, large or small, can operate without obeying a myriad of government rules and restrictions. Costs and profits can be affected as much by a directive written by a government official as by a management decision in the front office or a customer's decision at the checkout counter. Fundamental entrepreneurial decisions—such as what lines of business to go into, what products and services to produce, which investments to finance, how and where to make goods and how to market them, and what prices to charge—are increasingly subject to government control.[3]

The impact of social regulation, more than any other area of public policy, has made managers aware of the need to take public policy seriously. It is important to understand the impacts public policy has made on business and management to see the importance of this dimension to management. Business organizations have had to incorporate new values and objectives into their operating strategies. The environment in which managers perform their tasks has been and is being changed through public policy measures.

Thus the impacts that public policy can make on the corporation and management are significant. Specific public policies can cost substantial amounts of money, wipe out product lines overnight because of safety and health problems, involve the corporation in lengthy litigation, and other such matters. The corporation's response to public policy issues should not be a seat-of-the-pants or knee-jerk reaction, but rather a well thought-out and developed strategy based on research and analysis of the public policy problems facing the company. Such a response is much more likely to work in the company's best interest as well as in the interests of society as a whole.

The term or concept of public issues management has been developed to refer to an organized and systematic effort on the part of a corporation to respond effectively to issues of public concern in its external environment. Public issues management refers to a process whereby a strategy is developed for the corporation's involvement in the public policy process in regard to a specific public issue that affects the company. The concept implies that corporations take a responsibility to become involved with public issues and develop

[2]Adolph A. Berle and Gardiner C. Means, *The Modern Corporation and Private Property* (New York: Macmillan, 1932).

[3]Murray L. Weidenbaum, "Government Power and Business Performance," *The United States in the 1980s*, Peter Dunignan and Alvin Robushka, eds. (Stanford, Calif.: Hoover Institution Press, 1980), p. 200.

strategies on these issues in a manner comparable to the way strategies are developed for traditional business concerns.

> Issues management is a new, rapidly evolving strategic management and planning process used by a growing number of organizations. Its central focus is identifying current or emerging issues and trends that will affect organizational goals, developing and analyzing information on these issues and trends, and undertaking intelligent management strategies in response to these identified issues and their anticipated impacts.[4]

The term *public issues management* is something of a misnomer, as no corporation can manage the public policy process to attain a desired outcome on a specific issue with any degree of regularity. What can be managed is the corporation's response to an issue that is of concern to the company. The issues management process can help a company realize its business objectives by enabling it to anticipate and respond effectively to changes in its external environment. Issues management embodies "the deliberate recognition by company decision makers of the need for a systematic approach to public issues and to constructive participation in their resolution."[5]

DEFINITIONS OF PUBLIC ISSUES MANAGEMENT

Issues management is the capacity to understand, mobilize, coordinate, and direct all strategic and policy planning functions, and all public affairs/public relations skills, toward the achievement of one objective: meaningful participation in creation of public policy that affects personal and institutional destiny.

W. Howard Chase, "Issue Management Conference—A Special Report," *Corporate Public Issues and Their Management*, December 1, 1982, pp. 1–2.

Issues management is a program which a company uses to increase its knowledge of the public policy process and enhance the sophistication and effectiveness of its involvement in that process.

The Fundamentals of Issue Management (Washington, D.C.: Public Affairs Council, 1978), p. 1.

---

[4]Bart C. Weller, "The Process of Issues Management: Some Emerging Perspectives," The TrendTRACK Company, Boulder, Colorado, 1982, p. 4.

[5]Charles B. Arrington, Jr. and Richard N. Sawaya, "Managing Public Affaira: Issues Management in an Uncertain Environment," *California Management Review*, vol. XXVI, no. 4 (Summer 1984), p. 148.

Issues management is the process by which the corporation can identify and evaluate those governmental and societal issues that may impact significantly on it. The issues can then be assigned priorities for appropriate corporate response.

Richard A. Armstrong, "The Concept and Practice of Issues Management in the United States," Speech delivered to the National Convention, Public Relations Institute of Australia, Sydney, Australia, July 17, 1981.

Properly conceived and executed, issues management is a process to organize a company's expertise to enable it to participate effectively in the shaping and resolution of public issues that critically impinge upon its operations.

Charles B. Arrington, Jr. and Richard N. Sawaya, "Managing Public Affairs: Issues Management in an Uncertain Environment," *California Management Review*, vol. XXVI, no. 4 (Summer 1984), p. 148.

Issues management is an advanced process of strategic public affairs planning and action that goes beyond the conventional public affairs function. An effective issue management program—built into the total corporate strategic plan—enables a company to "manage," influence or control the development of public issues or trends that may affect it—rather than just react to the issues after they have developed.

National Association of Manufacturers, *The Public Affairs Manual*, p. 1.

The concept of public issues management first emerged in the corporate world through developments by the public relations or public affairs staff, as they attempted to respond to public policy issues that were affecting their organizations. This emerging activity received its name in 1976 from a veteran public relations officer, W. Howard Chase, who designed the basic issues management process model.[6] His company and others attempted to formalize earlier ad hoc approaches to public policy issues into a separate and distinguishable issues management activity. This activity was not intended as a substitute for existing activities but as a complement to fill a void in corporate activity.

Some companies created separate issues management units to engage in these activities. Others placed issues management activities in existing departments such as public affairs, government relations, corporate planning, or social responsibility. Thus many of the functions involved in public issues management were not necessarily new in themselves. Public affairs, which is most

---

[6]Robert L. Heath and Richard Alan Nelson, *Issues Management: Corporate Public Policymaking in an Information Society* (Beverly Hills: Sage Publications, 1986), p. 7.

likely involved in public issues management, has been a function in most corporations for many years. Many corporations, particularly the largest, have had Washington offices for some time that have been involved in the political process in some manner. What makes public issues management new, according to Richard A. Armstrong, President of the Public Affairs Council, is the following:

> What is new—is a new corporate attitude, or "mindset" which guides the Issues Management Program.
>
> What is new—is the extent of the corporate commitment in time and people to external issues and public affairs.
>
> What is new—is the concept that the external relations of a company is not a function to be delegated to a staff of specialists and then quietly forgotten.
>
> What is new—is the awareness of the need to expand the time frame in the corporation's early warning mechanism. Most companies today try to look ahead at least three years.
>
> What is new—is more capable and sophisticated research personnel. A host of new titles have appeared on the scene: Director, Public Affairs Research and Planning; Public Affairs Research Analyst; Policy Analyst; Director, Public Policy Planning; Government Research Coordinator, and many more.
>
> What is new—is the broadened arena for action. Corporate efforts today cannot simply be focused on the legislative process, rather they must try to reach the public and those interest groups mentioned earlier.
>
> Finally, not only new but so refreshing—business has decided to take the offense rather than simply defending itself. (Academics would call this being pro-active rather than reactive.) When a company can actually get involved in the policy-making process before the issues have become politically polarized, it can sometimes defuse them, or at least minimize their impact.[7]

The importance of public issues management to corporations is shown in Table 7.1, which reports the results of a survey of top practioners in the field. The data show that 73.8 percent of the respondents believe public issue management is either very important or extremely important in their organization. The reasons for the importance they attach to public issues management is perhaps even more revealing. Some business leaders and academics believe that the very survival of business and the business system is at stake and that business must develop better and more constructive responses to public issues than it has in the past or be faced with a further loss of credibility.

> In a world of uncertainties, where change is the one thing we can count on, businesses need the ability to anticipate and adapt successfully to change in

---

[7]Richard A. Armstrong, "The Concept and Practice of Issues Management in the United States," Speech delivered to the National Convention, Public Relations Institute of Australia, Syndey, Australia, July 17, 1981.

Table 7.1
Importance of Public Issues Management

Opinion	Number of Respondents	Percent
Extremely important	10	23.8%
Very important	21	50.0
Somewhat important	9	21.4
Not very important	2	4.8
Not important at all	0	—
	42	100.0%

Source: Rogene A. Buchholz, "Education for Public Issues Management: Key Insights from a Survey of Top Practitioners," *Public Affairs Review,* Vol. III (1982), p. 68.

both matters of public policy and their own market pursuits. Through a better understanding of public-policy genesis and development, organizations should be able to forsee public-policy changes and be responsive to them. Such an approach enables change—that is the key concept, change—to be accommodated with minimal disruption.[8]

The modern frontiers of professional management—corporate planning and external affairs—are those areas in which change is occurring most rapidly, where the least is known, where the most speculation occurs and where the opportunities for imaginative executive leadership are greatest. . . The manner in which organizations of all types, and large business corporations in particular, respond to commercial and social complexity is fundamental to their institutional legitimacy and their survival.[9]

Public issues management can be useful for a number of purposes in the corporation. These incllude (1) injecting public policy research into corporate decision making, (2) identifying emerging issues to give more lead time for coordinating internal and external responses, (3) actively monitoring issues and deflecting them before they become major problems or to transform emerging trends into corporate opportunities, and (4) providing a corporate-wide process for anticipating and dealing with issues. These are important purposes that should not be ignored by a management concerned with responding to public policy issues that impact the organization.[10]

According to David L. Shanks, Director of Corporate Public Relations and Advertising at Rexnord Corporation, proper management of public issues

[8]Graham Molitor, "How to Anticipate Public-Policy Changes," *S.A.M. Advanced Management Journal* (Summer 1977), p. 4.

[9]James E. Post, "The Challenge of Managing Under Social Uncertainity," *Business Horizons* (August 1977), pp. 51–52.

[10]Steven L. Wartick and Robert E. Rude, "Issues Management: Corporate Fad or Corporate Function?" *California Management Review,* vol, XXIX, no. 1 (Fall 1986), p. 130.

Table 7.2
Important Purposes of a Public Issues Management System

Purpose	Rank Score
Allows "management of" vs. "reaction to" public issues	1.9
Allows management to select issues that will have the greatest impact on the corporation	2.5
Inserts relevant issues into the strategic planning process	2.7
Gives the company ability to act in tune with society	3.6
Protects the credibility of business in the public mind	4.3
Provides opportunities for leadership roles	4.8

Source: Rogene A. Buchholz, "Education for Public Issues Management: Key Insights from a Survey of Top Practitioners," *Public Affairs Review,* Vol. III (1982), p. 70.

has many benefits, both protective and opportunistic. Public issues management (1) allows management to select issues that will have the greatest impact on the corporation, (2) allows "management of" instead of "reaction to" issues, (3) inserts relevant issues into the strategic planning process, (4) gives the company ability to act in tune with society, (5) provides opportunities for leadership roles, and (6) protects the credibility of business in the public mind.[11] Table 7.2 shows the ranking that top practitioners gave to these purposes in a recent survey. Rather than having to respond in knee-jerk fashion to issues that are already well formulated, a public issues management system provides the capability to anticipate issues and develop responses that are more likely to be consistent with the company's and society's best interests.

PUBLIC ISSUES MANAGEMENT SYSTEM The management of public issues involves a series of stages or steps that, taken together, constitute a public issues management system. Exhibit 7.1 shows the various stages of a typical public issues management system. There are many different models of the public issues management process, but this one seems to capture the essential functions involved in the activity and categorize them in a useful fashion.[12]

Identification The first stage of managing a corporation's response to the external environment is one of identifying those trends and issues that are likely to affect the

[11]James K. Brown, *This Business of Issues: Coping with the Company's Environments* (New York: The Conference Board, 1979), p. 72.

[12]See W. Howard Chase, *Issue Management: Origins of the Future* (Stamford, Conn.: Issue Action Publications, 1984), p. 37 for a description of the original Chase/Jones Issue Management Process Model. See also *The Fundamentals of Issue Management* (Washington, D.C.: Public Affairs Council, 1978), p. 2.

Exhibit 7.1
Public Issues Management System

I. Identifying Public Issues and Trends in Public Expectations
  - Scanning the environment for trends and issues
  - Tracking trends and issues that are developing
  - Developing forecasts of trends and issues
  - Identifying those trends and issues of interest to the corporation

II. Evaluating Their Impact and Setting Priorities
  - Assessment of impact and probability of occurrence
  - Assessment of corporate resources and ability to respond
  - Preparation of issue priorities for further analysis

III. Research and Analysis
  - Categorization of issues along relevant dimensions
  - Ensuring that priority issues receive staff coverage
  - Involving functional areas where appropriate
  - Using outside sources of information
  - Development and analysis of position options

IV. Strategy Development
  - Analysis of position and strategy options
  - Management decision on position and strategy
  - Integration with overall business strategy

V. Implementation
  - Dissemination of agreed-upon position and strategy
  - Development of tactics consistent with the overall strategy
  - Development of alliances with external organizations
  - Linkage with internal and external communication networks

VI. Evaluation
  - Assessment of results by staff
  - Management evaluation
  - Modification of implementation plans
  - Additional research

corporation. These trends and issues must be continually monitored or tracked for new developments. Forecasts must be developed to predict their probable development over the next several years. From this information, an initial screening can be made to identify those issues of greatest interest to the corporation because of their short-and long-term impacts. The purpose of this stage is to identify issues that will affect the corporation as early in their life cycle as possible.

Evaluation of Impact   Once issues have been identified, their potential impact on the corporation must be evaluated more thoroughly. The reason for this evaluation is to set some priorities for corporate responses. The typical corporation cannot respond to every public issue of interest—it probably does not have the resources—nor can it respond to every issue with the same level of involvement or effort. Priorities must be set according to the potential impact of the issue on the corporation, the issue's probability of occurrence, the corporation's ability to respond, and other relevant factors. Useful questions to ask at this stage include: (1) How large (in dollars, markets, products) will the impact of the issue be on the company? (2) How severely will the issue affect the ability of the firm to compete successfully for sales, investment funds, and employees? and (3) What can the organization and its various staff and line organizations do to affect the issue's outcome?[13] The result of this stage is a list of issues with priorities attached.

Research and Analysis

The next stage involves basic analysis and research on issues of highest priority. For this task, involvement of a public affairs staff devoted to public issues research is important. Involvement of functional areas—such as manufacturing when environmental issues are concerned or personnel when the issue is minority hiring—is also crucial. Outside sources can also be used at this stage, particularly consulting organizations, academia, or research centers such as the American Enterprise Institute for Public Policy Research or the Center for the Study of American Business.

Issues can be analyzed along certain dimensions that are of importance to the corporation. Public issues can be categorized according to type, for example, referring to the extensiveness and manner in which business is affected. An *operational* issue may affect one or more, but not all, operating units of the corporation. The issue may affect only manufacturing or marketing, or only certain geographic regions. Many environmental issues are of this nature, affecting only certain plants that are not in compliance with environmental standards or that manufacture products that are the subject of an emerging public concern. Strategies for these issues need not affect the entire corporation nor involve people from all corporate operations.

A *corporate* issue affects the corporation as a whole and can affect the way in which the entire entity functions. Issues such as corporate governance or public disclosure of information are of this nature. If the Securities and Exchange Commission, for example, were to require the disclosure of social information, this would affect all units of the corporation. Likewise, the involvement of employees in running the company, whether at the board level or at the shop floor, could affect all aspects of corporate structure and operation.

Finally, a *societal* issue affects the environment in which business functions. Such issues as national economic planning and regulatory reform fall in this category, as does the government's macro-economic policies. What the government does to combat unemployment and inflation affects capital mar-

---

[13]A. Sherburne Hart, "Identifying Issues," *The Public Affairs Handbook*, Joseph S. Nagelschmidt, ed. (New York: AMACOM, 1982), p. 78.

kets, stock prices, and the entire economic environment in which business functions. Issues that relate to trade can affect the entire international environment in which business competes. The issues in this category are in many ways more complex and involve more interests than issues in the other categories, making strategy development all the more difficult.[14]

Another way to categorize public issues is according to timing. It is of great interest to a corporate manager to have an idea of where an issue is with respect to timing. For example, a *latent* issue is one that is still not widely discussed in the media or by public interest groups or other stakeholders. But a scanning process might detect that pressures are building with respect to the issue or that trends are developing in society that may make the issue important in the near future. At this stage, corporations have a great deal of discretion in regard to their response, thus it is to their advantage to try and anticipate issues and catch them in the latent stage if at all possible. Perhaps some adjustment in corporate behavior at this point to meet public expectations will defuse the issue and keep it from going on to other stages.

An *emerging* issue is a public policy question with three essential characteristics: (1) its definition and contending positions are still evolving, but the issue is beginning to affect economic, social, or political interests in a manner likely to cause or result in conflict among the parties involved; (2) the issue is likely to be the subject of government action in the next three to five years because such conflict must usually be resolved through the political or public policy process; and (3) it can be acted on by affected corporations.[15] The issue is not fully politized at this point, but it is the subject of discussion by many groups and affected parties. Public opinion is being formed on the issue and the outlines of public policy on the issue are beginning to take shape. At this stage, business can engage in the discussion and help shape the debate and its outcome.

A *current* issue is being debated or otherwise acted on in local, state or federal government institutions. The issue is fully politized at this point and specific public policies to address the issue are being formulated and debated. Business activities at this stage are limited to some form of participation in the legislative process to give shape to the policy or policies that eventually result. Perhaps a specific bill can be defeated or perhaps business can have some influence on the content of the bill and its implementation.

The *institutionalized* stage refers to issues where public policy has already been formulated and whatever policies were approved are now being implemented. Most likely this implementation is being done by a government agency, perhaps a new one that was set up for the specific purpose of implementing a new area of public policy, or an old one that has been given some additional responsibilities. Business options at this stage are largely limited to

[14]Fran Steckmest, "Some Definitions and Examples of Public Policy Issues," presented at the Public Affairs Council Workshop, Washington, D.C., May 16-17, 1978, p. 3.

[15]*The Fundamentals of Issue Management* (Washington, D.C., Public Affairs Council, 1978), p. 3.

rearguard actions that consist of questioning the implementation of legislation in the courts as agencies issue new rules, for example, or working with the agencies to develop rules that are cost effective.

At this stage of the public issues management system, the corporation must do its homework and perform quality research on public issues comparable to the kind of effort devoted to technological issues in research and development laboratories. The development of a good priorities list is essential, as a corporation cannot do a thorough job of research and analysis on every public issue that is identified. Analysis is useful in deciding what to do about an issue, because the intent of this stage is not only to more thoroughly analyze the potential impact an issue can make on a corporation, but also to analyze the different positions and strategies that can be taken on the issue. The result is an analysis of the dimensions of an issue, including the pros and cons of different positions and strategies.

Strategy Development Emerging from this research and analysis phase is the development of different options that can be taken on an issue along with a recommended position that can be presented to management for consideration. The recommended position must reflect the best thinking of the corporation and be based on solid research rather than a hastily put together reaction that will most likely not work in the corporation's best interests. Management must eventually decide to go along with the recommendation or adopt one of the other options.

The choice of an option can also be put in terms of strategy formulation. There are many aspects to strategy development. Issues need to be categorized along relevant dimensions so the strategic implications will become more apparent. The choice of an overall strategy that reflects the nature of the issue as well as the objectives of the corporation needs to be made. Specific implementation strategies or tactics then need to be adopted that are consistent with the overall objectives. Because of its importance, this stage will be discussed more thoroughly in a later section of this chapter.

Implementation The choice of an overall strategy must then be disseminated to the appropriate people in the company who are responsible for implementation. They must develop specific tactics for changing corporate behavior, influencing public opinion, changing the thinking of public policy makers, developing a court case— whatever tactics are consistent with the strategy chosen. If other parties, such as a trade association, are involved, alliances must be built during this stage and action taken. Lobbying tactics must be developed and carried out if attempts at legislative influence are appropriate.

Linkages with internal and external communications networks must be developed as needed. For example, if grass-roots lobbying is called for, this must be communicated to the grass-roots network for it to be activated. If a change is appropriate in the way a company produces a product to reduce ecological damage, this must be communicated to the plant personnel who are in a position to make the necessary changes. External communications involves informing the public about what the company is doing to meet public expectations or engaging in a debate about the issue itself.

Evaluation of Strategy   Finally comes the all-important stage of evaluation. The tactics that are implemented must constantly be evaluated to ascertain whether they are achieving results. Some kind of evaluation system must be developed to determine whether the public issues management effort is a success. This evaluation is extremely difficult. For example, how much credit can any single corporate effort be given for the defeat of a bill in Congress? Or, if the bill passed when the objective was to defeat it, was this the fault of a single corporate lobbying effort? How can changes in public opinion be measured and attributed to a specific advocacy advertising program? What is the impact of a corporate economic education program?

These are very complex questions, and yet without some kind of evaluation by both the staff involved in public issues management and management iself, one is operating in the dark. The process of evaluation is important because the implementation tactics may have to be modified in light of the evaluation or additional research performed to develop different positions.

All through this public issues management system there are a number of key functions that have to be accomplished. Figure 7.1 shows these functions in boxes that correspond to the six stages of the public issues management system. According to a survey of public issues management practitioners completed in 1981, there have been significant improvements at almost every stage of this public issues management process. Table 7.3 shows that between 50 and 70 percent of the respondents believe there have been significant improvements in capability in the first five components. The relatively low percentage on the evaluation component is undoubtedly due to the difficulty of evaluating the results of the public issues management effort.

Figure 7.1
Six Steps to Successful Issues Management

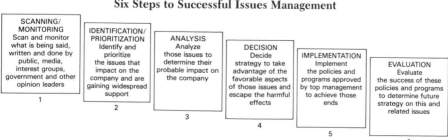

Source: Jon Johnson, "Issues Management: What Are the Issues," *Business Quarterly,* Autumn 1983, p. 3

Table 7.3
Significant Improvements in Capability
($N=42$)

Area of Improvement	Number of Respondents	Percent
Evaluating the impact of public issues on the corporation and setting priorities.	29	69.0%
Development of a strategy to respond to public issues of concern to the company.	27	64.3
Research and analysis of public issues identified as being important to the corporation.	25	59.5
Identifying public issues and trends in public expectations.	23	54.8
Implementation of strategy with respect to public issues.	21	50.0
Evaluation of the response to a public issue.	14	33.3
Other areas	10	23.8

Source: Rogene A. Buchholz, "Education for Public Issues Management: Key Insights from a Survey of Top Practitioners," *Public Affairs Review,* Vol. III (1982), p. 69.

ENVIRONMENTAL ANALYSIS   One of the most important elements in successful public issues management is the development of an ability to identify those public issues in the environment that will have an impact on the corporation. The earlier an issue can be identified in its life cycle, the more options business has open to it and the better chance business has to develop an effective response. Arrington and Sawaya call this the foresight function of issues management where public issues are identified, monitored, analyzed, and prioritized according to their impact on business operations.[16]

Early identification of issues can enable a corporation to be more interactive with society in helping to formulate public policy and change its performance, rather than being reactive (opposing every new piece of legislation or public demand), or accommodative (simply adapting itself to whatever legislation and regulation eventuate). The modern corporation must consider all factors in the environment that impinge on its operations, not just the more traditional economic and technological factors.

The need for early identification of social and political factors has become a must for many companies. Some have been confronted with a number of embarrassing situations that could have been avoided with a little forethought. Ignoring social and political trends has cost other companies a good deal of money because they have been forced to respond to public pressure or burdensome government regulation. In some cases, the very survival of the company may be at stake. Environmental analysis of public issues typically includes the functions of scanning, monitoring, forecasting, and assessment.

[16]Arrington and Sawaya, "Managing Public Affairs," p. 149.

Environmental Scanning   The first step in identifying issues is one of scanning the environment to look for developing issues that may affect the corporation. The process of scanning can best be compared to a radar scan used in presenting the weather report in a television newscast. The purpose of the radar scan is to discover storms that may affect a given area sometime in the near future. The purpose of environmental scanning is to discover issues that may affect a given corporation in the near future. Thus the scope of the search must be broad, focusing on particular areas of interest.

There are various ways to scan the environment to discover important public issues. Four different modes of scanning were discovered by Aguilar as a result of a field study of information-gathering practices of managers. These include: (1) undirected viewing, which refers to a manager's exposure and perception of information that has no specific purpose; (2) conditioned viewing, which involves purposefulness by the manager in being receptive to information and assessing its significance; (3) informal search, where the manager moves to a proactive orientation in seeking information for a specific purpose; and (4) formal search, where information is obtained for specific purposes and formal procedures and methodologies are emphasized.[17]

One method of categorizing the sources for gathering information in the scanning process for the social and political environments is shown in Exhibit 7.2. According to this scheme, sources are categorized into internal and external, then as personal and impersonal within each of these categories. *Internal sources* refers to those within the corporation itself and *external sources* refers to those outside the organization. *Personal sources* means the use of people as sources, whereas *impersonal sources* refers to the use of reports or studies.

The chief executive officer is an obvious source of environmental information, especially if he or she is politically involved and thus knows something about the current political scene in Washington or at the state level. Because of time pressures, the CEO cannot be part of a continual scanning process, but can be a good source of information if the right questions are asked when time is available. When the CEO brings up an issue, it is very likely to be of concern to the company. The CEO also has many contacts that may be useful for follow-up information.

The board of directors is another good source of information, especially when there is a public responsibility committee whose job it is to be concerned about such matters. Information about the political environment, such as legislation or regulation being considered, ought to be readily available from a corporation's Washington office. Other executives and managers are also good sources of information. They can be polled directly or asked to be part of a more

---

[17]Francis J. Aguilar, *Scanning the Business Environment* (New York: Macmillan, 1967), pp. 19–21.

Exhibit 7.2
Sources of Scanning Information

I. External
  A. Personal
    1. Consultants (Washington)
    2. Conferences (Public Affairs Council, trade associations, professional and scientific meetings, etc.)
    3. Executives and managers in other companies
    4. Government officials (Congressmen and regulators)
    5. Representatives of public interest organizations

  B. Impersonal
    1. Reports from trade associations
    2. Government publications (Congressional Record, Federal Register)
    3. Newspapers and magazines
    4. Trade and technical journals (Food and Chemical News) and books
    5. Special consulting and reporting services
    6. Publications of public interest organizations

II. Internal
  A. Personal
    1. Chief executive officer
    2. Board of directors
    3. Washington office
    4. Other executives and managers
    5. Staff specialists

  B. Impersonal
    1. Management reports and memoranda
    2. Accounting reports
    3. Planning reports and budgets

Source: Adapted from Francis J. Aguilar, *Scanning the Business Environment* (New York: Macmillan, 1967), p. 66. Copyright by The Trustees of Columbia University in the City of New York. Reprinted with permission.

sophisticated process such as a Delphi exercise. Finally, staff specialists who are involved in regulatory areas can supply information about their particular area of concern.

Impersonal internal sources include management reports and memoranda that may deal with issues in the political and social environments, accounting reports that show how resources are being allocated, and planning reports and budgets that show how much money is going to be spent on an area of concern, such as pollution control (e.g., pointing out the importance of that issue to the future of the company as assessed by managers who have control of the budgeting process). The budget represents the bottom line, in a sense, and reflects the values and priorities of the company.

Outside consultants are very useful sources of information about emerging social and political issues. These outside consultants frequently conduct research for the company to measure the effectiveness of a particular program in dealing with an issue of concern. They can bring an objective viewpoint to their analysis that may be lacking in the use of internal sources that have vested interests in programs and policies.

Conferences are a good place to pick up environmental information. Many corporate executives can be found attending conferences such as the Annual Meeting of the Academy of Management. Executives and managers of other companies may be good sources of information as are government officials in various positions. The information from these sources must be screened carefully, however, as it is more likely to be biased than information from other sources. Finally, representatives of public interest groups can be consulted on their current concerns, which they often are willing to express quite readily.

Impersonal external sources include reports from the general business and trade associations, such as the Business Roundtable, which publishes studies analyzing various aspects of the environment. Government publications are an obvious source of scanning information, particularly congressional hearings on such subjects as plant closings or antitrust reform. The Federal Register contains regulations that affect business, both regulations being proposed and those issued in final form. Finally, the census reports contain demographic information about population trends.

Newspapers and magazines are another important source of information. Some companies and industries have a rather elaborate system for monitoring these sources. The American Council of Life Insurance, for example, has a Trend Analysis Program that depends on the efforts of over 100 volunteer monitors who work for member companies. These volunteers regularly scan one or more publications from a list of close to 100 publications, and abstract any article in their assigned area that meets the following criteria: (1) the article involves an event or an idea that is indicative of either a trend or a discontinuity in the environment, and (2) it contains implications for the long-range concerns of society and the life insurance business. These abstracts are analyzed six times a year by an abstract analysis committee and may eventually find their way into a trend report for member companies.[18]

Trade and technical journals are also good sources of information. Some companies have a full-time employee who does nothing but monitor trade journals. Special counseling and reporting services can be useful sources of information. Finally, the literature distributed by public interest groups must not be overlooked, especially those that are known to be influential in political circles. This literature can be indicative of developing trends in society and of the interests of significant stakeholder groups.

Another way of categorizing scanning information is shown in Figure 7.2, which focuses on the public, media, thought-leaders, and government as key segments of the external environment that needs to be scanned and monitored. Thus there are a great many sources of information for political and social environments. Some of these sources will obviously be more important than

[18]Brown, *This Business of Issues*, pp. 22–25.

GROUPING	MONITORING DATA BASE	RESEARCH/ANALYSIS TECHNIQUES
1. PUBLIC • General • Key Segments	• Attitudes • Knowledge Level	• Surveys • Special Studies
2. MEDIA • Print • Electronic	• News • Editorials • Features	• Content Analysis • Contact Program • Editorial Briefings
3. THOUGHT-LEADERS • Academics • Activists	• Position Statements • Publications • Conferences	• Literature Search • Surveys • Contact Program
4. GOVERNMENT • Politicians • Civil Servants • Advisors	• Policy Statements • Background Studies • Legislation	• Legislative Review • Issue Analysis • Contact Program

Figure 7.2
A Scanning-Monitoring-Analysis System

Source: Jon Johnson, "Issues Management: What Are the Issues?" *Business Quarterly*, Autumn 1983, p. 3.

others, and it is best to have an overall framework in mind when making these judgments. The most important challenge in the scanning process is to make sense out of all the unconnected and ambiguous data that may be collected in the scanning process so that it is useful for planning purposes.

Environmental Monitoring   Environmental monitoring involves the tracking of trends and issues that have been identified in the scanning process. The purpose of monitoring is to discern whether certain trends are emerging into issues that need closer attention. Again, a comparison can be made with the weather report on television, where storms that may have been spotted by the radar scan are continually monitored to see where they are moving and how they are developing.

Monitoring almost always follows scanning to ensure that hunches and intuitive judgments made about trends and issues during the scanning process are either confirmed or not confirmed. Monitoring can be more focused and systematic than scanning because analysts generally know what they are looking for and can be more formal about gathering data that is relevant to their concerns. The outcome of the monitoring process includes: (1) a specific description of environmental trends and issues to be forecast, (2) the identification of trends and issues for further monitoring, and (3) the identification of areas requiring further scanning. Monitoring may identify trends or issues that were not included in the scope of the original scanning activity.[19]

[19]Liam Fahey and V. K. Narayanan, *Macroenvironmental Analysis for Strategic Management* (St. Paul: West, 1986), pp. 39–40.

Environmental Forecasting   Forecasting can be defined as the attempt to predict some future event or condition as a result of rational study and analysis of pertinent data. Forecasting in this sense is not an intuitive guess about the future, but is an educated guess based on actual data and analysis that provide evidence for a particular kind of development. To continue the analogy with a weather report, once the radar screen has discovered some storms in the area, a forecast will predict what will happen to these storms. Are they likely to hit an area or miss it entirely? Will they intensify or weaken before reaching a given area? Forecasting is very difficult at best, but if a few simple laws are followed (see box), one has a better chance of making accurate and relevant forecasts.

The first law of forecasting: Forecasting is very difficult, especially if it's about the future.

When presenting a forecast: Give them a number or give them a date, but never both.

A forecaster's best defense is a good offense, so: If you have to forecast, forecast often. But: If you're ever right, never let'em forget it.

Source: Edgar R. Fiedler, "The Three Rs of Economic Forecasting—Irrational, Irrelevant and Irreverent," *Across the Board*, Vol, XIV, No. 6 (June 1977), pp. 62–63. Copyright © 1977 The Conference Board.

Forecasting is nothing new to business, of course, but traditionally these activities have been limited to the economic and technological environments (see Figure 7.3). Economic forecasting at the macro level includes projections of future gross national product, consumption and investment expenditures, productivity projections, inflation, and balance of payments. The purpose of this level of forecasting is to get some idea of the general economic conditions with which business will be faced in the immediate future. For this purpose, many corporations subscribe to one or more of the econometric models that are available, sometimes adapting them to their own purposes.

Economic forecasting at the micro level involves forecasting related to the specific markets in which the company sells products—either mature markets that have been in existence for some time, markets that are newly developing, or potential markets the company may be considering. The purpose of this forecasting is to be more specific about the sales of particular products the company is already producing or considering. Micro forecasting also involves financial forecasts about the availability of money and credit to support the operations of the company.

Technological forecasting is concerned with state-of-the-art developments

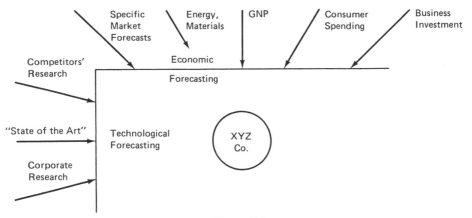

Figure 7.3
Traditional Environmental Forecasting

Source: Ian H. Wilson, "Socio-Political Forecasting: A New Dimension to Strategic Planning," *Michigan Business Review*, Vol. XXVI, No. 4 (July 1974), p. 19. Reprinted with permission.

in products and processes. Forecasters try to predict where new technological breakthroughs are likely to happen that will significantly alter corporate planning. Forecasts of completion dates for company research and development projects are also a part of this area, as well as attempts to assess competitors' technical competence and development activities. Technological change is one of the most visible and pervasive forms of change in society.

The traditional approach to environmental forecasting has been two-sided, based on the assumption that all other factors are equal. But the 1960s and 1970s taught many business organizations that all other things were not equal, and that it was precisely the social and political environments that were giving business the most trouble and affecting its profits and very survival. Ian Wilson, one of the early pioneers for a broader approach, proposed a four-sided model for environmental forecasting, including the political and social environments in addition to the economic and technological ones (see Figure 7.4).[20]

Forecasting the political environment involves, in its broadest sense, some assessment of business-government relations in the society as a whole. Crucial questions in this regard relate to the pro-business or anti-business posture that is likely to be taken by a particular administration, and what implication long-term conservative or liberal political trends in society have for business. The answers to these questions have significant implications for the kind of political strategies a business adopts. More specific forecasting of the political environment involves keeping track of legislation being considered by Congress, the stage of the political process legislation is in, what the likely

[20]Ian H. Wilson, "Reforming the Strategic Planning Process: Integration of Social Responsibility and Business Needs," *The Unstable Ground: Corporate Social Policy in a Dynamic Society*, S. Prakash Sethi, ed. (Los Angeles: Melville Publishing Co., 1974), pp. 247–248.

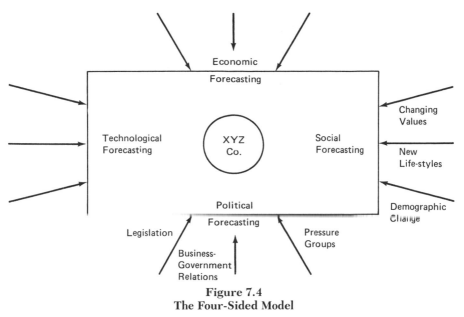

Figure 7.4
The Four-Sided Model

Source: Ian H. Wilson, "Socio-Political Forecasting: A New Dimension to Strategic Planning," *Michigan Business Review*, Vol. XXVI, No. 4 (July 1074), p. 20. Reprinted with permission.

outcome will be, and keeping aware of the various political pressures being applied by interest groups on issues of concern to the corporation.

The social environment is much more difficult to forecast. It is important, however, for business to attempt to predict major value changes in society that may give rise to new concerns and demands that will affect the corporation or the business system as a whole. Forecasting the social environment also means predicting whether current lifestyles are likely to continue or whether some major changes are probable. Finally, demographic trends are also important to follow, as shifts in population with respect to age or regional location can have major effects on the corporation.

An adequate forecasting system must include at least these four major environmental elements (see Table 7.4). It is not enough to focus on economic and technological aspects alone. Changes in government regulation and social expectations can affect profits as much as changes in technology or general economic conditions. Social and political forecasting is more and more becoming a part of the corporate scene and must be a part of an environmental analysis that is to include all factors of importance to the corporation.[21]

After developing the four-sided forecasting framework, Wilson goes on to enunciate certain principles that he believes should guide the forecasting effort. The forecasting system should be holistic in its approach—the economic, tech-

[21]"Capitalizing on Social Change," *Business Week*, October 19, pp. 105–106.

Table 7.4
Environmental Factors

Socio-Cultural	Economic	Technological	Political-Legal
Life-style changes.	GNP Trends.	Total federal spend-	Antitrust regulations.
Career expectations.	Interest rates.	ing for R&D.	Environmental pro-
Consumer activism.	Money supply.	Total industry spend-	tection laws.
Rate of family	Inflation rates.	ing for R&D.	Tax laws.
formation.	Unemployment	Focus of technologi-	Special incentives.
Growth rate of	levels.	cal efforts.	Foreign trade
population.	Wage/Price controls.	Patent protection.	regulations.
Age distribution of	Devaluation/	New products.	Attitudes towards for-
population	revaluation/	New developments	eign companies.
Regional shifts in	Energy availability	in technology trans-	Laws on hiring and
population.	and cost.	fer from lab to	promotion.
Life expectancies.		marketplace.	Stability of
Birth rates.		Productivity improve-	government.
		ments through	
		automation.	

Source: Thomas L. Wheelen and J. David Hunger, *Strategic Management* (Reading, MA: Addison-Wesley, 1984), p. 79. Copyright © 1984 by Addison-Wesley. Reprinted with permission.

nological, social, and economic environments should not be seen as separate or distinct from each other. The system should also be iterative in its operation, be designed to deal with alternative futures, provide for contingency planning, and be an integral part of the decision-making process of the corporation.[22]

In making an actual forecast, two concepts must be kept in mind: events and trends. Events can be defined as important specific occurrences in the social and political environments that may affect business. Such an event was the passage of legislation to raise the mandatory retirement age from sixty-five to seventy a few years ago—an action that took place very rapidly in the political environment. A trend, on the other hand, can be defined as a general tendency or course of events, that is, a whole series of events that seem to be leading in a certain direction. The aging of the population throughout the 1970s and worsening economic conditions are two trends in the social environment that built up pressure for changing the retirement age.

A forecasting system deals with both events and trends in some fashion. There are two approaches, according to Wilson, in developing a forecast of the future (see Figure 7.5). One can take scanning information and try to predict long-term trends—take a leap into the future, so to speak, and develop alternative scenarios. Then one can work backwards, through a process of deductive reasoning, to develop hypotheses on the implications of these various futures

[22]Ian H. Wilson, "Environmental Scanning and Strategic Planning," *Business Environment/Public Policy: 1979 Conference Papers*, Lee E. Preston, ed. (St. Louis: AACSB, 1980), pp. 160–161. Quoted with permission.

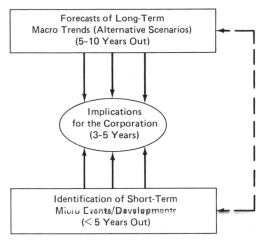

Figure 7.5
Approaches to Forecasting

Source: Ian Wilson, "Characteristics of Futures Research," materials prepared for Conference on Business Environment and Public Policy, Washington University Center for the Study of American Business, July 8–13, 1979, p. 2. Reprinted with permission.

for the corporation in the immediate present. The other approach is to focus on the specific events themselves and continue to monitor them, and then, through a process of inductive reasoning, create a future five years hence based on these events.[23]

These two approaches should be seen as complements to each other rather than as alternative methods of forecasting. Environmental scanning can contribute to both long-term macro forecasts and short-term micro analyses. The purpose of either approach is to identify emerging issues in sufficient time to allow an intelligent response by the corporation. The more lead-time a corporation can have with respect to a given issue, the more options it has open to develop strategies to respond.

Environmental Issues Assessment To be useful for planning purposes, the issues that have been identified as being of concern to the corporation must be ranked or prioritized. The corporation cannot concern itself with everything that has been discovered in the scanning process and forecast as having an impact. It must focus its effort on the issues that are likely to have the greatest impact. They key issues that the environment presents to the organization must be identified and these issues must be further analyzed as to their implications for the organization.

[23]Ibid., pp. 159–160.

One method of prioritizing issues is to lay the issues in a matrix arrangement (see Figure 7.6). The issues have to be analyzed by the forecasting group with the help of management. Decisions must be made about the probability of their occurrence—that they will be significant to large enough segments of society to be placed on the public agenda, and their potential impact on the specific company. Once placed in the appropriate cell of the matrix, the issues can then be categorized into high, medium, and low priority. Those issues falling into the top left-hand portion of the matrix should receive immediate management attention, those in the middle are not as crucial, but still need attention, and those falling in the lower right-hand corner can be put on the back burner for the time being. This assessment, however, must be done periodically, as conditions change quite rapidly. The key to this method, of course, is a correct analysis of the issues according to the two dimensions of the matrix. For this analysis, techniques such as probability analysis, trend impact analysis, cross-impact analysis, and simulation modeling may be useful.

Figure 7.6
Issues Priority Matrix

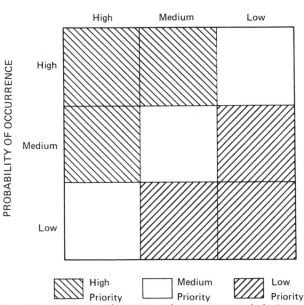

Source: James K. Brown, *This Business of Issues: Coping with the Company's Environments* (New York: The Conference Board, 1979), p. 32. Reprinted with permission.

DEFINITIONS OF PRIORITIES FOR ISSUES: TWO COMPANY EXAMPLES

High priority—those issues on which we need to be well-informed in order to provide knowledgeable counsel or take specific action.

Nice to know—those issues which are interesting but neither critical nor urgent enough to warrant spending a disproportionate amount of time and resources on.

Questionable—those unidentified or unframed issues that will become important as soon as something happens or somebody elevates them.

—Xerox

Priority A: issue is of such critical impact on PPG as to warrant executive management action, including periodic review of the issue and personal participation in implementing plans to manage the issue.

Priority B: the issue is of such critical impact on PPG as to warrant division general manager or staff department executive involvement.

Priority C: the issue has potential impact so as to warrant government and public affairs department surveillance, assessment and reporting.

—PPG Industries

From: James K. Brown, *This Business of Issues: Coping with the Company's Environments* (New York: The Conference Board, 1979), p. 33. Reprinted with permission.

There are less sophisticated methods of prioritizing issues, of course, that use rather broad definitions of categories (see box). The placing of an issue in one of these categories involves management judgment based on the best monitoring and forecasting information available. Different levels of attention are then given to the issues placed in each category. Another company rates issues on a ten-point scale, using the following five criteria. The scores on each of the criteria are totaled to arrive at an overall score that can then be used to prioritize the issues.

- Impact on Earnings: To be considered, an issue must have a quantifiable impact on the company's earnings, through regulation, external pressure, or media crisis.
- Ability to Influence: There must be a reasonable likelihood that the company's involvement in an issue will influence its outcome.

- Public Awareness: A relative judgment is made on the degree to which an issue is perceived as important by the company's various constituencies.
- Probability of Occurrence: How likely is it that, if no action is taken, a given issue will progress to its next life cycle stage?
- Timing: How soon is the issue likely to progress to the next life cycle stage?[24]

Regardless of the method used, the outcome should be some listing of issues in a priority scheme that can be useful for further analysis and planning. These priorities can then be factored into the issues management process of the corporation to develop a position with respect to an issue and strategies that will be effective in implementing that position. By way of summarizing the information presented in this section, Table 7.5 describes the distinctions among scanning, monitoring, forecasting, and assessment. Although it is useful to separate these activities for conceptual purposes, it must be remembered that, in practice, these activities are inextricably intertwined and influence each other.[25]

PUBLIC ISSUES AND STRATEGY FORMULATION Having created an agenda of issues that need further attention, a firm must then formulate and implement appropriate strategic responses for its high-priority issues. The firm's response to an issue should be a set of coordinated actions, some of which may be internally directed to change the corporation itself, while others may be externally directed to impact the environment in which the firm operates. Organizations enter the public policy arena to influence public policy and governmental policy and attempt to influence stakeholder expectations and perceptions of corporate behavior. Corporations can also change their policies and behavior in response to public issues that are significant.

Public issues management, which deals with public policy issues, is actually a subset of the strategic planning universe, which deals with the entire business environment. Strategic planning is the more inclusive of the two processes, but issues management contributes to and parallels strategic planning. Issues management addresses public policy issues that shape and are shaped by the total business environment. Strategic planning, which calls for alternative scenarios about external events and trends, must include consideration of public issues that are critical to the corporation.[26]

Public Issues Life Cycle The notion of a public policy agenda suggests that public issues have a life cycle—they go through a series of stages as they evolve from an issue that is of little

---

[24]Continental Illinois Corporation (now Continental Bank Corporation), "Management Insight," October 1981, p. 4.

[25]Fahey and Narayanan, *Macroenvironmental Analysis*, p. 43.

[26]Arrington and Sawaya, "Managing Public Affairs," p. 153.

Table 7.5
Distinctions Among Scanning, Monitoring, Forecasting, and Assessment

	Scanning	Monitoring	Forecasting	Assessment
Focus	Open-end viewing of environment Identify early signals	Track specific trends and events	Project future patterns and events	Derive implications for organization
Goal	Detect change already under way	Confirm/disconfirm trends	Develop plausible projections of future	Derive implications for organization
Scope	Broad, general environment	Specific trends, patterns, events	Limited to trends, patterns, and issues deemed worthy of forecasting	Critical implications for organization
Time Horizon	Retrospective and current	Real time	Prospective	Prospective and current
Approach	Unconditioned viewing Heterogeneity of stimuli	Conditioned viewing Selective stimuli	Systematic and structured	Systematic, structured, and detailed
Data Characteristics	Unboundable and imprecise Vague and ambiguous	Relatively boundable Gains in precision	Quite specific	Very specific
Data Interpretation	Acts of perception Intuitive reasoning	Weighing evidence Detailing patterns	Judgments about inferences	Judgments about inferences/implications
Data Sources	Broad reading Consulting many types of experts inside and outside of the organization	Focused reading Selective use of individuals Focus groups	Outputs of monitoring Collected via forecasting techniques	Forecasts, Internal strategies Competitive context, etc.
Outputs	Signals of potential change Detection of change under way	Specification of trends Identification of scanning needs	Alternate forecasts Identification of scanning and monitoring needs	Specific organizational implications
Transition	Hunches regarding salience and importance	Judgments regarding relevance to specific organization	Inputs to decisions and decision processes	Action plans
Organizational Outcomes	Awareness of general environment	Consideration and detailing of specific developments Time for developing flexibility	Understanding of plausible futures	Specific actions

Source: Liam Fahey and V. K. Narayanan, *Macroenvironmental Analysis for Strategic Management* (St. Paul: West, 1986), p. 37.

importance to one that receives major public attention and may eventually involve legislation and regulation as a social control mechanism (see Figure 7.7). This concept is an important one for management to grasp, as the development of effective strategies to influence public policy depends on an accurate assessment of the stage the issue is in at any given time in its development.

The life cycle begins with changing public expectations that create a gap between corporate performance and what the public expects from its institutions. These changes are most likely the result of structural changes in society that cause strains between expectations and what is actually happening in society. The seeds of a new public issue are sown when the gap becomes wide

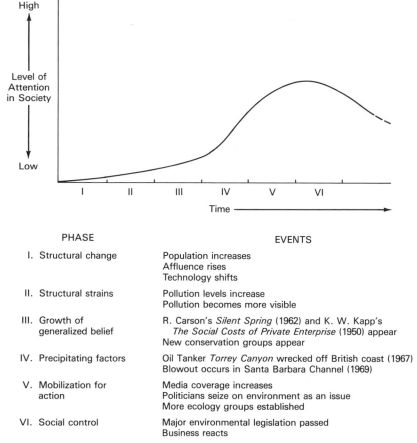

Figure 7.7
Application of The Life Cycle Concept

PHASE	EVENTS
I. Structural change	Population increases Affluence rises Technology shifts
II. Structural strains	Pollution levels increase Pollution becomes more visible
III. Growth of generalized belief	R. Carson's *Silent Spring* (1962) and K. W. Kapp's *The Social Costs of Private Enterprise* (1950) appear New conservation groups appear
IV. Precipitating factors	Oil Tanker *Torrey Canyon* wrecked off British coast (1967) Blowout occurs in Santa Barbara Channel (1969)
V. Mobilization for action	Media coverage increases Politicians seize on environment as an issue More ecology groups established
VI. Social control	Major environmental legislation passed Business reacts

Source: Grover Starling, *The Politics and Economics of Public Policy: An Introductory Analysis with Cases* (Homewood, IL: Dorsey, 1979), p. 141. Reprinted by permission of Brooks/Cole Publishing Company, Pacific Grove, CA 93950.

enough to affect significant numbers of people and cause extensive dissatisfaction with corporate performance. The issue begins to be discussed at grass-roots levels and people begin to form opinions. These new expectations may then become successfully politized. As the issue becomes widely discussed in the media and becomes a concern for interest group discussion, it may be picked up by some politicians to be introduced into the formal public policy process. Perhaps some major precipitating events will occur, such as a major oil spill or chemical disaster, that will galvanize the issue and harden public opinion. Thus the issue is brought before the public and is placed on the public policy agenda where it will most likely be the subject of some kind of action.

The legislative phase refers to the time period surrounding the enactment of legislation dealing with the issue and its implementation. The rules of the game for business are being changed in this phase with the formal enactment of legislative and regulatory requirements. New legislation and regulations may require considerable debate and bargaining and even be the subject of court rulings. But at this stage, the issue has become institutionalized as society has changed the contract between business and society and expressed its expectations in formal legislation and regulation.

The last stage, which has been called the litigation phase, is one of implementing the new rules of the game. During this period, there may be many negotiations between government and business regarding enforcement standards and timetables for meeting the new requirements. If government agencies do not believe business is successfully meeting the new rules and negotiations break down, the agencies may file suit in court to force compliance. In this stage, the adversarial relationship between business and government is most pronounced, and the opportunities for cooperation to meet public expectations are severely limited.

Generic Strategies   The particular model adopted and the number of stages involved are probably not as significant as simply recognizing the importance of the public issues life cycle and keeping this notion in mind when developing strategies.[27] With respect to strategy formulation in regard to high-priority issues, there are certain generic strategies or overall response patterns that can be described within which more short-term or specific strategies can be chosen. There are four such major response patterns to public issues (see Table 7.6) that can be described and that corporations have adopted at one time or another.

In the *reactive* response pattern, business does not treat a public issue as within the domain of its concern, at least as far as changing corporate behavior is concerned, and opposes any change that public policy would make in corporate operations. Business by and large adopted this pattern in the late 1960s regard-

[27]See James E. Post, *Corporate Behavior and Social Change* (Reston, Va.: Reston Publishing Co., 1978), p. 26, and Continental Illinois Corporation, "Management Insight," October 1981, p. 2 for other models of the public issues life cycle.

Table 7.6
Corporate Responses to Public Issues

Reactive	Accommodative	Proactive	Interactive
Fighting change	Adapting to change	Influencing change	Adjusting to and Influencing change

ing consumer legislation. Usually no attempt is made to anticipate public issues in this pattern, nor does business try to develop a constructive position about the issues. But business will use every means at its disposal to fight change by blocking any resolution of the issue that would change corporate behavior. The organization attempts to postpone public policy decisions with tactical maneuvers. Another word that has been used to describe this response pattern is *stonewalling*.

The *accommodative* response means that business simply adapts to the changes involved with a public policy measure as best as possible and attempts to resume as quickly as possible its main line of business. The company makes no attempt to fight or influence change in any manner, nor does it set up any kind of a mechanism to anticipate change. The concerns expressed in legislation and regulation are accepted as legitimate, and are accommodated with the appropriate operational and organizational changes.

In the *proactive* response, business develops some kind of a mechanism to anticipate those public issues that will affect the corporation most significantly. Rather than fighting change or simply accommodating to the changes a public issue may involve, the corporation attempts to influence change by changing the environment in which issues arise and are discussed. The goal of a proactive strategy is to prevent change from becoming necessary, if possible, or at least to minimize the effects of a particular public issue on the corporation. Business takes an initiative in this pattern and engages in independent behavior. It does not just respond to the actions of other parties. The firm tries to alter the expectations of stakeholders and change public opinion to reduce the gap between public expectations and perceptions of corporate performance.

In the *interactive* response pattern, the corporation recognizes the legitimacy of public policy as a process through which public expectations are expressed and the fact that business and society are related to each other complexly. This complexity involves the use of different strategies by the corporation to adjust to changing public expectations. This pattern emphasizes working out problems through mutual participation and adaption, without prior determination of outcomes or any clear "victory" or "defeat." Success involves the development or negotiation of an arrangement that commands the cooperation of all significant parties. As stated by James Post, a professor at Boston University:

Public Issues Management

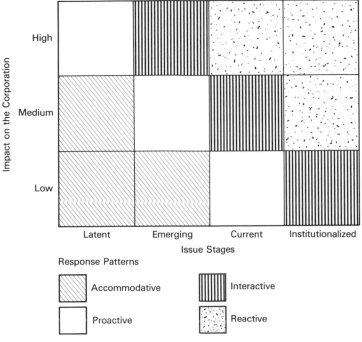

Figure 7.8
Strategic Dimensions of Public Issues

Source: Rogene A. Buchholz, William D. Evans, and Robert O. Wagley, *Management Responses to Public Issues: Concepts and Cases in Strategy Formulation* (Englewood Cliffs, NJ: Prentice Hall, 1985), p. 57. Reprinted by permission of Prentice Hall.

Sometimes action is taken to influence public opinion; at other times, to change corporate behavior. The two prerequisites for successfully using the interactive approach are a management commitment to anticipating external change and a willingness to adjust the corporation's normal operations to minimize the gap between performance and expectations. When consistently applied over time, an interactive approach tends to produce goals that the company and the public can accept.[28]

Public issues management comes into play in choosing an overall strategy or response pattern based on a systematic analysis of the issues and a discussion of alternatives. The analysis of issues and the choice of an overall strategy can be depicted in a matrix model (see Figure 7.8) that shows the relationship of the timing of an issue to its impact on the corporation. Whether an issue is emerging or current, and whether its impact is high, low, or medium, has some bearing on the choice of an overall strategy.

[28]James E. Post, "Public Affairs and Management Policy in the 1980s," *Public Affairs Review*, vol. I (1980), p. 8.

If an issue is latent and its impact on the corporation is judged to be low or high, or if an issue is emerging and its impact is judged to be low, an accommodative strategy might make the best sense. The cost to the corporation of adapting to the public's expectations may be relatively low in these cases. Such adaption may just satisfy public expectations enough to prevent the issue from reaching a further stage. For example, if business had adjusted its retirement policies to meet the expectations of an aging workforce a few years ago, government legislation on this matter may not have been necessary.

Latent issues that have a high impact, emerging issues that have a medium impact, and current issues that have a low impact would seem to demand a proactive strategy. Either the impact on the corporation is high enough to justify an expenditure of effort to try and prevent change, or the issue is so far along in its life cycle that a proactive strategy is necessary to try and minimize the effect of particular legislation that is being considered. Thus business is better off to try and influence the environment in which issues are being discussed or public policy formulated rather than simply accommodating itself to changing public expectations.

Issues that are emerging and have a high impact, current issues that have a medium impact, and institutionalized issues that have a low impact call for an interactive strategy. The issue will either have such a high impact or be so far along in its life cycle, that some kind of change on the part of the corporation is inevitable. But the nature of this change can still be affected by a proactive strategy, even if the issue is institutionalized. In this last stage of an issue, corporations can still work interactively with regulatory agencies to shape the particular regulations being written and make them more cost effective.

A reactive strategy may make the most sense when an issue is well along in its life cycle and the impact on a corporation is high as far as changes in corporate operations are concerned. Public expectations are already formalized at this point, and a reactive strategy is about all business has left. Thus it may make sense for business to challenge regulations in court, for example, either to buy time or to hope for a favorable court ruling that would overturn the regulation or modify it in some fashion.

Political Strategies

The choice of an overall or generic strategy is not the only strategic decision that business has to make with respect to a public issue. There is the matter of choosing political strategies (sometimes called *tactics*) to respond to issues of concern. Once business has chosen an overall or generic strategy and decided how to deal with changing public expectations, it has to decide on political strategies to accomplish these overall objectives. Shall it engage in advocacy advertising to influence public opinion? Should it lobby more effectively than in the past? Should the corporation form a Political Action Committee to try and influence an election or the vote of a representative? Should it file a lawsuit to try and prevent a rule from being implemented? The answers to these questions depend on the specific circumstances surrounding the issue and the resources the corporation has available. These political strategies (or tactics) must be consistent with the overall strategic pattern the corporation has decided to adopt. (Further discussion of this topic will be found in Chapter 8.)

Once a strategy is developed, it must be integrated with other strategic plans of the corporation in the development of a total corporate strategy. Nothing could be more important than the integration of public issues into a total corporate plan with respect to product development, capital expansion, hiring and promotion policies, and other corporate activities. Public issues management must be integrated forward into the strategic planning process as well as backward into operational planning. Yet it is on this dimension that most corporations have the greatest difficulty. Today, the company that shuts down a plant without recognizing that such a shutdown is not just a private matter but is indeed a public issue, is begging for trouble. The same can be said for many other issues that have been traditionally thought to be private in nature. Strategy must be developed with regard to any issue that has public dimensions and be integrated into overall corporate planning.

EVALUATING PUBLIC ISSUES MANAGEMENT

Evaluating the public issues managment effort poses, as the Conference Board points out, a conundrum. Evaluation is important as a basis for future planning and budgeting regarding the effort. Yet using either a management-by-objectives approach or a results-oriented evaluation can be very frustrating—so much so that many companies simply abandon the evaluation effort entirely. There are no reliable yardsticks, many executives believe, with which a company can measure the effectiveness of its public issues management effort. Some even believe that there is no need to evaluate the effort, since it is a job that simply must be done regardless of the results.[29]

> As is the case with many other staff functions whose impact on corporate profits is not immediately evident, external relations does not readily lend itself to measurement. This general difficulty is compounded in the case of external relations by the multitude of influences outside of management's sphere of control that can and do affect the issues and publics that corporate external relations programs are aimed at. In most areas, "results achieved," whether good or bad, cannot be attributed to corporate actions alone.[30]

Financial measures do not lead to a realistic bottom-line figure for a function as nebulous as public issues management. Other objective measures (e.g., a count of bills defeated or passed) say nothing about how much or how

[29]Phyllis McGrath, *Managing Corporate External Relations: Changing Perspectives and Responses* (New York: The Conference Board, 1976), pp. 68-69.
[30]Ibid., p. 64.

little one company's efforts had to do with the results. Subjective criteria based on the judgment of those being evaluated are not likely to offer much credibility.[31] Yet a company must expect some payoffs from the activity or it will not be continued. There are a number of payoffs that may stem from a successful public issues management program (see box).

PAYOFFS FROM ISSUES PROGRAMS

(1) Competitive advantages—in marketing, products, corporate image
(2) Salutary changes in corporate behavior.
(3) Avoidance of serious mistakes made in the absence of issues programs
(4) Ability to detect issues and develop corporate responses to them while they are in an emerging stage, when a company has more options and will incur less cost in confronting them.
(5) Enhancement of the firms credibility.
(6) Reduced vulnerability to "the slings and arrows of outrageous fortune."
(7) Indirect benefits—for example, greater management confidence in its decisions; improvements in planning; acceptance by management that the future will be different from the past.

Source: James K. Brown, *Guidelines for Managing Corporate Issues Programs* (New York: The Conference Board, 1981), p. 33.

Corporations that do evaluate the effort on a more systematic basis generally use one of two approaches: (1) evaluation on the basis of set objectives or (2) evaluation on the basis of activities carried out. Regarding the first approach, the two objectives of public issues management most frequently mentioned were to improve business credibility and to develop a positive corporate image. The former is the most global objective, as the restoration of public trust usually refers to not just one company or even one industry, but to the total business community. The attainment of a positive corporate image relates to the degree of public acceptance of the company.[32] The following are among some of the results looked for in accomplishing this objective.

- Accurate and objective coverage by the media.
- The ability to conduct the regular business of the corporation without interference, and the continued growth of the company.
- A sound environment for advancing the marketing and investment objectives of the company.

---

[31]Patti Nelson Andrews, "The Sticky Wicket of Evaluating Public Affairs: Thoughts About a Framework," *Public Affairs Review* (1985), p. 95.

[32]McGrath, *External Relations*, p. 64.

- Some perceptible degree of change in external attitudes to the company.
- Some degree of success in anticipating problems; a minimum of surprises from the company's publics.[33]

Judgment about attainment of these objectives is based on informal or formal feedback. Informal feedback includes the feedback a CEO gets when he or she comes into contact with business peers, from other people who are not part of the business community, and even from family and friends. Senior management also obtains feedback from employees, customers, educators, and government officials. The opinion survey is most frequently used to determine whether or not the company's message is reaching its targeted publics.[34]

Evaluation on the basis of activities focuses on what the public issues management group is doing. This evaluation can get as specific as measuring the number of contacts with legislators, the number of internal communications issued, or the number of people involved in the grass-roots lobbying program. Meeting budgeted forecasts is an activity measure used in some corporations.[35] Focusing on such activities is more of an input-oriented measure, however, and say nothing about the results of such activities in terms of actual benefits for the company.

Companies could also adopt a process orientation to the problem of evaluation. The process approach would focus on the system the company uses to participate in the formulation of public policy that will affect the company. This approach asks questions about the effectiveness of the process. Does the analysis that leads to company positions accurately capture details of present and prospective line operations? Does the overall process for developing and representing company positions avoid redundance? Are line managers and executive management sufficiently involved in position development and advocacy? Are external issues of concern sufficiently addressed by the issue management process? Are issues and their resolution taken into appropriate account in company planning?[36]

The formulation of objectives and policies was found to have a positive correlation to perceived success in external affairs, according to one study, even though only 57 percent of the respondents indicated their companies had established such policies and objectives. Over 72 percent of the firms had a formal evaluation mechanism, however, suggesting that many firms are evaluating their external affairs effort without formal objectives. Again, the existence of an evaluation procedure was linked to a higher level of perceived success.[37] Thus evaluation and setting of objectives may be important factors in the process, at

[33]Ibid., p. 65.

[34]Ibid., pp. 65–66.

[35]Ibid., pp. 66–67.

[36]Arrington and Sawaya, "Managing Public Affairs," p. 152.

[37]W. Harvey Hegarty, John C. Alpin, and Richard A. Cosier, "Achieving Corporate Success in External Affairs," *Business Horizons*, vol. 21, no. 5 (October 1978), pp. 70–72.

least as far as perceived success of the public issues management effort is concerned.

There are several obstacles to a successful public issues management effort. According to W. Howard Chase, these include: (1) the ignorance of managers of the evolving literature in public issues management and of their inexperience in the management of public policy issues; (2) the fear and resistance to innovation at both senior- and middle-management levels; (3) the tendency among professional societies and organizations to institutionalize, homogenize, or degrade their original objectives; (4) the proclivity of CEOs to delegate responsibility for external relations and public policy considerations to upper middle-management without regard to past experience; and (5) what Chase calls the "Neanderthal Urge" to fight fire with fire.[38]

Despite the difficulty of evaluating the public issues management effort and the existence of serious obstacles to its success, the public issues management effort is indispensable to most corporations. Some effort needs to be made to deal with social and political issues that affect corporations. An issues management function will have to be developed to handle this task and develop strategies that will give corporations some control over this part of their environment. The public issues management effort has beomce professionalized over the years to perform these tasks. Today, there is even a professional association of issues managers, called the Issues Management Association, that brings together people from U.S. and Canadian companies who perform issue management activities. Created in 1982, this organization has over 400 members, consisting of corporate managers, trade association managers, public sector managers, consultants, and academicians.

SELECTED REFERENCES

AGUILAR, FRANCIS JOSEPH. *Scanning the Business Environment.* New York: Macmillan, 1967.

BROWN, JAMES K. *This Business of Issues: Coping with the Company's Environments.* New York: The Conference Board, 1979.

CHASE, W. HOWARD. *Issue Management: Origins of the Future.* Stamford, Conn.: Issue Action Publications, 1984.

COATES, J. F. *Issues Identification and Management: The State of the Art of Methods and Techniques.* Palo Alto, Calif.: Electric Power Research Institute, 1985.

EYESTONE, R. *From Social Issues to Public Policy.* New York: Wiley, 1978.

FAHEY, LIAM, and V. K. NARAYANAN. *Macroenvironmental Analysis for Strategic Management.* St. Paul: West, 1986.

---

[38]Chase, *Issue Management,* p. 96.

Fox, J. Ronald. *Managing Business-Government Relations.* Homewood, Ill.: Irwin, 1982.

Freeman, R. Edward, and Daniel R. Gilbert, Jr. *Corporate Strategy and the Search for Ethics.* Englewood Cliffs, N.J.: Prentice-Hall, 1988.

Gollner, A. B. *Social Change and Corporate Strategy.* Stamford, Conn.: Issue Action Publications, 1983.

Heath, Robert L., and Richard Alan Nelson. *Issues Management: Corporate Public Policymaking in an Information Society.* Beverly Hills: Sage Publications, 1986.

Heath, Robert L. and Associates. *Strategic Issues Management.* San Francisco: Jossey-Bass, 1988.

Marcus, Alfred, A., Allen M. Kaufman, and David R. Beam. *Business Strategy and Public Policy. Perspectives from Industry and Academia.* New York: Quorum Books, 1987.

McGrath, Phyllis. *Action Plans for Public Affairs.* New York: The Conference Board, 1977.

————*Managing Corporate External Relations: Changing Perspectives and Responses.* New York: The Conference Board, 1976.

————*Redefining Federal Corporate Relations.* New York: The Conference Board, 1979.

Nagelschmidt, J. S., ed. *The Public Affairs Handbook.* New York: AMACOM, 1982.

Post, James E. *Corporate Behavior and Social Change.* Reston, Va.: Reston Publishing Co., 1976.

Schipper, F., and M. M. Jennings. *Business Strategy for the Political Arena.* Westport, Conn.: Greenwood Press, 1984.

Tombari, Henry A. *Business and Society: Strategies for the Environment and Public Policy.* New York: Dryden, 1984.

8

CORPORATE POLITICAL STRATEGIES

⟸ **IDEAS TO BE FOUND** ⟹
IN THIS CHAPTER

- Influencing Public Opinion
- Public Policy Formulation
- Public Policy Implementation
- Business and the Political Process

Since public policy is formulated through a political process, corporations must be active in this process to have some influence on the outcome, just as they are active in the exchange process to determine the value of the goods and services they provide. Corporations have values with respect to public goods and services as well, and these values have to be registered through some kind of political activity in order to have an impact on public policy. Nonparticipation in the political process means an implicit acceptance of other groups' priorities and solutions whether or not other alternatives more amenable to business interests might have been available.[1]

Participation in public policy is both a basic responsibility of corporate executives and a management function which, like any other, must be approached with systematic business discipline. Corporations must establish public policy objectives, set priorities, implement a working plan and set guidelines for measuring their success. In the world of today, the diverse

[1]Mike H. Ryan, Carl L. Swanson, and Rogene A. Buchholz, *Corporate Strategy, Public Policy, and the Fortune 500: How America's Major Corporations Influence Government* (Oxford: Basil Blackwell Ltd, 1987), p. 16

activities we call government and public relations, lobbying and issue advertising, must all be part of an integrated management strategy.[2]

The methods that corporations have for participating in the public policy process will be discussed in a framework that corresponds with the various stages of the public policy life cycle. The first stage concerns the formation of public opinion on specific issues that affect business or attitudes toward business in general. By helping to shape public opinion, corporations can exercise a broad influence in the society as a whole. The second stage is public policy formulation, a critical area when Congress or the executive branch is considering specific legislative proposals or holding hearings on issues of concern to business. The corporation has various ways by which it can participate in this stage of public policy formulation. The last stage occurs after legislation is passed, when regulations are being written and court decisions made on specific issues that affect business.

Obviously, these stages overlap—activities useful at one stage may also be effective at another—but certain activities seem more appropriate at one stage than another and will be discussed accordingly. The purpose of the public issues management system described in the previous chapter is to select the political activities or tactics that will be effective in accomplishing the overall strategy with respect to a public issue. Knowledge of the uses and limitations of the various political strategies is essential in making this choice.

INFLUENCING PUBLIC OPINION

The first stage of the public policy life cycle can be called the stage of public opinion formation. At this stage, the concern of the corporate strategist is with the emergence and development of public opinion. The primary focus is on emerging issues of concern to business. In this first stage, the major strategic approach available to corporations for influencing the public policy process is communicating its view on public issues to the public at large. Participation in the public policy debate gives the company the opportunity to present alternatives that could obviate the need for specific regulation altogether. From a corporation's point of view, the effect of a good communication strategy is that it reduces the need for other more expensive and potentially troublesome strategic options further along in the public policy life cycle. Once a corporation has determined its position on a particular public issue, this viewpoint should be expressed through a cohesive, coordinated communication strategy established at the highest levels of the company.

Communication has long been an operational concern of corporations as evidenced by the vast amounts of time, money, and effort spent on advertising

[2]David Rockefeller, "Free Trade in Ideas," at the Wharton School, Philadelphia, January 19, 1978, as quoted in W. Howard Chase, *Issues Management: Origins of the Future* (Stamford, Conn.: Issue Action Publications, Inc., 1984), pp. 30–31.

and public relations. More recently, corporate communication has been considered a major component of a political strategy. Many people in business believe it is important to identify key issues in society that may affect business and to engage in a debate about these issues before they are picked up by the formal political system. At such an early stage, the options that business has to deal with an issue are broadest and thus have the greatest potential of being very effective. Some argue that when government gets involved with an issue, it is too late for business to have much effect on the outcome. Government is reactive, they believe, and when it does finally begin to consider an issue, such as hazardous waste disposal, society has already made up its mind and the general outlines of policy on that issue have already been formed.

In any event, the use of communication as a political strategy has become more important, reflecting changes in the external environment of the corporation regarding public concern over corporate activities and a concomitant increase in government scrutiny and regulation. Corporations have a choice of various methods to participate at this stage of the public issue life cycle and attempt to influence public opinion on a specific issue of business and the free enterprise system in general. These methods include speaking out on issues to public groups, using the annual report to communicate about public policy issues, using advocacy advertising to engage in the debate about controversial issues, using image advertising to improve public perceptions of a company or industry, and using economic education programs to improve public knowledge about the economic system.

Speaking Out on Issues

One such method is the attempt of business to get involved in speaking out on issues that concern the company's interests. Management at some companies spends a good deal of time taking advantage of opportunities to speak to civic groups, participate in conferences, speak to high school and college classes, write articles for business journals or newspapers, meet with the media, and similar opportunities to get its viewpoint before the public. Some corporations have changed from a posture of keeping quiet on issues and working behind the scenes to one of raising their voices in public and becoming much more visible. This strategy not only involves top management at headquarters, but management at all levels in communities where company facilities are located.

The success of this method of influencing public opinion depends a great deal on how well business has done its homework. The position that management takes on an issue must be factually correct and defensible. Those who "go public" can expect to be questioned, sometimes hostilely, by their audience. If the homework is done well, however, and the business people involved have communications skills to articulate a business position and engage in debate, this can be an effective way to influence public opinion and gain credibility with the public. Increased communications with the public can be a positive factor in shaping public opinion with respect to business and the business system. Instead of sending out a public relations representative who has neither the knowledge or authority to say anything meaningful about corporate policies or operations, management itself should get involved in speaking to the public. The corporation is often better represented by someone who can respond confidently to unanticipated questions.

The leading role in this type of corporate advocacy is played by the chief executive officer of the company. The example of the top corporate officer sets the pattern for the total organizational effort. A Conference Board survey of 395 CEOs of major manufacturing, financial, and utility firms found that 26 percent of the CEOs described themselves as public communicators who spoke out widely on public issues. Another 21 percent were company spokespeople who took their views to the top levels of government and made them known to shareholders and customers, but did not beam their opinions at the general public.[3] Thus there is some evidence to suggest that a good many CEOs are taking this role of speaking out on issues seriously.

There are problems, however, with this approach. One problem is the speaker's credibility. For whom is the manager speaking? What group does his or her position represent? Who is the corporation? Agreement on a position may be reached by the management of a corporation, but is management alone the corporation? What about shareholders, customers, and employees? These constituencies, if indeed they are a legitimate part of the corporation, will undoubtedly have different views on an issue. How, then, can these diverse views be represented in a single "corporate" position? A public issues management system can be useful in establishing the legitimacy of a particular viewpoint.

A second problem concerns the kinds of issues in which business gets involved. If these issues are only those in which the company has a significant stake, the company can be criticized as pursuing only its own narrow self-interest at the expense of the public interest. This may only contribute more to the credibility problem that business already has with the public. To gain credibility, it is argued, business must concern itself with broader interests rather than just its own self-interest. It must seek to understand the concerns of other groups in society outside the business community and engage in debate about a broad range of issues that have a bearing on the quality of life. The Conference Board survey mentioned earlier found that over half of the executives in the sample were prepared to go beyond issues directly affecting their companies and speak out on broad public policies affecting the society as a whole.[4]

Finally, there is a question of how much influence business can have over public opinion with this method no matter how credible the message or the speaker. Most managers have a recognition problem the same as many public

[3]"Study Classifies 40% of Chief Executives 'Political Activists'," *The Wall Street Journal*, March 26, 1980, p. 12.

[4]"Political Activists," *the Wall Street Journal*, March 26, 1980, p. 12.

officials. Who knows them? And worse yet, how many people seriously listen to their opinions? To overcome this problem, managers might direct their efforts to the opinion leaders in society or in a community—those people who are influential in molding public opinion on an issue. Channels of communication must be chosen that are effective in reaching audiences where the message can have a significant impact.

The Annual Report The annual report represents the "official" publication of the corporation, having gone through a rigorous course of review and approval before being published. Therefore, it provides a source of ratification and legitimization as far as corporate communication is concerned that is not available for most other channels. It provides a means of directing corporate public policy statements to anyone who might find them useful and interesting at a low incremental cost to the organization. Most corporations print two or three times the number of annual reports that would be required for shareholders alone. In addition to shareholders, annual reports are typically distributed to suppliers, customers, financial analysts, brokers, librarians, business editors, government officials, academicians, students, and any other individual or group showing interest in the company.

Anyone who has the slightest interest in a corporation can easily obtain its annual report. Therefore, companies wishing to communicate their position on some public issue may reach a wide audience at a low cost by putting that information in their most important, widely distributed, and legitimate public document. The annual report can be used as a multipurpose tool—to report on financial information to shareholders and to communicate a corporate position on public policy issues to a larger audience that it wants to influence. The use of the annual report to communicate public policy positions should be encouraged.

A survey based on 1980 annual reports showed that over half (53.6 percent) of the Fortune 500 firms engaged in some form of public policy commentary. This finding was the result of an exhaustive content analysis of all Fortune 500 annual reports for that year. Over half (53.6 percent) of those companies that used the annual report as a channel for public policy commentary took a proactive approach in suggesting alternative courses of action to resolve public issues. The rest (47.8 percent) described the impact that specific issues would make on their company but did not concern themselves with policy making. Larger companies were more likely to engage in a proactive strategy.[5]

Almost all (99 percent) of the issues covered in the annual report were national in scope rather than regional, and the great majority (86 percent) of the public policy commentary was located in the chairperson's or president's letter. About two-thirds of the firms covered two or fewer issues in the annual report, choosing to focus their efforts on those issues of greatest concern. The public

[5]Ryan, Swanson, and Buchholz, *Public Policy*, pp. 73–76.

issues of greatest concern had to do with economic conditions, government regulation, inflation, energy policy, and tax policy.[6] These issues are not surprising, given the conditions that existed at the end of the 1970s. These findings thus suggest that the annual report is being used to some extent to communicate public policy information in the hopes of influencing the debate about issues of concern to the corporation.

Advocacy Advertising   This method has been defined as a form of advertising in which business takes a public position on controversial issues of public importance, aggressively stating and defending its viewpoint and criticizing those of opponents. Advocacy advertising is "concerned with the propagation of ideas and elucidation of controversial social issues of public importance in a manner that supports the position and interests of the sponsor while expressly denying the accuracy of facts and downgrading the sponsor's opponents."[7] Such advertising is designed to reach a general audience or, in some cases, a more targeted segment of the public, with messages regarding public policy issues. Advocacy advertising can be used to deal with specific issues, such as a national energy policy (see Exhibit 8.1) or general issues, such as public attitudes toward free enterprise or capitalism.

Advocacy advertising might be used for a number of reasons. One reason may be to counteract public hostility caused by ignorance or misinformation. Surveys indicate that the public has a grossly distorted view of after-tax profits, believing that business sometimes makes twenty-eight cents on a dollar of sales rather than the four cents average business as a whole actually makes.[8] Such misperceptions, if allowed to continue unchecked, can lead to a great deal of public hostility toward business that has taken place in the last decade.[9] Advocacy advertising can attempt to counter this hostility by presenting businesses' side of the story in as factual and objective a manner as possible.[10]

Advocacy advertising can also be used to counteract the spread of misleading information by critics and fill the need for greater explication of complex issues. Business often believes that its critics oversimplify many issues, whether it is hazardous waste disposal or nuclear safety, thus creating false impressions

---

[6]Ibid., pp. 77–82.

[7]S. Prakash Sethi, "Advocacy Advertising as a Strategy of Corporate Response to Societal Pressures: The American Experience," *Business and Its Changing Environment*, proceedings of a conference held at UCLA, July 24–August 3, 1977, p. 56.

[8]See "America's Growing Antibusiness Mood," *Business Week*, June 17, 1972, pp. 100–103.

[9]See Ibid.; Also Seymour Martin Lipset and William Schneider, "How's Business? What the Public Thinks," *Public Opinion*, vol. 1, no. 4 (July–August 1978), pp. 41–45; Daniel Yankelovich, "On the Legitimacy of Business," *Issues in Business and Society*, 2nd ed., George A. Steiner and John F. Steiner, eds. (New York: Random House, 1977), pp. 76–79; Seymour Martin Lipset and William Schneider, *The Confidence Gap* (New York: The Free Press, 1983).

[10]S. Prakash Sethi, "Advocacy Advertising and the Development of an Effective Corporate External Communications Program," *Private Enterprise and Public Purpose*, S. Prakash Sethi and Carl L. Swanson, eds. (New York: Random House, 1977), pp. 76–79.

Exhibit 8.1

NEEDED: A NATIONAL ENERGY DEBATE

(The following is excerpted from a talk delivered by Allen E. Murray, chairman and chief executive officer, at Mobil's annual meeting in Seattle May 7.)

There have been many warnings of a U.S. oil crisis to come, including three recent reports by the Department of Energy, the National Petroleum Council, and the American Petroleum Institute. All three included a laundry list of the steps the U.S. government could take to avert future shortages and gasoline lines. Some seem reasonable and necessary. Others, like an oil import fee, I consider counterproductive. But I'm not going to debate these possible solutions today.

Instead, I'd simply like to point out some aspects of the topic that are often overlooked. For one thing, the issue is worldwide, and not just a U.S. problem to be solved by U.S. measures. OPEC produces 40% of the Free World's oil every day and the facts of life are such that this nation will never again be able to do without imported oil, some of it from OPEC. The U.S. is not alone in this. Almost every Free World industrialized nation is in the same situation.

Second, I'd like to point out that what's really under discussion is worldwide availability of *energy*—not just oil. Any energy source will help us. For instance, natural gas can substitute for home heating oil. Nuclear can replace heavy industrial oil for generating electricity. The technology exists to convert coal to gasoline. Canadian gas, French nuclear plants and Wyoming coal can all make our oil outlook more secure.

Third, any rational discussion of our energy future requires a long range commitment. Energy is an enormous business, and it will take years to affect the direction in which we are going. Current proposals, such as the decontrol of natural gas, removal of the windfall profits tax and opening up more areas for exploration have merit—but they are only stopgap measures. While they should be done, they aren't long range solutions. Finally, solving any issue of this magnitude requires trade-offs and a clear agreement on national goals. When we object to the level of oil imports, have we thought through the alternatives? Are we willing to burn more coal? Should we have more nuclear plants? Should we use higher prices to force energy savings? What is it we really want?

These issues are going to affect our entire lives. They will affect our environment, our national security, our federal and local budgets, our trade balance and the quality of our lives for generations to come.

We need a national debate. A debate where all the alternatives are discussed. A debate where we must eventually agree—although it won't be easy—on where we want the United States to be twenty or fifty years from now. A debate that sets a framework for action.

Our government owes this to us. Stopgap—often politicized—measures are not enough.

How will Mobil be affected? Regardless of the options chosen, there will be plenty of opportunities ahead for enterprising, flexible, efficient multinational companies who can bring consumers all over the world the energy they want and need. This is, of course, the kind of company we already are. But sensible policies would make our work easier and more productive. They would also make everybody's economic future infinitely more secure.

Reprinted with permission of Mobil Corporation.

in the minds of the public. Through advocacy advertising, business can present its side of the issue to counter-balance information given to the public by its opponents. In the process of presenting another side to an issue, the issue itself receives greater exposure and explication than would otherwise be the case.[11]

Another use of advocacy advertising is to foster values of the free-enterprise system, which many businesspeople believe have been eroded by the growth of a welfare state with "cradle-to-the-grave" security, and ever-expanding government regulation that saps industrial initiative and creativity. By reinforcing traditional values and beliefs, perhaps free enterprise can be restored and the autonomy of business preserved.[12] This use of advocacy advertising is more ideological in nature and attempts to build support for the business system and elicit commitment to the values of that system.

There are a great many problems with this role of advocacy advertising, however, not the least of which is a possible incongruity between the message and the reality. When business goes hat in hand to Washington and asks for protection from foreign competition or a loan guarantee for a failing business, it does not present an image of having confidence in the free enterprise philosophy it often espouses. There is more danger in this usage of advocacy advertising than perhaps any other. The public is quick to see through an ideological shell game.

Finally, advocacy advertising can be used to counteract inadequate access to and bias in the news media. Businesspeople contend that their access to the television news media is inadequate when compared with the amount of time devoted to discussing the viewpoints of the opposition. Television shows such as *60 Minutes* came in for particular criticism. One company went to great lengths to create its own version in rebuttal of the *60 Minutes* program about the company, much of it footage that *60 Minutes* chose not to air to the public.[13] Thus the media is often seen as an adversary of business. According to Louis Banks, a former editor of *Fortune:*

> We are fed a daily diet of authoritative ignorance, most of which conveys a cheap-shot hostility to business and businessmen. Here is where the nation sees a persistently distorted image of its most productive and pervasive activity, business. . . . The reporters and the editors in the general media are woefully ignorant of the complexities and ambiguities of corporate operations, and being so, are easy targets for politicians or pressure group partisans with special axes to grind at the expense of business.[14]

[11]Ibid., pp. 404–406.

[12]Ibid., pp. 406–407.

[13]See "Illinois Power Pans '60 Minutes'," *The Wall Street Journal*, June 27, 1980, p. 18.

[14]Louis Banks, "Media Responsibility for Economic Literacy," speech given at the Annual John Hancock Awards for Excellence in Business and Financial Journalism, "A Bicentennial Examination of the Free Market System," John Hancock Mutual Life Insurance Co., Boston, October 28, 1975, as quoted in Sethi, "Corporate External Communications," p. 407. See also Louis Banks, "Taking on the Hostile Media," *Harvard Business Review*, vol. 56, no. 2 (March–April 1978), pp. 123–130.

There is some evidence to suggest that media personnal are more liberal and Democratic than the public at large. While basically supportive of private enterprise, they also show a strong preference for welfare capitalism, supporting assistance to the poor in the form of income redistribution and guaranteed employment. The media show a clear preference for post-buorgeois goals such as citizen participation and a humane society.[15] Because of differences like this, questions have been raised about journalism's qualifications as an objective profession.

The key issue, however, according to Michael Jay Robinson, writing in *Public Opinion*, is whether this liberal bias that exists in the minds of media personnal finds its way into their news reporting. After analyzing more than 6,000 news stories and testing almost every dimension of press behavior in a media analysis project at George Washington University which focused on network and wire coverage of the 1980 national political campaign, Robinson stated that there was no liberal bias in the reporting of this campaign. His conclusion was that in "looking at domestic press content, it seems fairly clear that most hard news reporting, whatever its shortcomings, reflects the canons of objectivity more often than the political opinions of the newspeople themselves."[16]

Advocacy advertising can be used to counteract this bias and distorted presentation, to the extent it exists, and influence public opinion toward a more positive image of business. The corporation can offer its technical knowledge and experience on particular public issues to rebut false impressions created by the media. The net effect can be to broaden the debate about an issue by letting the public hear another side to the story in rebuttals to media charges.[17]

The right of corporations to speak out on public issues in this manner was upheld by the Supreme Court in a 1978 decision. This ruling struck down a Massachusetts law, upheld by a state court, that made it a criminal offense for any bank or business incorporated in the state to spend money to influence a vote on referendum proposals in the state other than those materially affecting the property, business, or assets of the corporation. The specific instance in the case concerned a referendum to win voter approval for a graduated, rather than a flat-rate, income tax, which the law stated did not materially affect corporations. This law was challenged by a few banks and corporations in Massachusetts. The majority of the Supreme Court held that the type of speech the companies wanted to engage in was at the heart of the protection offered by the

[15]S. Robert Lichter and Stanley Rothman, "Media and Business Elites," *Public Opinion*, vol. 4, no. 5 (October–November 1981), pp. 42–46.

[16]Michael J. Robinson, "Just How Liberal Is The News? 1980 Revisited," *Public Opinion*, vol. 6, no. 1 (February–March, 1983), p. 60. See also Albert R. Hunt, "Media Bias Is in Eye of the Beholder," *The Wall Street Journal*, July 23, 1985, p. 28.

[17]Sethi, "Corporate External Communications," pp. 407–410.

First Amendment to the Constitution, which was aimed at promoting a free discussion of public issues.[18]

Some pitfalls in the use of advocacy advertising must be mentioned. First, a high level of intellectual integrity must be maintained if business expects community or government officials to give serious consideration to what is admittedly a partisan position. To help accomplish a positive impact, S. Prakash Sethi recommends that the sponsoring corporation should openly identify itself with the message and not hide behind such innocuous sounding names as the "Citizens Committee for Better Economic Environment."[19]

Second, there must be a congruence between the message of advocacy advertising and business performance. If, for example, a corporation's advertising is directed toward promoting the values associated with free enterprise, competition, and laissez faire, and then is subsequently found guilty of price fixing or making payments to government officials of a foreign country, its advertising efforts are very likely to be counterproductive and the company's credibility questioned even more severely. Corporations who use advocacy advertising must not only concentrate their fire on corporate critics, but must also speak out against abuses of power by corporations that adopt practices that are illegal or harm the broader public interest.[20]

Then there is the matter of how advertising expenditures are treated with regard to taxation. The Internal Revenue Service prohibits writing off expenditures to influence public opinion about legislative matters. Pure image advertising (see next section) would seem to fall outside this ruling, but sometimes the distinction between image advertising and advocacy advertising is not altogether clear. Sethi recommends that the emphasis in a corporation should not be on what ad expenses can be squeezed into the deductibility area, but on what expenses must stay out because they fall into the gray area and therefore may become controversial.[21]

Finally, there is a possible danger of shareholder suits over wastage of corporate assets by using corporate resources to further views with which some shareholders might disagree. Minority shareholders, for example, might resort to lawsuits to challenge corporate expenditures made for improper purposes or merely to further management's own interests. This could be very embarrassing and troublesome for corporate management and negate any benefits advocacy advertising might provide the company.

In a 1975 article, O'Toole presented guidelines for the use of advocacy

[18]*First National Bank of Boston* versus *Bellotti*, 435 U.S. 765. Rehearing denied 438 U.S. 907. See also "A Right-to-Speak Ruling Business May Regret," *Business Week*, May 15, 1978, p. 27; and "Corporation's Right to Disseminate View on Political Issues Backed by High Court," *The Wall Street Journal*, April 27, 1978, p. 4.

[19]Sethi, "Advocacy Advertising as a Strategy," p. 77.

[20]Ibid., p. 79.

[21]Ibid., pp. 78–79.

advertising that are still relevant in today's world. These include: (1) sponsoring companies should communicate clearly so that the indentity of the company becomes part of the message; (2) the dialogue with the public should begin long before the company is under siege, thus making its advertising seem completely self-serving; (3) the campaign should be based on a healthy respect for the readers' intelligence; (4) the position of the company must interest readers and relate to their interests; and (5) measurements should be used to test the effectiveness of the advertising campaign.[22]

Abuses of advocacy advertising would probably lead to some form of regulation or forced disclosure of financial records to assess how much corporations spend to influence public opinion. But properly used, advocacy advertising can serve the corporate objective of reducing public distrust of its actions and performance. Advocacy advertising can contribute to improved understanding on the part of the public as to what can reasonably be expected of business in fulfilling a society's expectations. To be successful, "advocacy advertising should be an integral part of the total corporate communication program and designed to communicate the firm's public policy positions. The communication must bear a close relationship to the activities of the corporation, the vision of society and its role that the corporation wishes to project, and societal expectations regarding corporate performance."[23]

Image Advertising This type of advertising does not deal directly with public issues, but instead seeks to better the image of a particular company or industry by presenting it as being genuinely concerned about the environment, health and safety, or some other issue of social concern. The purpose of image advertising is to change the public's perception of business performance through information the public might not otherwise have available. The distinction between image ads and advocacy ads, as stated earlier, is not always clear. The real purpose of an oil-company ad trumpeting its commitment to environmental cleanup might be to influence public opinion about the windfall profits tax rather than to sell gasoline.

Image ads have the potential of changing unfavorable public opinion toward business and allaying criticism while differentiating the sponsor from its competitors. They try to build basic recognition, awareness, and identity of a company in the public's mind. The content of image advertising typically follows several themes, including productivity, energy, ecology, social responsibility, consumerism, technology, financial performance, labor relations, product quality, name change, and other corporate activities.[24] Direct image advertise-

[22]James E. O'Toole, "Advocacy Advertising Shows the Flag," *Public Relations Journal*, no. 31 (November 1975), pp. 14–16.

[23]S. Prakash Sethi, "Corporate Political Activism," *California Management Review*, vol. XXIV, no. 3 (Spring 1982), p. 42.

[24]Robert L. Heath and Richard Alan Nelson, *Issues Management: Corporate Public Policymaking in an Information Society* (Beverly Hills: Sage Publications, 1986), p. 27.

ments carefully and clearly differentiate the image of the sponsor and its products or services from those of its competitors. Indirect image ads deal with social, financial, or economic issues surrounding corporate responsibility of goodwill efforts.[25] The purposes of image advertising include the following.

1. To educate, inform, or impress the public with regard to the company's policies, functions, facilities, objectives, ideals, and standards.
2. To build favorable opinion about the company by stressing the competence of the company's management, its scientific know-how, manufacturing skills, technological progress, product improvements, and contribution to social advancement and public welfare.
3. To build up the investment qualities of the company's securities or to improve its financial structure.
4. To sell the company as a good place in which to work, often in a way designed to appeal to college graduates or to people with certain skills.[26]

Examples of image ads are Dow Chemical's efforts to inform the public that the company lets its employees engage in projects to improve human welfare such as conducting laboratory research on ways to grow more grain for starving children. Phillips Petroleum attempts to project the image that it does more than just produce and market oil and natural gas—it is also a good public citizen that aids community projects such as those designed to curb drunk driving.[27] The Chemical Facts of Life ads of Monsanto Corporation (see Exhibit 8.2) try to better the image of the industry by educating the public about issues related to the use of chemicals in daily life. It is hoped that this information will have some positive influence on public opinion with respect to that industry in general and companies in the industry doing the advertising. Monsanto spent $4.5 million on its ad campaign in 1977, and has since equalled or exceeded that amount each year, seeking to improve the image of the company and the industry.[28] Companies as a whole spent more than $725 million on image advertising in 1985, which was more than triple the amount spent twelve years earlier.[29]

Economic Education This method of influencing public opinion is based on the assumption that much of the American public is economically illiterate. The credibility problem business has and the support given for regulation that adversely affects business

[25]Ibid., p. 31.

[26]T. F. Garbett, *Corporate Advertising: The What, the Why, and the How* (New York: McGraw-Hill, 1981).

[27]National Wildlife Federation, "Image-Makers: Corporate Ads with an Environmental Twist," *Conservation Exchange*, vol. 4, no. 3 (Fall 1986), p. 7.

[28]"Cleansing the Chemical Image," *Business Week*, October 8, 1979, p. 73.

[29]National Wildlife Federation, "Image-Makers," p. 7.

Exhibit 8.2

Without chemicals, life itself would be impossible.

Some people think anything "chemical" is bad and anything "natural" is good. Yet nature is chemical.

Plant life generates the oxygen we need through a chemical process called photosynthesis. When you breathe, your body absorbs that oxygen through a chemical reaction with your blood.

Life is chemical. And with chemicals, companies like Monsanto are working to help improve the quality of life.

Chemicals help you live longer. Rickets was a common childhood disease until a chemical called Vitamin D was added to milk and other foods.

Chemicals help you eat better. Chemical weed-killers have dramatically increased the supply and availability of our food.

But no chemical is totally safe, all the time, everywhere. In nature or in the laboratory. The real challenge is to use chemicals properly. To help make life a lot more livable.

For a free booklet explaining the risks and benefits of chemicals, mail to:
Monsanto, 800 N. Lindbergh Blvd., St. Louis, Mo. 63166. Dept. A3NA

Name _____

Address _____

City & state _____ Zip _____

Monsanto

Without chemicals,
life itself would be impossible.

Source: *Monsanto Speaks Up About Chemicals* (St. Louis, Mo.: Monsanto Company, 1977), p. 14. Reprinted with permission.

performance is based on an ignorance of how business actually operates and how the economic system functions. Many people simply do not understand the role of profits; concepts such as efficiency and productivity have no meaning, and the way a market system allocates resources is poorly understood. Many of the problems business has with the public and with government thus stem from an ignorance about business and the economic system rather than hostility toward business or the system (see Exhibit 8.3).

More and more companies are developing extensive educational programs directed at various segments of the public, including their own employees, educators, high school students, and shareholders.[30] These programs can include speakers dealing with various economic subjects, videotapes, and reading materials prepared by the company itself. According to a recent *Business Week* article, nearly 3,000 corporations, including more than half of the top 500, distribute educational materials to classrooms across the country.[31] In addition to corporate activities, there are "think tanks" around the country that try to make sure that both scholars and school children have a sound knowledge of and reverence for the free market system.[32]

The three major objectives of these programs are to (1) improve understanding of economic principles, (2) improve audience attitudes toward business in general, and (3) explain the free enterprise system.[33] Whether these objectives are actually attained, however, is difficult to ascertain since the impact of these programs is often measured subjectively, making the success claimed open to question. A study that measured the impact of the American Economic System campaign, an educational undertaking of the Advertising Council, showed that information is not the critical determinant of attitudes toward business. These attitudes mirrored the nation's economic health. When times were good and people felt economically secure, they tended to look favorably on business. When times were bad, people became less tolerant of the imperfections inherent in every institution, including business. The authors concluded that such attitudes cannot be changed by educational campaigns supplying information about the economic system.[34]

Paul Weaver, writing in *Fortune*, believes that most of the activities that go by the name of economic education have little to do with economics in the strict sense of the word.[35] They are programs of indirect corporate advocacy,

[30]Myron Emanuel, Curtis Snodgrass, Joyce Gildea, and Karn Rosenberg, *Corporate Economic Education Programs: An Evaluation and Appraisal* (New York: Financial Executives Research Foundation, 1979), p. xv.

[31]"Industry's Schoolhouse Clout," *Business Week*, October 13, 1980, pp. 156–157.

[32]See Trevor Armbrister, "Think Tanks with Clout," *Reader's Digest*, January, 1982, pp. 179–180.

[33]Emanuel, Snodgrass, Gildea, and Rosenberg, *Economic Education*, p. 338.

[34]Karen F. A. Fox and Bobby J. Calder, "The Right Kind of Business Advocacy," *Business Horizons* (January–February 1985), pp. 7–11.

[35]Paul H. Weaver, "Corporations Are Defending Themselves with the Wrong Weapon," *Fortune* (June 1977), pp. 186–196.

Exhibit 8.3

AMERICANS FLUNK ECONOMIC TEST

If you think large corporations keep more than 11 percent of their revenues as profits, that the government regulates interest rates on savings accounts, or that the Federal Trade Commission suggests retail prices, you're wrong.

But, before you fret about what that might mean to your ability to win at Trivial Pursuit, you should know you've got company.

A recent survey found that, despite a surge of interest in business and economic news, most Americans don't understand some of the most basic concepts of the economy and commerce.

The survey, released last month, polled 1,006 people nationwide and was conducted by the New York City-based polling firm Research & Forecasts Inc. for the Hearst Corp. It showed that:

• Sixty-one percent of Americans wrongly believe that unemployment statistics are determined by the number of people collecting unemployment benefits. In fact, it also includes those who have exhausted their benefits, but are still seeking jobs.

• Only 26 percent, the study found, know that each percentage point in the unemployment rate represents about 1 million people.

• About 40 percent believe that more than half of the nation's work force is unionized. Only 18 percent know that roughly 20 percent are in unions.

• Nearly 50 percent believe incorrectly that corporations kept more than 11 percent of revenues as after-tax profits last year. Only 16 percent know profits were typically 10 percent or less of revenues, while 37 percent either didn't answer or didn't know.

• A majority do not know what the Gross National Product is. Forty-eight percent incorrectly identify it as the value of goods and services purchased by federal, state and local governments. It is actually the total value of all U.S. generated goods and services.

"The pattern that I see in the responses is that the closer the question got to personal experience, the more they knew," said Frank Walton, head of the research project and executive vice president of Research & Forecasts. But there were some inconsistencies in that pattern.

While 75 percent could quote the present average rate for adjustable home mortgages (it was about 14 percent when the survey was taken in late summer and early fall), 52 percent wrongly believed that federal and state regulators set interest rates on savings accounts (savings institutions set their own rates).

Before starting the survey, the research group studied newspapers, magazines and television reports over six months to determine the most commonly used business and economic terms, Walton says. His conclusion: "The terms being frequently used are not understood by most people."

WHAT PEOPLE DON'T KNOW ABOUT BUSINESS

Some misconceptions:
• That large corporations keep more than 11 percent of their revenues as profits.
• That the government regulates interest rates on savings accounts.
• That unemployment statistics are determined by the number of people collecting unemployment benefits.

And did you know:
- That each percentage point in the unemployment rate represents about 1 million people.
- That only about 20 percent of America's work force is unionized.
- That import quotas on foreign goods generally lead to higher consumer prices.

Source: *Dallas Times Herald*, November 24, 1984, p. B-1. Reprinted with permission of Knight-Ridder Newspapers.

according to Weaver, and their purpose is political persuasion. Yet there is no evidence to suggest that economic education has made any headway in changing the political character of a community or nation, because it rests on the basic misconception that Americans are economically illiterate. According to Weaver:

Opinion polls do not reveal any great economic illiteracy on the part of the American people. What they do show is that many Americans don't like the profit motive, job insecurity, or other features of a market economy. Giving these people information isn't going to dispel their misgivings.[36]

Americans like private enterprise and the efficiency of big business. They have not lost confidence in the economic system of this country. But people do question the honesty, dependability, and integrity of business leadership. They believe that business serves its own self-interest by profiteering at the expense of the rest of society. They see businesspeople as greedy and indifferent to the human consequences of their actions. In general, the public is bothered by the seemingly cynical, self-interested abuse of power by those at the summit of business.[37]

Thus there is a potential backlash in the use of educational materials. Some experts expect that the debate over industry-produced materials will emerge as a major antibusiness rallying point, going hand-in-hand with the debate over advertising aimed at children. Some observers believe the government must step in to protect the "captive audience" in the classroom from being exposed to what are admittedly biased educational materials.[38] The self-interested use of educational materials may only reinforce existing stereotypes of U.S. businesspeople and lead to further deterioration of the public's attitudes toward business. Educational materials are no substitute for sound business performance that is in line with the expectations of society.

[36]Ibid., p. 186.
[37]Yankelovich, "On the Legitimacy of Business," p. 78. See also Lipset and Schneider, "How's Business?" p. 47.
[38]"Industry's Schoolhouse Clout," *Business Week*, p. 157.

PUBLIC POLICY FORMULATION

The second stage of the public policy life cycle is called the stage of public policy formulation. At this stage the concern is with specific legislative proposals that have been introduced into Congress that will directly or indirectly affect the business firm. The issues at this stage have become politicized and have taken on form and substance as proposed legislative enactments. The primary strategic objective of the corporation is to oppose or support bills, depending on their impact, or change them in some way so that they are more acceptable. While communication strategies are still useful at this stage, a new element is introduced into the public policy life cycle. The focus is now on the office holder who will be dealing with the issue as it takes form as a formal legislative or regulatory enactment.

Communication strategies are useful for attempting to influence emerging issues—those that are currently being debated in society, which is in the process of forming opinions about a common course of action with respect to an issue of concern. The stage of public policy formulation deals more with current issues—those that are the subject of government action where there are already strongly held opinions about what needs to be done. While some options may be closed to business at this stage, business must get involved in the political process to have some influence on the outcome of the legislative process and to engage in more formal public policy formulation. Because of the influence of government on business, it is important for managers to become students of public affairs and learn how to influence the political process appropriately.

Principle strategic options utilized by corporations at this stage involve some kind of contact with office holders and candidates for political office. Such contact can be achieved through participating in general business or industry and trade associations designed to enhance the "voice" of business, lobbying to obtain access to legislators and ensuring that the firm's point of view is heard and understood, and building a constituency to promote grass-roots lobbying efforts on the part of shareholders and other corporate constituents.

Of growing significance at this stage is the use of political action committees (PAC) monies as a means of influencing the electoral process. Although individuals may contribute to the candidate of their choice, the inherent limits of single contributions, particularly since they represent the viewpoint of a single person, do not always provide the needed leverage to offset the impact of other single contributors. As a consequence, the pooling of individual contributions and the distribution of those funds through a PAC has come to be viewed as a principle strategic option for corporations interested in influencing the formulation of public policy into acceptable legislative mandates.

General Business Associations

There are several nationwide organizations that are composed of corporate members representing all or most industries in the country. These groups can organize the resources of many business organizations across the nation to get involved in public policy formulation. They can help business organizations to identify issues being considered in government, gather information about issues, assess the political climate, coordinate the strategies of the various companies that are concerned about a given issue, lobby on behalf of their membership, and perform other functions related to this stage of public policy formulation. Individual business organizations can use these general associations to pursue their interests at the level of the federal government. The most prominent organizations of this type are the National Association of Manufacturers (NAM), the Chamber of Commerce of the United States, the Business Council, the Business Roundtable, and the National Federation of Independent Business.[39]

National Association of Manufacturers. The NAM moved its headquarters to Washington, D.C., in 1074 and reorganized itself in the process. With a membership of about 13,500 manufacturing firms, the NAM is the senior national business organization and claims to be the "voice of American industry." The organization is currently structured into four divisions covering various regions of the country. The functions of the NAM are to provide early information to its membership at the formative stages of legislative development and activate corporate grass-roots programs. The current emphasis of the NAM is to provide services for its membership, particularly for those small companies who do not have the resources to hire their own representation in the nation's capital. The NAM restructured its activities in Washington into fourteen policy committees, each of which is headed by a registered lobbyist who follows a major issue through all the branches of government. The areas these committees cover include international economic affairs, taxation and fiscal policy, government regulation and competition, and industrial relations. The organization also conducts meetings for member companies to bring together corporate executives with the legislators from their region of the country. The NAM's member firms account for 75 percent of the nation's industrial capacity.[40]

Chamber of Commerce of the United States. The Chamber has a membership of 154,000, most of whom are corporations, but which also includes municipal and state chambers of commerce and trade associations. The organization has numerous committees, task forces, and panels involving business, professional, and educational representatives. Its policy concerns are much broader than the NAM and its budget is much larger. The

[39] A survey conducted by Louis Harris & Associates Inc., based on interviews with 600 high-level officials from the 1,200 corporations that constitute *Business Week's* Corporate Scorecard, asked how effectively the business viewpoint had been advanced by some of these general business associations. Only 16 percent of these executives rated the Business Roundtable as very effective in this regard compared with 10 percent for the Chamber, 7 percent for the NAM, and only 2 percent for the NFIB. See "Executives Take a Dim View of Their Image-Makers," *Business Week*, March 7, 1983, p. 14.

[40] *NAM: Industry's Voice in Washington* (Washington, D.C.: NAM, undated).

membership relies on the Chamber's assistance in the legislative field in testifying before Congress on behalf of business, lobbying or talking with government leaders, going to court for business, keeping track of the legislative agenda, and speaking out for business whenever possible. This latter function is accomplished through a number of publications such as *Washington Report*, *Voice of Business*, and *Nation's Business*. The Chamber also conducts a far-reaching grass-roots program to mobilize its constituency with respect to an issue. Finally, the Chamber engages in business education by holding legal workshops for corporate executives, conducting executive development programs, and offering a communications education program to teach executives how to use the media, especially television, effectively.[41]

The Business Council. Membership in the Business Council is limited to sixty-five chief executive officers of the top industrial, retail, transportation, and financial corporations in the country. Thus it serves as a link between big business and the government. It mainly serves as an advisory role and scrupulously avoids lobbying activities. The Council's influence primarily depends on the personal prestige of its members, and since it does not engage in formal lobbying, it tends to exert more influence with the executive branch than with Congress. Council members are frequently appointed to high executive or advisory positions in every administration. Though the Council never formally takes a position on an issue, when a consensus does develop it is often expressed through the Business Roundtable, with whom there is considerable overlapping of membership.[42]

The Business Roundtable. The Business Roundtable was formed in 1972, but it has had a tremendous impact that in many ways has eclipsed the older organizations. The Roundtable was formed partly because many leaders of large business corporations believed their interests were not being adequately represented by the NAM or the Chamber because their membership was so diverse and consisted largely of smaller business corporations. The Roundtable's membership consists of heads of large companies. The organization presently has a membership of about 200 chief executive officers, representing a wide diversity of industries and regions of the country.

The unique feature of the Roundtable is the fact that the chief executive officer of a company is the person who is involved. These CEOs, of course, have direct personal access to the highest levels of government. The Roundtable has an office in New York and Washington, but these offices have very small staffs in comparison to the other general business associations. The Roundtable occasionally hires outside help for research and public relations efforts, but the bulk of its work is done through task forces that cover such issues as taxation, consumer

---

[41]Phyllis S. McGrath, *Redefining Corporate-Federal Relations* (New York: The Conference Board, 1979), pp. 86–87.

[42]Sar A. Levitan and Martha R. Cooper, *The Public Good and the Bottom Line* (Baltimore, Md.: Johns Hopkins, 1984), pp. 30–31.

Exhibit 8.4
The Business Roundtable Task Forces, 1987

Accounting Principles	Roger B. Smith
	General Motors
Antitrust and Government Regulation	John D. Ong
	BF Goodrich
Construction Cost Effectiveness	John F. Bookout
	Shell Oil
Corporate Responsibility	H. Brewster Atwater
	General Mills
Employment Policy	James E. Burke
	Johnson & Johnson
Environment	David M. Roderick
	U.S. Steel
Federal Budget	Robert D. Kilpatrick
	CIGNA
Health, Welfare & Retirement Income	John J. Creedon
	Metropolitan Life
International Trade and Investment	James D. Robinson III
	American Express
Taxation	Charles W. Parry
	Alcoa
Tort Policy	Robert H. Malott
	FMC

Source: The Business Roundtable, February 1987. Reprinted with permission.

interests, energy, environment, regulation, antitrust, and the like. Each task force is headed by the CEO of a member company (see Exhibit 8.4), who can draw on the research capabilities of his or her own company or the companies of the other task force members. This help is of no cost to the Roundtable itself.[43]

These task forces research issues in their domain and eventually draft a position paper. When the task force reaches a consensus, the issue then goes to a policy committee that works out any differences that remain on the issue and then formally releases a position paper to the media, government officials, and other interested parties. The positions of the Roundtable do not always reflect the interests of its entire membership. For example, the Roundtable opposed the government loan guarantee for Chrysler Corporation, and Chrysler subsequently canceled its membership.

These position papers form the basis for further lobbying efforts on the part of Roundtable membership. The CEOs of member corporations can use this research for their own speeches or in contacts with individual policy makers. Most of the Roundtable's efforts go into lobbying and related research efforts. The Roundtable also spends some of its resources promoting internal

[43]"Business' Most Powerful Lobby in Washington," *Business Week,* December 20, 1976, pp. 60–61.

self-reform on the part of corporations as exemplified in its statement on boards of directors.[44] It also engaged in a one-shot campaign of advocacy advertising on behalf of the free enterprise system.

The Business Roundtable has thus far been highly effective and its advice and counsel on a wide range of issues is sought by the administration and Congress alike. The enthusiasm of its membership is probably responsible for a large degree of its success, along with its resistance to becoming bureaucratized. This helps the organization to be flexible and respond to issues more quickly than larger organizations like the NAM and the Chamber, which have a great deal of organizational inertia to overcome. Another reason for the Roundtable's success is its pragmatic and positive approach to problems and acceptance of government involvement. Two Roundtable guidelines are pivotal in this regard:

> A recognition that the adversarial relationship of business and government is exaggerated and counterproductive; that in most instances business and government seek the same ends; that the means to the end, not the end itself, is usually the principal concern; and that business and government must work together to find the best way to achieve agreed goals.
> A recognition that the Roundtable will receive better support for its views, and make a greater contribution to society, if it registers "positive ideas and objectives," and avoids the negative posture on important issues that critics of American capitalism often present as the stereotype stance of the business community.[45]

National Federation of Independent Business. The NFIB is the largest organization representing small business, with a membership of about 470,000 firms. There are no limits as to size—almost two-thirds of its members employ fewer than ten people and over 80 percent of its members employ fewer than twenty people. The organization lobbies Congress and all fifty state legislatures to make sure that the interests of small business are considered during the law-making process. In addition, the NFIB deals directly with the President and administrative agencies to try and see to it that once a law is passed, its implementation is as painless as possible for the small businesses affected. The positions the NFIB takes on issues are based on a vote of the membership on a specific issue. These votes, called "mandates," are reported to members of Congress and officials in the executive branch. The mandates are binding on the organization, and its lobbyists cannot commit the

[44]See *The Role and Composition of the Board of Directors of the Large Publicly Owned Corporation* (New York: The Business Roundtable, 1978).

[45]Donald J. Watson, "The Changing Political Involvement of Business," paper presented at the Conference on Business and Its Changing Environment, UCLA, July 31, 1978, p. 7. See Doug Bandow, "A Corporate Lobby Pulls Its Punches," *The Wall Street Journal*, July 23, 1986, p. 18, for a criticism of the Roundtable's pragmatic approach.

NFIB to policy compromises. The NFIB also operates a political action committee at the national level.[46]

Industry and Trade Associations   Industry and trade associations perform many functions for their membership, including development of industry standards, conducting educational programs, and industry-wide advertising. Increasingly, politics is becoming the major focus of these organizations, which perform many of the same political functions for their membership as do the general business associations mentioned earlier. Many members simply do not have enough strength of their own in Washington and must rely on their trade association for political activity. These political activities include testifying at congressional hearings on matters affecting the industry, appearing in proceedings before government agencies and regulatory bodies on issues of concern to the industry, contributing to precedent-setting cases before the courts, raising political contributions, making industry information available to the courts, and serving on various advisory committees.

The nation's capital now contains 1,500 association headquarters with more to come. Many of these have recently moved their headquarters from New York City to Washington, reflecting the focus on politics. The budgets and membership of some of these associations are large and managers of these associations can make up to $150,000 a year, reflecting their increasing importance. These industry and trade associations stand between business and government, interpreting the government's actions and attitudes to their business constituency and bringing the interests of business before government officials.

Lobbying   Lobbying involves efforts by political professionals or business executives to establish linkages with key people who are in the process of formulating public policies. Lobbying by business has both an offensive and a defensive function. The offensive function consists of getting a company's views on pending legislation across to senators, members of the House of Representatives, their aides, and committee staff members. Lobbying is designed to monitor legislation, to provide information to policy makers on the anticipated effects of proposed legislation, and to attempt to influence the decisions of legislators and key advisors. The defensive function of lobbying is geared to avoiding embarrassing investigations of and attacks on a company or an industry. This function is accomplished by providing additional information and presenting the other side of the story at an early stage of a committee's deliberations.

The nature of lobbying has changed from what it was in the past. The job demands, as never before, homework on issues and legislators.[47] *Time* magazine

[46]Levitan and Cooper, *The Public Good*, p. 41.
[47]"The Swarming Lobbyists," *Time*, August 7, 1978, pp. 15–16.

reported: "Instead of cozying up to a few chairmen or a powerful speaker, the lobbyist must do tedious homework on the whims and leanings of all the legislators. . . . Lobbying now demands, as never before, highly sophisticated techniques, a mastery of both the technicalities of legislation and the complexities of the legislator's backgrounds, and painstaking effort."[48] Many yearn for the simpler, splashier days of the trade. As stated by one longtime corporate lobbyist: "My job used to be booze, broads, and golf at Burning Tree. Now it is organizing coalitions and keeping information flowing."[49]

The success of lobbying depends a great deal on finding where the real power lies in government.[50] In past years, this was not too difficult since powerful committee chairpersons existed and a few key members of Congress exercised great influence over their colleagues. But while power as a whole has become centralized in Washington, it has also become more diffused with the change in the committee structure of Congress, which has weakened the power of committee chairpersons. Diffusion of power has also resulted from the election of independent-minded legislators who do not necessarily adhere to the party line, the increasing importance of congressional staffs in drafting legislation, and the growing regulatory bureaucracy that implements the legislation. These changes may have made a lobbyist's job more difficult, but they do not mean that policy makers have been liberated from the influence of special interests.

New forms of lobbying have recently appeared, including the practice of inviting members of the House and Senate to speak before various groups and paying them a handsome honorarium. However, not only are the politicians invited to speak, they are also expected to listen to concerns of the groups who invited them and are paying the honorarium. An analysis by Common Cause showed that the amount of honoraria paid by all interest groups reached a record $7.2 million in 1985, up from $5.4 million in 1984 and topping the previous record of $6.1 million set in 1983. This total is likely to increase as Senators now allow themselves to keep honoraria totaling 40 percent of their salary as compared with 30 and as little as 15 percent in previous years.[51]

These honoraria have an odd legal status. Rules in both the House and Senate prohibit members from taking any gifts valued at $100 or more from lobby groups. But they can legally accept as much as $2,000 for an appearance before these same groups. Sometimes they make more than one such paid visit in a single day, earning a good deal of money in the process. The Common Cause study found that the ten top Pentagon suppliers paid a combined

[48]Ibid., p. 16.

[49]"New Ways to Lobby a Recalcitrant Congress," *Business Week*, September 3, 1979, p. 148.

[50]See Dan H. Fenn, Jr. "Finding Where the Power Lies in Government," *Harvard Business Review*, vol. 57, no. 5 (September–October 1979), pp. 144–153.

[51]Brooks Jackson, "Lobbyists Who Pay Lawmakers $1,000 an Hour Have Found an Effective Way to Communicate," *The Wall Street Journal*, June 25, 1986, p. 58.

total of $236,163 in 1985, 77 percent of which went to members of the defense appropriations subcommittees or to the armed services committees of Congress.[52] Such fees used to come largely from the traditional lecture circuit of colleges and universities and local civic and religious groups. But the largest growth in recent years has come from trade associations and companies who want special consideration from Congress on legislation that affects their interests.[53]

Constituency Building

Lobbying only in the nation's capital has its limitations. Corporations have turned increasingly to grass-roots lobbying on the assumption that rank-and-file legislators in the new political environment may be more sensitive to expressions of political sentiment from their home districts. Grass-roots lobbying takes place in the legislator's home district rather than in Washington, and involves building a constituency that will support corporate interests on a particular issue. Thus constituency building refers to corporate efforts to identify, educate, and motivate individuals who may be affected by public policies that have an impact on the corporation.[54]

The so-called natural constituency of a corporation includes employees, shareholders, suppliers, dealers, and community residents where the corporation has a significant presence. Many companies attempt to keep constituents informed on relevant issues and encourage their participation in the legislative process, often through letters or phone calls to elected representatives as legislation is being considered.[55] They are putting a good deal of money and energy into organizing employees and shareholders into a concerted voice powerful enough to capture the attention of legislators.

A company gets into grass-roots programs because such efforts represent a force in the community that is largely untapped. A great deal of political power within the corporation itself potentially can be mobilized to influence government. The first task in mobilizing this political power is to identify a network of individuals who share the interests of the company—in other words, to build a constituency. Employees are a natural source of people who share company interests and at the same time vote locally and may even have personal relationships with local legislators. Shareholders constitute another source of people who identify with corporate interests and can be made part of the corporation's

---

[52]Ibid.

[53]Brooks Jackson, "Interest Groups Pay Millions in Appearance Fees to Get Legislators to Listen as Well as to Speak," *The Wall Street Journal*, June 4, 1985, p. 58. See also Brooks Jackson and Edward F. Pound, "Legislative Lucre: Fees for Congressmen from Interest Groups Doubled in Past Year," *The Wall Street Journal*, July 28, 1983, p. 1.

[54]Gerald D. Keim and Carl P. Zeithaml, "Corporate Political Strategy and Legislative Decision Making: A Review and Contingency Approach," *Academy of Management Review*, vol. 11, no. 4 (1986), pp. 59–60.

[55]Ibid.

political constituency. There are about 27 million shareholders, and when spouses are added, that makes more than 50 million people. Some research has found that 96 percent of these shareholders voted in a recent election compared to 53 percent of the general public.[56]

Such numbers add up to a major political force to support corporate interests on public policy matters. Individual shareholders, who are usually the silent partners in big business, may become the political activists of the decade, according to Gerry Keim of Texas A&M University. In a survey of 3,000 stockholders from five major corporations within the Fortune 500, the following results were discovered.

84 percent felt corporate executives should continue to speak out on public policy issues; while 7 percent disagreed; and the remainder had no opinion.

64 percent of the shareholders supported corporate positions on policy issues; 6 percent disagreed.

90 percent wanted their companies to provide them with analysis of public policy issues; 10 percent disagreed.

57 percent wanted companies to provide voting records of politicians, 22 percent disagreed.[57]

These results suggest shareholders can be mobilized to support the political interests of business. If only a small percentage of these stockholders can be mobilized to become politically active, the public policy process, says Keim, would reflect more accurately the interests of business.[58] Characteristics that shareholders possess that are suggestive of their value as grass-roots lobbyists include: (1) individual shareholders often are affected directly by public policies that influence the corporation; (2) individual shareholders can be identified easily by the corporation, thereby facilitating the communication process; (3) individual shareholders represent a large number of people; and (4) the wide geographical dispersion of individual shareholders creates opportunities to influence a large number of elected officials.[59]

Grass-roots programs vary among corporations, but some of the typical elements include the organization of political education or discussion groups for employees and stockholders, presentation of management's views on issues that concern the company, and mailings of political information along with the company's position on certain legislative issues to employees and stockholders.

---

[56]Gerald Keim, "Firms Silent Partners May Turn Political Activists," *Dallas Morning News*, July 5, 1981, p. 2H.

[57]Ibid.

[58]Ibid.

[59]Barry D. Baysinger, Gerald D. Keim, and Carl P. Zeithaml, "An Empirical Evaluation of the Potential for Including Shareholders in Corporate Constituency Programs," *Academy of Management Journal*, vol. 28, no. 1 (1985), p. 185.

Once a network of people is developed who will support company interests, it needs to be kept informed about public policy developments. It can then readily be mobilized to respond to an issue by contacting its local elected officials and making their views heard. Research shows that companies who maintain regular communications with their constituents can expect these constituents to be more positive about corporate political activity and involvement.[60]

Not all potential constituents can be motivated, however, to be politically active, nor are they necessarily interested in the same issues. According to Keim and Baysinger, "Effective constituency building efforts must thus identify the politically active subset of constituents and must utilize appropriate members of this group on the basis of the relevance of a particular issue."[61] Shareholders, for example, may be more interested in issues that affect capital formation and the development of new technologies, whereas employees may be more interested in equal employment opportunity or job safety issues.

Lobbying efforts at both the Washington and grass-roots levels are believed to be effective and perform a useful function in the formulation of public policy by government. The professional lobbyist in Washington can supply a practical knowledge that is vital in the writing of workable legislation. Potential consequences of certain provisions in the law can be pointed out that may otherwise be overlooked. The lobbyists in Washington are eager to point out such hazards and do so at no public expense. Grass-roots lobbying lets a congressional representative know what his or her immediate constituencies believe about an issue, and makes for a closer link of accountability between elected officials and the people they represent.

Campaign Contributions

Another way to exercise influence at the stage of public policy formulation is to contribute money to candidates for political office. This can be done to help elect people who will be favorable to business interests or who will then owe business some favors because of the help given them in their campaigns. Society has been concerned about this kind of involvement since the beginning of the century, and has passed legislation to limit the financial participation of businesss in the election process.

The Tillman Act of 1907 made it illegal for business to make contributions to campaigns involving the election of federal officials. The objectives of this act were to (1) destroy business influence over elections, (2) protect stockholders from the use of corporate funds for political purposes to which they had not given their assent, and (3) protect the freedom of the individual's vote. The Corrupt Practices Act of 1925 broadened this concept by defining corporate contributions to include not only monetary contributions, but anything of

---

[60]Ibid., pp. 180–200.

[61]Gerald D. Keim and Barry D. Baysinger, "Corporate Political Strategies Examined: Constituency-Building May Be the Best," *Public Affairs Review*, vol. III (1982), p. 85.

value—a definition that markedly affected future contributions activities. The Labor-Management Relations Act of 1957 extended these same restrictions to labor unions. Finally, in 1972, Congress passed the Federal Election Campaign Practices Act, which requires that candidates for federal office and their potential committees must make public the names and addresses of their supporters who contribute more than $100 to the campaign. The act also limits the contributions an individual can make to all candidates for federal office to $25,000 per year and $3,000 per candidate per campaign ($1,000 each in primaries, runoffs, and general elections).

Thus both business and labor unions are prohibited from making contributions to federal political campaigns from company or union funds. Some states also prohibit contributions to state elections. However, a new phenomenon that has appeared in recent years with respect to campaign contributions is the development of political action committees (PACs). The labor movement had already initiated something called political action committees in the 1930s, which utilized voluntary contributions from union members for campaign contributions rather than union funds. In 1955, the AFL-CIO formed a Committee on Political Education (COPE) to administer these funds, which became the model for more formal committees. The legal status of these committees was unclear, however, and unions favored formal legislation permitting the formation of PACs using separate funds for campaign purposes. Thus an amendment was added to the Federal Election Campaign Act of 1971 that institutionalized PACs and established their legality for not only labor unions, but for business corporations and trade-professional associations as well.

In subsequent years, the role of PACs was clarified and strengthened through a series of legislative, judicial, and regulatory decisions. Because of ambiguities in the language of the 1971 Act, the Sun Oil Company sought an advisory opinion from the Federal Election Commission as to whether the right to operate a PAC included the right to use general treasury funds to pay PAC operating expenses.

In response to this request, the Federal Election Commission issued a historic advisory opinion, now called the SUNPAC decision, upholding the right of a corporation to establish and administer a separate, segregated fund out of which political contributions could be made. This opinion set forth rules and limitations for such funds, including the following:

1. General treasury funds can be expended for establishment, administration and solicitation of contributions to the PAC—if it is maintained as a separate segregated fund.

2. A company can make political contributions in a federal election, if made solely from PAC funds which are obtained voluntarily.

3. A company can control disbursement of funds from a separate segregated fund.

4. A company can solicit contributions from its shareholders and employees.

5. A company can accept contributions to its PAC from any source that would not otherwise be unlawful.[62]

In 1976, the Supreme Court in *Buckley* v. *Valeo* upheld the Federal Election Campaign laws ruling that limitations on contributions, record-keeping requirements, and public financing of presidential elections were constitutional. But it also ruled that expenditure limitations were unconstitutional, except in presidential elections, ruling that both candidates and citizens acting independently can spend as much as they wish. The Court also ruled that the Federal Election Commission was unconstitutional because of the manner in which the commission was appointed.

This action necessitated amendments to the Federal Election Campaign law to reconstitute the Federal Election Commission. With regard to PACs, the 1976 amendments specifically provided for: (1) "crossover," where hourly employees may be solicited twice a year only, in writing at their residence, provided there is confidentiality of contributions of $50 or less; (2) solicitation of executive and administrative personnel and shareholders without limitations; (3) a cloudy definition of executive or administrative personnel; (4) solicitation guidelines, requiring corporations to inform solicitees of the political nature of the particular action and the solicitees' right to refuse without reprisal; and (5) anti-proliferation rules stating that political committees that are established, administered, or controlled by a single organization will be treated as a single political committee and there will be an aggregation of their contributions.[63]

These developments, in a sense, opened the door for PAC growth. From 1974 to 1979, the number of PACs tripled from 608 to 1,900. In 1980, there were 2,551 PACs, and by 1982, the number had grown to 3,149, a fivefold increase in eight years. This growth continued into future years as there were 4,347 active PACs in the 1983–84 campaign, and 4,568 during the 1985–86 season. In 1980, PACs gave $55.2 million to House and Senate campaigns; in 1974, by way of contrast, PACs then in existence contributed only $12.5 million.[64] Total contributions of PACs in the 1982 races reached a staggering $189 million, including $87.3 million for federal races. PAC contributions to federal candidates totaled $113.0 million in 1984 and reached the level of $139.5 million in the 1986 races.[65]

These figures include PACs not only from business, but also from industry and trade associations and similar organizations. Regarding business PACs alone, in 1974 there were only 89 corporate PACs in the country—by 1976

---

[62]*Business' Political Awakening: PAC Overview* (Washington, D.C.: Fraser/Associates, 1979), p. 6.

[63]Ibid., p. 7.

[64]Ibid., p. i; Federal Election Commission, Press Release, February 21, 1982, p. 1.

[65]"Record $189 Million Was Raised by PACs for 1982 Election," *The Wall Street Journal*, January 6, 1983, p. 5; "PACs Contributed Record $87.3 Million to '82 Federal Races," *The Wall Street Journal*, April 29, 1983, p. 15; Federal Election Commission, Press Release, May 21, 1987, p. 1.

there were 433, by 1979 there were 812, and by 1980, there were 1,251 corporate PACs. These numbers increased to 1,521 in 1984 and to 1,576 during the 1985–86 election.[66] There were names such as Back Pac, Peace Pac, and Cigar Pac. Beer distributors had a committee named Six Pac and Whataburger called its PAC, most appropriately, Whata Pac.[67]

These PACs solicit money form individuals including employees, stockholders, and others, which is different from using corporate funds for contributions. A company, however, must not use coercion to solicit these contributions. An individual is not to be penalized for refusing to contribute or rewarded for participating. Should such incidents occur, the chairperson and treasurer of the PAC would be subject to criminal prosecution. The operation of a PAC is usually monitored by the company's legal counsel. The folowing methods are generally used to solicit contributions from employees:

> Letters from the CEO or PAC chairman
> Individual contacts
> Solicitation meetings
> Solicitation brochures
> Management newsletter

The legal definition of a PAC is a fund that receives political contributions from more than fifty people and receives or spends more than $1,000 a year. Such organizations must file regular reports with the Federal Election Commission. The maximum annual contribution that an individual can make to a PAC is $5,000 per election. The ceiling on the contribution a PAC can make to any one candidate for federal office is also $5,000 per election. Such relatively small amounts are not likely to buy a candidate's vote for any corporation, but they can open the door to future corporate influence.

The typical PAC organization is shown in Figure 8.1. The law permits a company itself to pay the costs of administering the PAC, including expenses for salaries, rent, postage, and the like. Contributions to candidates, however, must be made out of the voluntary contributions of individuals. Each PAC is required to have a chairperson and treasurer, and a number have set up contributions committees. The officers of the PAC on these contributions committees must often decide where the money will go, but some companies allow the contributors to designate the party they wish their money to reach and most are open to suggestions from contributors.

In 1986, corporate PACs contributed a total of $49.4 million to political campaigns, ahead of labor's $31.0 million. Trade association PACs reported $34.4 million, while PACs organized by other groups contributed $5.3 million.

---

[66]*Business' Political Awakening*, p. i; Federal Election Commission, Press Release, February 21, 1982, p. 1; December 1, 1985, p. 1; May 21, 1987, p. 1.

[67]"Running With the Pacs," *Time*, October 25, 1982, p. 20.

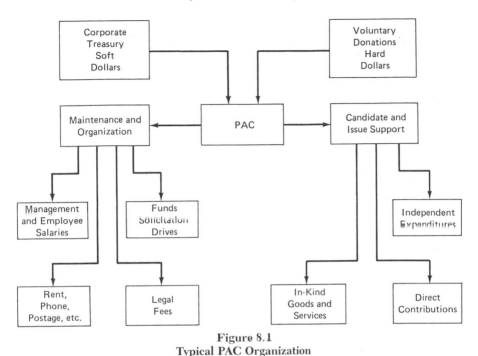

Figure 8.1
Typical PAC Organization

Source: Business' Political Awakening: PAC Overview (Washington D.C.: Fraser/Associates, 1979), p. 16.

Nonconnected organizations contributed another $19.4 million to the 1986 campaign. These amounts add up to a total of $139.5 million contributed by the PACs to the 1986 election.[68] The top ten corporate and association contributors are shown in Exhibits 8.5 and 8.6. These figures show that the amount given by the top ten associations far outweighs the top ten corporate contributors.

During the first few years of contributions by business PACs, it was clear that more money was being given to Democratic candidates than Republican candidates, a surprising development for many corporate leaders. The reason for this development seems to be that PACs were supporting incumbents more than challengers, and there simply were many more Democrats in that position. This trend began to change with the 1980 election, and continues into later years, as the data for 1986 (Table 8.1) show that corporate contributions favored Republicans, indicating a shift to more ideologically supported efforts. Still, the labor PACs gave a significantly higher proportion of their money to Democratic candidates than business PACs did to Republican candidates. Even if a challenger is more closely aligned ideologically with a company's position, it is a fact of political life that incumbents win most elections.

There has been a good deal of concern in government about the growth and impact of PACs, especially those of business and professional organizations.

[68]Federal Election Commission, Press Release, May 21, 1987, p. 2.

Exhibit 8.5
Leading Corporate PAC Contributors to the 1986 Elections

1. American Telephone & Telegraph Co. Inc. (AT&T PAC)	$799,760
2. Philip Morris Political Action Committee (PHIL-PAC)	559,505
3. UPSPAC	480,524
4. Tenneco Employees Good Government Fund	447,250
5. Lockheed Employees PAC	430,858
6. Rockwell International Corp. Good Government Comm.	428,675
7. General Dynamics Corp. Voluntary Pol. Contribution Fund	378,908
8. Textron Inc. Political Action Committee	373,050
9. American Family PAC	360,825
10. AMOCO PAC	340,900

*Source:*Federal Election Commission, Press Release, May 21, 1987, p. 14.

Exhibit 8.6
Leading Trade/Membership/Health PAC Contributors to the 1986 Elections

1. Realtors Political Action Committee	$2,738,338
2. American Medical Association PAC (AMPAC)	2,107,492
3. Nat'l Assn of Retired Federal Employees PAC (NARFE-PAC)	1,491,895
4. Build PAC of the National Association of Home Builders	1,424,240
5. Association of Trial Lawyers PAC (ATLA)	1,404,000
6. National Association of Life Underwriters PAC	1,087,859
7. Dealers Election Action Committee of the National Automobile Dealers Association (NADA)	1,059,650
8. American Bankers Association BANKPAC	934,440
9. NRA Political Victory Fund	909,549
10. American Dental PAC	761,675

Source: Federal Election Commission, Press Release, May 21, 1987, p. 23.

The House voted to prevent any PAC from giving a House candidate more than $6,000: the previous limit was $10,000. The House also voted to bar any House candidate from accepting more than $70,000 from PACs in any two-year period between elections. The House measure also provides that candidates who dip into their own pockets to finance their campaign cannot later reimburse themselves from PAC funds for any more than $35,000. Formal legislation has been introduced to place a limit on the amount of PAC contributions a candidate for either the House or Senate may accept.[69]

[69]David Shribman and Brooks Jackson, "Conservative Support Adds Momentum to a Move by Congress to Limit PAC's Influence in Elections,"*The Wall Street Journal*, November 22, 1985, p. 54; Brooks Jackson, "Senate Votes to Limit PAC Donations, Toughen Disclosure of Gifts to Parties," *The Wall Street Journal*, August 13, 1986, p. 46; and "Is Congress Ready to Bite the Hands That Feed It?" *Business Week*, June 1, 1987, pp. 102–103. Despite these efforts at reform, there are always new ways invented to circumvent restriction on PAC donations. These include the giving of "soft" money to state party organizations, the contributions made by independent PACs, and establishing policy foundations. See "Campaign Reformers Just Can't Catch Up With PACs," *Business Week*, January 20, 1986, pp. 24–25, and "What's In For Presidential Hopefuls: Think Tanks," *Business Week*, May 12, 1986, pp. 60–62.

Table 8.1
Committee Contributions to Federal Candidates (in millions of dollars)

Types of Committees	Number of Active Committees	Number Making Contributions to Federal Candidates	Contributions to Federal Candidates	Senate	House	Democrat	Republican	Other	Incumbents	Challengers	Open Seats
Corporations	1902	1576	49.4	21.6	27.7	19.2	30.2	.005	37.7	3.9	7.8
Labor organizations	418	259	31.0	7.9	23.1	28.7	2.3	.004	17.9	7.6	5.5
Nonconnected	1251	566	19.4	8.1	11.3	11.2	8.2	.016	9.8	4.9	4.7
Trade/membership/ health	783	586	34.4	10.5	24.0	16.8	17.5	.002	26.5	3.0	4.9
Cooperatives	57	51	2.7	.7	1.9	1.5	1.1	0	2.2	.2	.2
Corporations without capital stock	157	114	2.6	1.1	1.5	1.3	1.3	.0003	2.0	.3	.3

Source: Federal Election Commission, press release May 21, 1987, p. 2.

PACs have been widely criticized for distorting the political process in favor of special interests. They have further weakened party discipline, because Democrats and Republicans alike have become more dependent on PAC funds and less dependent on party support. In the 1986 election, for example, it was estimated that 43.5 percent of a Democratic candidate's spending in a House race came from PAC contributions. The comparable figure for House Republican incumbents was 35.2 percent.[70] The PACs who contribute money to politicians clearly want something in return; they don't give money out of generosity. What they are buying is influence in the political process, making politicians beholden to them rather than the party. There is some evidence to suggest that the PACs are successful in this effort.[71]

Besides making it appear that Congress is up for sale, PACs are also accused of driving up the cost of campaigning. The desire to buy more and more television time, because PAC money is available, only increases PAC dependency. Candidates become hooked on lavish campaign expenditures just as people become hooked on drugs. In 1974, the average cost of campaigning for the House was $50,000; in 1980, the average was $150,000; and in 1982, races costing $500,000 were not uncommon. In 1986, winners in the House spent an average of $340,000 on their campaigns, up 17 percent from the previous election and about four times the average spent a decade earlier. Senate winners spent an average of $3 million each—five times more than they spent a decade earlier. The availability of PAC money is believed to be largely responsible for this increase.[72]

PACs are not only operative at the federal level. Much attention was devoted to the state level in the 1982 elections as deregulation and federalism gained favor in Washington, pushing the economic stakes at the state level higher and higher. The number of PACs in Texas, for example, rose to 1,400 in 1982 from 1,000 two years previously, and PACs contributed $2.8 million to the 1982 primaries. In California, PACs tripled in number from 1976 to 1982, and gave $17.7 million to candidates for state office in 1982, representing two-thirds of total campaign gifts in the state.[73]

A study conducted by the Center for Research in Business and Social Policy at the University of Texas at Dallas showed that the public generally perceived PACs to be a "bad" thing by a 2.5 to 1 ratio. The study was based on a

[70]Brooks Jackson, "PAC Contributions to Candidates Rise 32% in 1986 Races," *The Wall Street Journal*, August 1, 1986, p. 36.

[71]See Albert R. Hunt, "Special-Interest Money Increasingly Influences What Congress Enacts," *The Wall Street Journal*, July 26, 1982, p. 1; Brooks Jackson, "Tax-Revision Proposals Bring Big Contributions From PACs to Congressional Campaign Coffers," *The Wall Street Journal*, August 9, 1985, p. 36.

[72]"Running with the PACS," p. 21; Brooks Jackson, "New Congress Relied Heavily on PAC Donations, But Much of Spending Had Little Effect on Results," *The Wall Street Journal*, December 24, 1986, p. 32.

[73]"Corporate Pacs Turning Attention to the State as Deregulation Gains," *The Wall Street Journal*, October 28, 1982, p. 31.

sample of 1,007 people representing a scientifically selected and statistically valid cross section of the U.S. population. Data were collected by the Roper organization in face-to-face interviews conducted in respondents' homes.[74]

When people perceived PACs as having a great deal of influence on the outcome of the elections, they considered PACs to be a "bad" thing by a margin of 4.4 to 1 in almost all demographic and socio-economic characteristics. Even business executives, who might be expected to be supporters of PACs, held attitudes towards PACs consistent with the rest of the population. There was also no relationship between a person's political philosophy and his or her attitude toward PACs. It did not matter whether a person was conservative or liberal, Democratic or Republican, PACs were generally perceived negatively.[75]

Despite these attitudes towards PACs, however, a Lou Harris poll of 600 business leaders showed that 213 of them believed that business is much better organized now than five years ago to deal with politics. In many cases, this favorable reaction resulted from the formation of a PAC organized by the company to assist in the election of candidates who favored the company's interest. Some 44 percent of these executives believed that, compared with five years ago, business is generally getting its money's worth out of political campaign contributions. In distributing PAC money, 87 percent of the executives polled said they gave money to candidates who agreed with the views of the company, whether they were Republican or Democrat.[76]

A survey of Fortune 500 firms and their PAC activities in the 1980 election campaign showed that only 56 percent established a PAC in that year. These 280 PACs made a total of 19,373 contributions totaling $11,350,183. Two-thirds of these contributions went to incumbents rather than challengers for congressional seats. Very few of these corporations gave the maximum allowed by law (less than 1 percent) and the average contribution was only $592.20, suggesting that corporations are buying access to legislators rather than votes by giving token sums to as many candidates as possible. If electoral success is measured in terms of supporting winners, these PACs were successful—over 80 percent of their contributions went to winners and 70 percent of the candidates they supported won their elections. This study was based on contribution information filed with the Federal Election Commission for the 1979–80 election cycle.[77]

[74]S. Prakash Sethi and Nobuaki Namiki, *Public Perception of and Attitude Toward Political Action Committees* (Dallas: University of Texas Center for Research in Business and Social Policy, 1982), p. 1.

[75]Ibid., pp. 7–15.

[76]"How Business Is Getting Through to Washington," *Business Week*, October 4, 1982, p. 16.

[77]Ryan, Swanson, and Buchholz, *Public Policy*, pp. 127–159. See Joanna Banthin and Leigh Stelzer, "Political Action Committees: Fact, Fancy, and Morality," *The Journal of Business Ethics*, no. 5 (1986), pp. 13–19, for a criticism of this rational investment approach. The authors argue that their data support the principled approach where groups with interests, including business, identify congressmen who share their commitments and help them get elected. The focus of the principled approach is on the person and not the office. See also Marick Masters and Barry D. Baysinger, "The Determinants of Funds Raised by Corporate Political Action Committees: An Empirical Examination," *Academy of Management Journal*, vol. 28, no. 3 (1985), pp. 654–664.

Of further interest is the finding that larger firms in the Fortune 500 are the most active in terms of using the PAC option as a political strategy. Firms in the top quartile (more than $3 billion in sales) had 36.9 percent of the PACs and made 59.7 percent of the contributions. By way of contrast, firms in the bottom quartile (less than $723 million in sales) had only 12.9 percent of the 280 PACs and gave only 5 percent of the contributions. Firms in the top half of the sales rankings had 67 percent of the PACs accounting for 85 percent of the contributions, while firms in the bottom half of the rankings had only 33 percent of the PACs accounting for 15 percent of the contributions to candidates for federal office.[78]

PUBLIC POLICY IMPLEMENTATION

The last stage of the public policy life cycle is called the stage of public policy implementation because at this point the statutory legislation has been enacted and regulations are being promulgated that will impose costs and changes in operations on the corporate community. Since the issues have become bureaucratized with the emphasis being on administrative decision making, the primary objective of business is to obtain regulations it can live with, and transfer the regulatory costs, to the extent possible, onto the consumer or other parties.

At this stage, many options for business are closed, or, at best, limited. The firm's strategic response is no longer solely in the hands of the firm's managers. The firm's legal counsel is a primary actor in this stage of strategy development. During this stage, regulations are being written to implement the statutes passed by Congress. It is important for business to continue involvement at this stage of the public policy process because business may get a bill passed and then see it modified beyond recognition as it is finally implemented by a government agency that issues regulations. Thus business must continue to have contact with regulatory agencies to help implement legislation, if possible, or appear at hearings before agencies to present their case. Disputes over implementation of the law can also be resolved through the courts, where the firm's interest is represented by attorneys in a narrowly focused, adversarial litigation proceeding. Firms can also choose a strategy of noncompliance at this stage and accept whatever penalties this strategy might involve.

Another option available to companies at this stage is to generate a new public policy issue. This forces the problem back to the first stage of the public policy life cycle in the hopes of changing public opinion with resultant changes in the enabling legislation and implementing regulations. Something like this happened during the late 1970s as business became subjected to more and more regulation. While business lost many individual battles over specific pieces of legislation and regulation, the whole issue of government regulation in general was thrown back into the discussion stage. Regulation was a major

[78]Ibid., p. 129.

factor in the presidential election of 1980, at which time a candidate was elected who promised to cut back on regulations that were hampering business.

Contact with Regulatory Agencies   Continual contact with government agencies is important. Industry has much of the technical information needed if reasonable and workable regulations are to be developed. Experts in environmental affairs, for example, need to work with EPA professionals to reach realistic compromises on pollution standards, timetables, and the kind of pollution control equipment the company has to install to be in compliance. These relationships between corporate and regulatory staffs are difficult to keep in balance. Because of its dependence on information from companies, an agency can be criticized as being captured by the industry it is supposed to regulate. Further complications arise when government officials leave the federal service for higher-paying jobs in industry. Both parties need to remember that they operate in a fishbowl, and thus need to be circumspect and above-board in their relationships.

Much of the work at this level is done through advisory committees. There are thousands of businesspeople who at the government's request provide data and advice to help shape public policy. Many of these committees are created by Congress to perform a specific task, such as the Federal Paperwork Commission created in 1977 to prepare recommendations for easing the burden imposed by government reports. Others are set up by Congress to see how well legislation is being implemented. Agencies themselves can set up committees to maintain objectivity and take the heat off the agency on a controversial issue. Finally, other committees are established by presidential order to advise the President on public policy matters.[79] Service on any of these advisory committees can be seen as a way of influencing public policy.

Some agencies have encouraged companies and industries to make counterproposals to the regulations they have proposed, recognizing that managers and engineers probably know better than rule writers how to meet requirements in specific situations. Managers know that no one regulation will exactly fit their situation. A regulation, once issued, is often too inflexible to allow managers much leeway in meeting the requirements in ways that make sense for their operations. Thus the EPA has introduced the concept of "controlled trading," which encourages managers to take the initiative in proposing new ways to meet pollution standards. Instead of writing rules and enforcing them, controlled trading makes it possible for business to propose smarter alternatives before government moves on to enforcement. Thus if business does not like an EPA regulation, it can make a counterproposal, which will probably be accepted if it meets the same standards.[80]

[79]"Advisory Committees: The Invisible Branch of Government," *Industry Week*, February 23, 1976, p. 44.

[80]William Drayton, "Getting Smarter About Regulation," *Harvard Business Review*, vol. 59, no. 4 (July–August 1981), pp. 38–52.

Contact with congressional committees becomes important if a major piece of regulatory legislation is up for revision. Legislation undergoing revision gives business a chance to make important changes. These changes may improve the implementing regulations by making them more cost-effective. Business cannot usually expect to bring about a comprehensive change in the basic statutory framework supporting an area of regulation, but it can at least hope to make some important incremental changes in the language of the statute and the nature of the public policy requirements. When public policy legislation is up for revision, business thus has another chance to change the legal framework that has been designed to respond to an issue of concern to the public.

Judicial Procedures Business can try to block regulatory requirements in court or contest enforcement activities of government agencies. In some cases, business first has to take its case to a special court, such as the Occupational Safety and Health Review Commission, in order to contest an enforcement action. But most such cases can be taken directly to the regular court system. Many of the standards proposed by OSHA have been the subject of court proceedings. Some of these, such as the benzene standard and the cotton dust standard, have gone all the way to the Supreme Court for a final ruling.

Business has a number of grounds on which it can challenge a standard. Business can challenge the way a rule was made, claiming that a rule was promulgated without sufficient notice and opportunity for comment, as required by the APA, or that an agency did not follow procedural requirements specifically contained in the statute it is implementing. Before a product can be banned by the Consumer Product Safety Commission, for example, it must present facts showing that the product presents an unreasonable risk of injury.[81]

The substance of a rule can also be challenged by questioning the agency's authority to regulate a particular kind of activity, or by trying to prove that a rule is not based on substantial evidence, thereby making it arbitrary and unreasonable. Business may also challenge the application of a regulation, claiming that its activities are not covered by the regulation. If the regulation as written does not clearly refer to the situation at hand in the charged violation, it may not apply.[82]

Regulations must also be enforced in a reasonable manner. If a regulation does not prescribe a particular method for implementing a standard, the agency may not impose an impractical or unfeasible manner of achieving the required result if a business is reaching the desired standard of performance with another method of control. Finally, business can insist upon fair and unbiased agency adjudications, which involves adequate notice and a fair hearing with unbiased

---

[81]McNeill Stokes, "Fighting Agency Enforcement," _Conquering Government Regulations: A Business Guide_, McNeill Stokes, ed. (New York: McGraw-Hill, 1982), pp. 147–153.

[82]Ibid., pp. 153–159.

administrative law judges. Unreasonable delay in holding a hearing may prejudice the party against whom an agency action is brought. Witnesses may no longer be available or evidence may have been destroyed in the normal course of business if the delay is too lengthy. The case may be set aside if adjudicatory procedures are not appropriate.[83]

Recently, business has adopted another strategy in regard to judicial procedures. It has begun to file "friend of the court" briefs with the Supreme Court, an activity which is a relatively new approach for business. These friend of the court briefs are nothing new to some groups, as labor unions and civil rights groups have for years been telling the Court how they believe issues ought to be resolved. There were more such briefs filed in the Bakke civil rights case, for example, than for any case in history.

Yet business's purpose in filing such briefs is different from these groups. Traditionally, such briefs are filed after the Supreme Court has agreed to hear a case, presenting a particular point of view on the case for the Court to consider. Business, however, places more emphasis on calling attention to cases before the Court has decided to hear them. The objective is to argue that a particular case is of greater importance to business than the justices might realize. Business believes that early briefs of this nature will increase the chances of the case being heard. Increased activity of this sort stems from an awareness of the importance of the Supreme Court in adjudicating disputes affecting business interests.[84]

Creating a New Issue

A particularly effective strategy at this stage of an issue life cycle is to try and create a new issue that will mitigate the adverse effects of the old issue and force the problem back to the first stage of discussion. Using this strategy, a corporation that has lost the battle with regard to a specific issue or a host of issues can perhaps redefine the issues so as to create a new issue in the mind of the public and place this new issue on the agenda to be debated. If the corporation is then able to successfully convince the public that this new issue needs attention, many of the burdens of the old issue can perhaps be mitigated or even removed entirely.

The best illustration of this strategy is the proliferation of government regulation that took place in the 1960s and 1970s, as the government responded to public concerns related to the environment, safety and health in the workplace, equal opportunity, and consumer protection. By and large, business opposed all legislation dealing with these matters, but lost the battle in most cases, as new legislation was passed dealing with these concerns, new agencies were created, new regulations were issued, and additional responsibilities were given.

[83]Ibid., pp. 159–170.
[84]"Business Starts Pushing More at High Court," *The Wall Street Journal*, April 23, 1982, p. 33.

Thus business was faced with the institutionalization of a host of new laws and regulations to change its behavior regarding social problems. Business has learned to work with regulatory agencies in a more cooperative manner over the years in order to have some effect on the regulations they issue and make them more cost-effective. Business has fought numerous court battles to try and prevent specific regulations from being issued and enforced. But perhaps its most effective strategy was to create a new issue that included the effects of all these regulations and make regulation a public policy issue in and of itself.

In the 1970s, several studies were done, with business support, that demonstrated the impact that regulation was having on the economy. Regulation was costing business conservatively $100 billion a year in direct costs to simply comply with existing regulations. Besides these direct costs, it was argued that regulation affected productivity, had an adverse impact on employment and capital formation, and diverted management attention from running the business.

Besides these comprehensive studies that dealt with the costs of regulation, there were numerous citations of anecdotal evidence related to conflicting regulations, the ambiguity of the language, difficulties of enforcement, the trivial concerns of some regulations, and the unnecessary adverse impacts on particular business organizations. What all of these studies and concern about regulation did was to make regulation itself the problem and draw the public into a discussion of adverse impacts of regulation despite their support for the goals of regulation. Thus a whole new issue was created that threw all the specific regulations business was concerned about back to the first stage, in a sense, to be discussed in the debate about regulation in general.

Then a new administration was elected that had as one of its main concerns a reduction of the regulatory burden on business as one of the specific elements of its more general goal of getting government off the backs of the people. The Reagan administration proceeded to reduce the regulatory burden on business without changing any of the statutory framework. By the power of appointment, the issuance of an executive order requiring benefit-cost analysis, and through control of the agency budgets, the administration was able to change the entire regulatory effort and reduce the regulatory burden on business. Thus business was able to mitigate the effects of specific regulations in the institutional phase by creating a whole new issue and helping to elect an administration more sympathetic to its views about the proper role of government.

Noncompliance   It may seem strange to include noncompliance as a strategy for business at this stage, but on closer reflection and based on even a cursory knowledge of corporate law violations, it is obvious that this is indeed a strategy. Given the current number of violations in the news media, the use of this strategy may be on the increase. In any event, corporations can choose to violate laws and regulations if they deem such action to be in their interest. Although a law violator obviously hopes to never be caught, the risk of getting caught is probably taken into account and weighed against the penalty or penalties that might result. This is not to suggest that all corporate violations of the law are deliberate—most are probably not intended or are more in the nature of accidents. But a significant number of violations may be the result of conscious deliberation on the part of corporate executives who believe the benefits to be obtained from violating the law outweigh the costs that might accrue to themselves and the corporation. It would be naive to think otherwise.

Addording to Clinard and Yeager, corporate crime is any act committed by a corporation that is punishable under some form of law, whether it be administrative, civil, or criminal.[85] Corporate crime is a form of white-collar crime, yet it might more appropriately be called organizational crime that occurs in the context of complex relationships and expectations among boards of directors, executives, and managers, on the one hand, and among parent corporations, corporate divisions, and subsidiaries, on the other.[86] Corporate crime is enacted by aggregates of discrete individuals, and thus is not comparable to the action of a lone individual.

The corporation obviously cannot be jailed as can an ordinary citizen, but it can be fined. Thus the corporation is treated as a person at least to this extent. Most corporate crime is handled by quasi-judicial bodies or regulatory agencies that use administrative and civil enforcement measures. These measures include warning letters, consent agreements or decrees not to repeat the violation, orders to compel compliance, seizure or recall of commodities, administrative or civil monetary penalties, and court injunctions to refrain from further violations.[87]

There are many pressures that impinge on a corporate executive that contribute to his or her willingness to engage in corporate law violations. Most businesspeople probably bring to the job roughly the same sense of morality that exists in the society at large, that is, a desire to be honest and fair and abide by the ethical standards of society. But the pressures of the business world often cause them to violate these ethical standards and make compromises in order to survive and get ahead. The reward system of the corporation shapes their behavior to a large extent, and the ultimate test of effectiveness in a competitive system is profit, not morality.

Obedience to one's superior, loyalty to the corporation, and the desire to get ahead in salaries and bonuses are common justifications that are offered to justify unethical and illegal behavior on the part of corporate executives.[88] The rewards that executives are offered include high salaries that are augmented by bonuses based on profits, deferred compensation plans, and extensive perks.

[85]Marshall B. Clinard and Peter C. Yeager, *Corporate Crime* (New York: The Free Press, 1980), p. 16.

[86]Ibid., p. 17.

[87]Ibid., p. 16.

[88]Ibid., pp. 274–275.

Failure to retain or to gain such rewards can be disastrous to the self-image of executives and their personal lives.[89] Thus managers are under intense pressure to take unethical or even illegal shortcuts to meet profit objectives and reap the rewards the corporation has to offer. It is all too easy to justify law violations in the name of the corporation when one is under such pressure and has a strong sense of loyalty to the corporation and the management team.

Given the current state of affairs with regard to corporate law violations, there is a great deal of interest in developing more effective procedures to deter corporate crime and mitigate its effect on society. There is a need for more understanding of the pressures and incentives that lead to corporate crime, which will help in designing effective policies to control and prevent such behavior. Thinking of corporate law violations as a strategic response to a changing environment may aid in understanding the role noncompliance plays in the total picture of possible corporate responses in the institutional stage of an issue life cycle.

BUSINESS AND THE POLITICAL PROCESS

Table 8.2 presents a strategic management model of the public policy life cycle that summarizes the strategic options that a firm might employ at each stage. The concept of a life cycle for public issues is important because different corporate strategies are called for at different stages. The options that are open to business for some kind of a response to the issues are different at each stage, which makes it necessary for corporations to concern themselves with "goodness of fit" between the life cycle of a public issue and the response of a corporation. The development of an appropriate plan that takes this life cycle into account is important for the development of corporate strategy. For the corporate strategist, the question is not whether to participate in the public policy process, but how to participate effectively and appropriately.

Table 8.3 depicts the focus and the key actors at each stage of the public policy life cycle. In the first stage, the issue is an idea that is being discussed. The issue is of concern to some people and may involve a change in corporate performance. The key actors in society in championing this issue are public interest groups who seek to enlist broader support for their interests. These groups can use various strategies, including protests, boycotts, demonstrations, media coverage, and the like to gain attention and have their concerns placed on the public policy agenda. If corporations want to participate at this stage, they must become involved in the discussion at some point.

In the second stage, the issue has been translated into particular kinds of legislation that are being considered to deal with the concerns raised in the first stage by requiring some kind of change in corporate behavior. The key actors at

[89]Ibid., p. 276.

Table 8.2
A Strategic Management Model for Public Policy Issues

The Strategic Process/ Public Policy Life Cycle	Strategic Options
Stage I: Public Opinion Formation	Communication Strategies Direct Meetings Press Releases Special Media Presentations TV and Radio Talk Shows Annual Report Advocacy Advertising Image Advertising Economic Education Programs
Stage II: Public Policy Formulation	Participation Strategies General Business Associations Industry/Trade Associations Lobbying Honorariums Constituency Building Campaign Contributions
Stage III: Public Policy Implementation	Compliance Strategies Cooperation with Agencies Legal Resistance Judicial Proceedings Creating a New Issue Non-Compliance

Source: Mike H. Ryan, Carl L. Swanson, and Rogene A. Buchholz, *Corporate Strategy, Public Policy and the Fortune 500: How America's Major Corporations Influence Government* (Oxford: Basil Blackwell, 1987), p. 45.

Table 8.3
The Public Issues Life Cycle

Stages	I	II	III
Nature of Issue	Idea	Legislation	Law
Key Actor in Society	Public Interest Groups	Office-Holders	Regulators

Source: Mike H. Ryan, Carl L. Swanson, and Rogene A. Buchholz, *Corporate Strategy, Public Policy and the Fortune 500: How America's Major Corporations Influence Government* (Oxford: Basil Blackwell, 1987), p. 46.

this stage are elected office holders who introduce and debate the legislation and who eventually vote to support or defeat the legislation. For corporations to be involved at this stage means they must relate to these office holders and their staffs in some fashion.

The third stage focuses on law or the implementation of legislation that has been previously enacted. The original issue has now become institutionalized and the idea has been translated into specific legislation that has become the law of the land. The principal actors at this point are the regulators in government agencies who are writing and enforcing rules to bring corporations into compliance with legislation. Corporations can choose to work with these regulators to write and interpret rules so as to take corporate interests into account, they can challenge particular rules in the courts, or they can adopt a strategy of noncompliance.

The actors at each stage of the public policy life cycle form what has come to be called the infamous *iron triangle*. The iron triangle consists of (1) the public interest groups who have a significant stake in a particular issue or issues; (2) the regulatory agency who has responsibility for implementing legislation that has been passed with respect to the issue or issues of concern; and (3) the particular subcommittee or committee of Congress that had primary responsibility for shaping the legislation and continues to exercise an oversight function regarding the regulatory agency. This iron triangle has been held to be virtually impregnable by some commentators, particularly if each of the three parties has the same interest in the issue. Thus it is important for business to recognize the significance of this triangle and its implications for the formation and implementation of public policy.

SELECTED REFERENCES

Business' Political Awakening: PAC Overview. Washington, D.C.: Fraser/Associates, 1979.

EMANUEL, MYRON, CURTIS SNODGRASS, JOYCE GILDEA, and KARN ROSENBERG. *Corporate Economic Education Programs: An Evaluation and Appraisal.* New York: Financial Executives Research Foundation, 1979.

EPSTEIN, EDWIN M. *The Corporation in American Politics.* Englewood Cliffs, N.J.: Prentice-Hall, 1969.

HACKER, ANDREW. *The Corporation Take-Over.* New York: Harper & Row, 1964.

HEATH, ROBERT L. and RICHARD ALAN NELSON, *Issues Management: Corporate Public Policymaking in an Information Society.* Beverly Hills: Sage Publications, 1986.

LEVITAN, SAR A., and MARTHA R. COOPER. *The Public Good and the Bottom Line.* Baltimore, Md.: Johns Hopkins Press, 1984.

MCGRATH, PHYLLIS. *Redefining Corporate-Federal Relations.* New York: The Conference Board, 1979.

RAYMOND, A., ITHIEL DE SOLA POOL, and LEWIS ANTHONY DEXTER. *American Business and Public Policy: The Politics of Foreign Trade.* Chicago: Aldine-Atherton, 1972.

ROSE, ARNOLD M. *The Power Structure: Political Process in American Society.* New York: Oxford University Press, 1967.

RYAN, MIKE H., CARL L. SWANSON, and ROGENE A. BUCHHOLZ, *Corporate Strategy, Public Policy, and the Fortune 500: How America's Major Corporations Influence Government.* Oxford: Basil Blackwell, 1987.

SCHUMPETER, JOSEPH A. *Capitalism, Socialism, and Democracy.* New York: Harper & Row, 1947.

SETHI, S. PRAKASH. *Advocacy Advertising and Large Corporations.* Lexington, Mass.: Lexington Books, 1977.

INDEX

Drayton, William, 251
Dresser Industries, 173
Duties, 100
Dye, Thomas R., 29, 39, 48, 104–06

Ecology movement, 4
Economic education, 227–31
Economic forecasting, 197
Economic management, 71–72
Economic roles, 36
Economic sanctions, 168–75
　costs, 170
　results, 174–75
　types, 168–69
Economic value system, 33–34, 94–95
Education and values, 91
Eells, Richard, 161, 164
Egalitarianism, 74–75
Elbing, Alvar O. and Carol J., 90
Elder, Shirley, 107–08
Elite theory, 103–04
Elkins, Arthur, 4
Employment Act of 1946, 71–72
Energy, 55–57
Entitlement programs, 4
Entitlements, 73, 93, 99–100
Entrepreneurs, 57
Environmental analysis, 192–204
Environmental assessment, 201–204
Environmental forecasting:
　approaches, 200–01
　conceptual basis, 197–99
　defined, 197
　principles, 199–200
Environmental monitoring, 196
Environmental Protection Agency, 81–
　82, 113, 251
Environmental scanning:
　definition, 193
　models, 193
　sources of information, 193–96
Equal Employment Opportunity Commis-
　sion, 81–82, 139
Equal opportunity, 3
Equal rights, 3
Establishment, 102–03
Ethical decision, 96

Ethical standards, 4
Ethics, 95–102
　definition, 96
　and public policy, 95
　and values, 96
European Economic Community, 159
European Free Trade Association, 158
Exchange process, 32–33
Executive branch, 129–132
Executive office of the President, 131
Executive orders, 131, 141
Export Administration Act:
　amendments, 173–74
　penalties, 171–72
　problems, 172–73
　provisions, 171
　uses, 172

Fahey, Liam, 196, 204–05
Federal Communications Commission, 64
Federal Election Campaign Practices Act,
　242
Federal Election Commission, 242–43
Federal Energy Regulatory Commission,
　64
Federal judicial system, 133–36
Federal Power Commission, 64
Federal Register, 140
Federal Trade Commission, 82, 139
Federal Trade Commission Act, 62
Feminist movement, 3
Fenn, Dan, 142, 144, 146–47, 238
Fiedler, Edgar R., 197
First National Bank of Boston v. *Bellotti*,
　225
Food and Drug Administration, 81, 139
Ford, Henry, 65
Forecasting (see Environmental forecast-
　ing)
Foreign Corrupt Practices Act:
　accounting provisions, 165
　antibribery provisions, 165
　parties, 166
　penalties, 166–67
　implications, 167
Foreign payments controversy, 160–68
　defense, 163

263